T0221112

Symmetric Cryptography 1

SCIENCES

Computer Science, Field Directors –
Valérie Berthé and Jean-Charles Pomerol

Cryptography, Data Security, Subject Head – Damien Vergnaud

Symmetric Cryptography 1

Design and Security Proofs

Coordinated by
Christina Boura
María Naya-Plasencia

WILEY

First published 2023 in Great Britain and the United States by ISTE Ltd and John Wiley & Sons, Inc.

ISTE Ltd
27-37 St George's Road
London SW19 4EU
UK

www.iste.co.uk

John Wiley & Sons, Inc.
111 River Street
Hoboken, NJ 07030
USA

www.wiley.com

Any opinions, findings, and conclusions or recommendations expressed in this material are those of the author(s), contributor(s) or editor(s) and do not necessarily reflect the views of ISTE Group.

Library of Congress Control Number: 2023930945

British Library Cataloguing-in-Publication Data
A CIP record for this book is available from the British Library
ISBN 978-1-78945-146-7

ERC code:
PE6 Computer Science and Informatics
 PE6_5 Cryptology, security, privacy, quantum cryptography

Contents

Chaoyun LI and Bart PRENEEL

Orr DUNKELMAN

Gilles VAN ASSCHE

Chapter 5. Modes of Operation   73
Gaëtan LEURENT

Chapter 6. Authenticated Encryption Schemes   87
Maria EICHLSEDER

Preface

Christina Boura[1] and María Naya-Plasencia[2]
[1]*University of Paris-Saclay, UVSQ, CNRS, Versailles, France*
[2]*Inria, Paris, France*

Symmetric-key cryptology is one of the two main branches of modern cryptology. On the one hand, it comprises primitives and constructions for providing security services such as confidentiality, integrity and authentication, the particularity being that the same secret key k is used at both sides. On the other hand, it studies and provides cryptanalysis and proof techniques for analyzing the security of the above constructions. Even if in general keyless, some hash functions are also considered as part of this family of algorithms because of the similarities in their construction and analysis with the other symmetric-key primitives.

Symmetric-key algorithms are essential for communication security as they are built on simple operations (e.g. XOR, logical AND and so on) and for this reason they can achieve a high speed in both software and hardware implementations. They are in particular much faster and lighter than public-key algorithms, having at the same time much shorter encryption keys. The security and efficiency of modern communications is heavily based on symmetric algorithms and for this reason symmetric-key cryptology is a very important and constantly developing branch of modern cryptography.

The first widely deployed symmetric-key algorithm was the block cipher data encryption standard (DES), whose design dates backs to the 1970s. Since then, tens if not hundreds, of new symmetric-key algorithms were designed either with the aim to be broadly deployed or with some specific design criteria or use case in mind.

From a historical point of view, the first widely used symmetric schemes were undoubtedly block ciphers and stream ciphers. The first ones encrypt a message by first dividing it into blocks of fixed size and then treating each block separately. The second ones encrypt one bit (or one word) at a time, by XORing each bit (or word) of the message with a bit of a stream, called keystream, derived from the key. Both types of primitives aim at providing confidentiality and are still extremely popular, even if an important part of the design space has been taken more recently by tweakable block ciphers and cryptographic permutations. The symmetric algorithms to ensure data authentification are known as message authentication code (MAC) functions. While keyless, hash functions are also considered as symmetric-key constructions aiming for integrity and play an important role in some cryptographic protocols. Finally, authenticated encryption (AE) schemes can provide both confidentiality and authenticity of data and their popularity constantly increases.

The goal of this project is to reflect the current scientific knowledge and present the most trending orientations on the design, security proofs and cryptanalysis of all the above symmetric-key schemes.

This book is divided into two volumes. The first volume is composed of 14 chapters, where the first nine chapters are dedicated to the description of the most important design principles for stream ciphers, (tweakable) block ciphers, cryptographic permutations, hash functions as well as for their inner components. The five remaining chapters are reserved to the presentation of the most important security proof techniques.

Chapter 1 introduces the main generic design goals, criteria and strategies for building robust symmetric constructions. This chapter starts by discussing the most important building blocks deployed in symmetric cryptography. As encryption schemes, MAC functions and authenticated encryption schemes usually support messages of arbitrary length, modes and constructions for building variable-length schemes are discussed next. This chapter examines then how to choose the adequate number of rounds for an iterated construction and gives some criteria that should be taken into account when designing a cipher's round function. Finally, a number of ciphers that inspired both designers and cryptanalysts are presented.

Chapter 2 gives an overview of the main design principles for stream ciphers. It discusses first the most important generic constructions as well as attacks against them and gives an overview of the different stream cipher competitions and standards. This chapter focuses next on feedback shift register (FSR)-based constructions as well as on software-oriented constructions based on large tables. Next are presented stream ciphers that are constructed based on block ciphers and large permutations. The chapter concludes with a discussion on authenticated encryption based on stream ciphers and with a treatment of low-complexity stream ciphers that are optimized for use in advanced cryptographic protocols.

Chapter 3 is dedicated to block ciphers. It presents notably the two most popular constructions for these primitives: the Feistel construction and the substitution permutation network (SPN). To expand the master key to a series of subkeys, an algorithm called key-schedule should be used, and for this reason the design of these algorithms is next discussed. This chapter analyzes also some generic attacks against block ciphers and gives some positive results concerning their security. Finally, two particular classes of block ciphers are discussed: tweakable block ciphers, where an extra argument called the tweak is used to diversify the encryption function and algebraic block ciphers, essential for the encryption of data in some emerging scenarios and applications.

Chapter 4 presents the most important design approaches for building secure cryptographic hash functions and extendable output functions (XOFs). It first discusses some necessary generic requirements for a hash function to be secure. The random oracle model is then defined as the model that hash functions and XOFs should follow and is accompanied by a discussion on how the security claim of a hash function or an XOF should be formulated. Next, the most popular hash function constructions are presented, notably the Merkle-Damgård construction. The weaknesses of this construction and different ways to repair it are presented. A focus is given next on how to build robust compression functions for hash functions that follow this principle. Then, the indifferentiability framework used to prove that a construction is secure against generic attacks is discussed. The sponge construction and the KECCAK family are introduced next. Finally, the principle of tree hashing that permits efficient hashing of long messages in multi-processor environments is presented.

Cryptographic schemes are usually designed with a bottom-up approach. We first start with primitives that operate on small message blocks and achieve a well-defined security notion and then choose a mode of operation to deal with messages of arbitrary length. Chapter 5 describes the main modes for encryption and authentication and discusses their security.

Authenticated encryption offers the combined security properties of an encryption scheme and a message authentication code. Gradually, authenticated ciphers take over classical encryption schemes as from one side authenticity of data is an important security requirement and from the other side it has become more clear over the years how to securely build such schemes. Chapter 6 is dedicated to the design of authenticated encryption schemes. It details the relevant security notions before presenting the most promising design strategies for building authenticated ciphers. Dedicated designs are next discussed, and an overview of different authenticated encryption designs used as Internet standards or issued from some cryptographic competitions is given.

The next two chapters are dedicated to the construction of linear and nonlinear layers for an important class of symmetric-key primitives. Chapter 7 discusses the construction of the so-called maximum distance separable (MDS) matrices that are linear layers with optimal properties used in many SPN ciphers. A part of this chapter is notably focused on the construction of MDS matrices with a low implementation cost that are particularly relevant in the context of lightweight cryptography.

Nonlinearity, essential for the security of cryptographic constructions, is typically achieved by the mean of small nonlinear permutations, called S-boxes. Chapter 8 gives an overview of the most important properties cryptographic S-boxes should verify and presents some classical S-box constructions.

Chapter 9 discusses what it means for a primitive to be trustworthy. It presents notably what the typical lifecycle of a primitive is from the design phase to the final deployment and the role played by cryptanalysis. Next is analyzed what happens when an algorithm fails to adhere to a typical deployment process, in the cases notably of some proprietary algorithms or of backdoored designs. Examples of primitives found to have hidden properties are given next. The chapter is concluded by presenting some rules of thumb to follow when choosing a primitive to deploy.

Once a primitive has been designed, it is important to prove it secure against advesaries. The second part of this volume is dedicated to security proofs in symmetric cryptography. Chapter 10 is concerned with how to formalize security of cryptographic primitives. It first discusses the most common adversary models and what it means for an attack to be successful under these models. As we want an encryption function to look like a function that responds randomly for each input, a theoretical function that behaves ideally in this respect and called the random oracle is introduced. The central notion of distinguishing advantage is then presented and analyzed. Finally, typical security claims for both stream ciphers and block ciphers are given.

Chapter 11 is dedicated to the security of modes of operation. The most important modes are introduced (see also Chapter 5) and are analyzed from a security point of view. Then a concrete example of how one can prove the security of a particular mode is given. More precisely, it is demonstrated how to formally argue that the counter mode, based on advanced encryption standard (AES), is a secure stream cipher.

Chapter 12 investigates the provable security of message authentication and authenticated encryption. It starts by formalizing a message authentication code and discusses its security definition. Then the notion of universal hash functions is introduced and an example of the provable security result of Wegman-Carter-Shoup authenticator is given. Finally, the security of authenticated encryption is introduced and an example of the provable security result of Galois/counter mode is shown.

Chapter 13 is an introduction to the H-coefficients technique, a proof method allowing to upper bound the advantage of a computationally unbounded adversary in distinguishing between two random systems. This chapter presents next the

Even-Mansour construction that defines a block cipher from a single permutation and shows how to apply the H-coefficients technique to prove its security in the random permutation model.

Chapter 14 presents the χ^2-method, a proof technique that can help to obtain tight and simplified proofs for certain constructions. This technique is notably applied to prove the pseudo-random function (PRF)-security of the truncated random permutation construction. In addition, the proof of the PRF-security of the sum of two random permutations is given and some additional applications are discussed.

Finally, the specifications of four popular, standardized and widely employed symmetric schemes: DES, AES, PRESENT and KECCAK are given in the appendix, as many chapters of both volumes refer to them.

The second volume is dedicated to the most important cryptanalysis techniques for symmetric ciphers. It also discusses some promising future directions for the domain.

The field of cryptography is a domain that has never stopped evolving since the appearance of the first commercial cryptographic applications in the 1970s. Due to this constant evolution, providing a complete survey of all the design trends, cryptanalysis techniques or proof methods is an extremely difficult task. We believe however that this book offers a good starting point to all readers interested in learning about the most important and promising results of the field, in particularly to all those wishing to learn how to design and analyze a secure symmetric cipher. We believe that the two volumes of this work will be helpful to researchers, master's and PhD students studying or working in the field of cryptography as well as to all professionals working in the field of cybersecurity.

July 2023

PART 1

Design of Symmetric-key Algorithms

1

Introduction to Design in Symmetric Cryptography

Joan DAEMEN
Radboud University, Nijmegen, The Netherlands

1.1. Introduction

This chapter gives a bird's-eye view of design in symmetric cryptography. It tries to set the scene by focusing on some dominant design trends.

In our treatment, we have somewhat neglected stream ciphers. For an overview of stream cipher design, we refer to Chapter 2.

Symmetric cryptography covers schemes for encryption, data authentication and authenticated encryption (AE) where sender and receiver share a secret key. Functions for data authentication are called *Message Authentication Code (MAC) functions*. It also usually includes cryptographic hash functions that are a building block in many protocols and that have many unkeyed applications.

The presence of a key in the former allows for an elegant and easily motivated split of the design effort into two layers: one that covers primitives and one that covers modes. In mainstream cryptography, these primitives are most often *block ciphers*.

1.2. Cryptographic building blocks

In this section, we describe the most important building blocks deployed in symmetric cryptography. First, we discuss those with fixed input and output length:

block ciphers, tweakable block ciphers and cryptographic permutations. Then, we briefly describe differentially uniform functions.

1.2.1. *The block cipher and its variants*

A block cipher can be seen as a mini-encryption scheme only able to encipher a plaintext of some specific length into a ciphertext of the same length, and this taking a secret key. The length of the plaintext/ciphertext is called the block length n and is typically 8 or 16 bytes.

The standard security goal is that a block cipher instance with a fixed key is hard to distinguish from a random n-bit permutation by an adversary that does not know the key. This hardness is expressed by a *distinguishing advantage* that ranges between 0 and 1. Designers of a block cipher usually claim an upper bound on this advantage as a function of the resources of the adversary. Such a bound cannot be proven but the claim serves as a challenge for cryptanalysts and, in the absence of attacks breaking the claim, as a security specification when *using* the block cipher. The resources of the adversary split naturally into two categories: data and computation. The data complexity of an attack is the amount of data exchanged with the keyed primitive and the computational complexity is the amount of computation an attack requires. The latter must be expressed in some well-defined unit of computation for the claim to be meaningful.

If the adversary can query only the *encryption* operation of the block cipher, we call this pseudorandom permutation (PRP) security. If the adversary can additionally query the *decryption* operation, we call this strong PRP (SPRP) security.

We may wonder what is the point of defining PRP security, as decryption would always require the decryption operation of the block cipher. Additionally, the setup of SPRP security seems futile as an adversary that can ask for decryption does not need to break the cipher to find out the plaintext. The answer lies in the fact that block ciphers are deployed in a so-called *mode of use* to support input of arbitrary length. A good mode of use comes with a proof for an upper bound of the success probability of an attack as a function of the resources of the adversary. PRP security is relevant in modes that do not require the inverse block cipher and SPRP for the other modes.

Often block cipher publications do not come with an explicit security claim. In that case, one silently assumes that the block cipher is designed such that exhaustive key search is the most efficient distinguishing attack, both in the PRP and SPRP case. This implies that the advantage cannot be above the success probability of exhaustive key search. This is $N2^k$, where k is the length of the key in bits and N is the computational complexity expressed in the number of executions of the block cipher under attack.

(S)PRP security at the level of exhaustive key search is usually the design goal of a block cipher, of course next to efficiency and possibly other criteria.

Some block ciphers take an additional input called a *tweak* and are hence called *tweakable* block ciphers. Their security goal is, when keyed with a fixed and unknown key, to be hard to distinguish from a family of random permutations, where the members are indexed by the tweak. Here also both PRP and SPRP flavors exist. The tweak input is very useful in that it can be used for domain separation, resulting in modes with simpler security proofs.

Instead of adding an input to a block cipher, we can go the other way and remove the key input. The result is a *cryptographic permutation*. Many consider its security goal to *have no structural properties* that a random permutation would not have. Unlike (S)PRP security of a block cipher, this cannot be formally defined and we cannot attribute security to a cryptographic permutation independent of the construction it is used in. However, when building a cryptographic primitive from a permutation using a construction like the sponge (Bertoni et al. 2007), keyed duplex (Bertoni et al. 2011b) or Even-Mansour (Even and Mansour 1991), the security of the resulting primitive can be formally defined.

1.3. Differentially uniform functions

MAC functions and AE schemes often feature keyed functions (traditionally called *function families*) that can be proven to be ϵ-universal (Stinson 1995). These keyed functions take as input a variable-length input and return a fixed-length output. Roughly speaking, a function is ϵ-universal if an adversary faced with an instance of the function with a uniformly selected secret key has a maximum probability of ϵ of guessing two inputs with the same output. Functions that can be proven to be ϵ-universal with very small ϵ can be built by using simple algebraic functions such as polynomial evaluation over a finite field (den Boer 1993; Bierbrauer et al. 1993). The two best known such functions are used in the Galois/Counter (GCM) mode (McGrew and Viega 2004; NIST 2007) and Poly1305 (Bernstein 2005). The former operates over a field with characteristic 2, $\mathbb{F}_{2^{128}}$ and the latter over the prime field $\mathbb{F}_{2^{130}-5}$. For a treatment of the security of MAC functions based on differentially uniform functions, we refer to Handschuh and Preneel (2008).

1.4. Arbitrary-length schemes

Encryption schemes, MAC functions and AE schemes usually support messages of arbitrary length, possibly with some upper bounds.

1.4.1. *Modes and constructions*

Variable-length schemes are often built from a fixed-length primitive like a block cipher, a tweakable block cipher or a cryptographic permutation by means of a *mode* or *construction*. They may have *provable* security in the form of a proof that a distinguishing advantage (e.g. IND-CPA, -CCA or -CCA2, see Chapter 10) or attack success probability (e.g. forgery) is below some limit, under the assumption that the underlying primitive is ideal. Here, *ideal* means that the underlying primitive is modeled as a random permutation, or in the case of a tweakable block cipher a family of random permutations.

In the case of a primitive that has a dedicated key input, the security objective of the primitive is exactly to be hard to distinguish from an ideal counterpart. According to the triangle inequality, the sum of the (proven) bound for the mode and the (claimed) bound for the primitive forms upper bounds for the distinguishing advantage or attack success probability of the scheme. If the primitive is a cryptographic permutation, the triangle inequality cannot be applied. This is because a security definition such as (S)PRP requires a key input to be meaningful. A cryptographic permutation cannot be hard to distinguish from a random permutation as it is fully specified. Still, the mode or construction can be proven secure and this proof is meaningful in the sense that it says something of the existence of generic attacks.

The terms "mode" and "construction" are apparently used to indicate the same concept. Still, there seems to be an implicit convention. The term "mode" is used most often for cases where the triangle inequality applies and "construction" for cases where it does not. We speak of counter mode, cipher block chaining (CBC) mode and output feedback (OFB) mode of block ciphers, but we speak of the sponge construction and the duplex construction of cryptographic permutations. We also speak of construction when the primitive does have a dedicated key input, but that input takes non-secret data. Examples here include the Merkle–Damgård construction (see Chapter 4) or the Davies–Meyer construction (see Chapter 4), both used in hashing. It makes sense to follow this convention.

In short, most (authenticated) encryption schemes, MAC functions and hash functions make use of fixed-length primitives and these primitives are designed to behave *sufficiently close to ideal*. More specifically, they should be such that there are no attacks against the schemes better than *generic attacks*. This has become known as the *hermetic* design approach (Bertoni et al. 2011a). This approach allows cryptanalysts to concentrate on the primitive without much consideration of the mode or construction it is used in.

1.4.2. *Dedicated schemes*

There are many schemes that do not adopt this hermetic approach. The most prominent such schemes are *dedicated stream ciphers* that take a short key and a short diversifier and return an arbitrary-length keystream. While stream ciphers can be built as modes of block ciphers, such as counter mode or OFB mode, or constructions of cryptographic permutations, such as SALSA (Bernstein 2008), there are many designs that have no building blocks that can be considered cryptographic per se. Examples of dedicated stream ciphers can be found in the eSTREAM portfolio (see https://www.ecrypt.eu.org/stream/).

Similarly, there are hash functions that are not built around a primitive. Examples include CELLHASH (Daemen et al. 1991b), PANAMA (Daemen and Clapp 1998), RADIOGATÚN (Bertoni et al. 2006) and the SHA-3 candidate FUGUE (Halevi et al. 2014). A design that offers both stream encryption and hashing without an underlying cryptographic primitive is SUBTERRANEAN (Claesen et al. 1993; Daemen 1995), recently refurbished to the NIST lightweight competition candidate SUBTERRANEAN 2.0 (Daemen et al. 2020).

1.4.3. *Modes and constructions versus primitives*

In the hermetic approach, the design of schemes splits nicely into two separate disciplines: primitives on the one hand and modes and constructions on the other hand.

Modes and constructions consist of splitting up the variable-length input, padding and the application of domain separation bits and calling the underlying primitive(s). One can make the difference between sound and unsound constructions. For example, the sponge construction has excellent indifferentiability bounds (Bertoni et al. 2008), while the Merkle–Damgård variant used in the SHA-1 and SHA-2 functions has a useless indifferentiability bound and requires a dedicated construction when being used for MAC computation like HMAC (Bellare et al. 1996; NIST 2008).

While there is a certain degree of sophistication in the design of modes and constructions, it has become mostly routine and the pitfalls are by now well known. Moreover, once a (correct) proof is obtained, no more analysis of the mode or construction seems needed. However, for some modes and constructions proven bounds are not tight, and advances in proof techniques lead to improved bounds. This is particularly the case in the active field of beyond-birthday-bound proofs.

The situation is very different for the primitives. There appears to be no limit to the range of possible attacks, and there is little hope that a proof of security can be constructed. The best we can do is to analyze the security of a (candidate) primitive against all known attacks. This is called *cryptanalysis*.

1.5. Iterated (tweakable) block ciphers and permutations

Most (tweakable) block ciphers and cryptographic permutations are iterated: they consist of the repetition of a simple round function. The processing steps applied to the main input are called the *data path*. In block ciphers, each round typically takes a round key and in tweakable block ciphers additionally a round tweak, sometimes as a combined value called a round *tweakey* (Jean et al. 2014). The round keys and tweaks are derived from the cipher key and tweak by means of a (key, tweak or tweakey) schedule. These schedules are often, similar to the data path, iterated.

In lightweight ciphers, the round keys are often just copies of the cipher key with a round-specific constant added to it (see e.g. NOEKEON (Daemen et al. 2000)).

There are of course exceptions and variants to this iterated approach. For example, in data encryption standard (DES) (NIST 1999) and advanced encryption standard (AES) (NIST 2001), the last round is slightly different from the other ones. In the AES contest submission SERPENT (Biham et al. 1998), there are eight different rounds, and in the NIST lightweight competition submission SATURNIN (Canteaut et al. 2020), there are three different rounds. The AES contest submission MARS (Burwick et al. 1999) is a rare example of a block cipher with different *types* of rounds.

1.5.1. *Cryptanalysis and safety margin*

All iterated block ciphers and permutations have in common that they can be made stronger against quasi all attacks by increasing the number of rounds. An exception to this rule are so-called slide attacks (Biryukov and Wagner 1999) and variants that exploit symmetry between the rounds and were applicable to some older weak designs.

Results in cryptanalysis are often incremental, in that they build on earlier work. As time goes by after publication of a primitive, the state of cryptanalysis advances and attacks become more and more powerful. In general, it is hard to predict how the security of a primitive will evolve over time. An excellent example of a cipher whose security strength melted away is FEAL (Shimizu and Miyaguchi 1987) (see section 1.6.2). But also the standard block cipher DES was for a long period widely believed to have a security strength close to that of its key length, until differential cryptanalysis was published that could recover the key with complexity arguably below that of exhaustive key search (Biham and Shamir 1990).

An example of a very bad break was that of the hash function MD5 (Rivest 1992). Very quick after its publication, this function was widely adopted in protocols to secure the Internet in the early 1990s, despite signs of weaknesses as reported by den Boer and Bosselaers (1993). In 2005 and the following years, it was demonstrated that MD5 offers almost no collision-resistance, a property essential when used in cryptographic signatures (Wang and Yu 2005).

These historical examples have taught us to build in some safety margins.

In iterated primitives, the safety margin consists of taking more rounds than needed when taking into account the state of cryptanalysis at time of design. One does this as follows:

1) Apply all known and relevant attack techniques to reduced-round versions of the cipher.

2) First apply them to single-round versions, then to two-round versions and so on to determine for how many rounds the technique can lead to an attack that breaks the security claim.

3) Then take the number of rounds that is needed to offer resistance against these attacks and add some rounds.

The decision of how many rounds to add is a tricky one. It is based on an expectation of advances in cryptanalysis that are per definition unknown and is hence a rather intuitive matter. In the version of RIJNDAEL with a 128-bit key, we based the 10 rounds on the square attack (Daemen et al. 1997) that broke six rounds at the time of publication and four rounds of safety margin. In retrospect, it seems this was a good compromise between performance on the one hand and security assurance on the other.

In KECCAK (Bertoni et al. 2014), we based the 24 rounds on the existence of zero-sum distinguishers (Boura and Canteaut 2010) for a high number of rounds in the KECCAK-f permutation and the desire to have a *hermetic* design. In retrospect this was an overly conservative choice and looking at the state of cryptanalysis more than a decade after publication, taking 12 rounds would still give a comfortable safety margin.

Examples of where an appropriate safety margin was chosen are the SHA-2 hash functions (NIST 2002) and examples of where the safety margin melted away are obviously DES, FEAL, MD5 but also SHA-1 (NIST 1995; Stevens et al. 2017).

1.5.2. *Designing the round function of primitives*

In iterated primitives, the focus of the design effort is on the round function. In a nutshell, the round function shall offer a good compromise between computational cost and cryptographic strength. It shall achieve the required security, for example, PRP security in the case of a block cipher, with a number of rounds that has a low computational cost.

Of course, computational cost depends strongly on the platform and a round function can perform well on one platform but badly on others. We often aim for designing a round function that leads to a cipher with a low computational cost on a wide range of platforms. If one specializes for platforms with strong restrictions, one speaks of *lightweight cryptography*.

As time proceeds and confidence grows in cryptographic primitives, we often see devices are equipped with dedicated hardware for these primitives, for example dedicated AES instructions such as AES-NI on Intel and later also in AMD and ARM processors. In that context, one can see the energy consumption per processed bit in dedicated hardware implementations as the computational cost measure relevant in the long term. In the design, we can also take into account aspects such as the vulnerability of implementations against side-channel or fault injection attacks. Important side channels are computation time, power consumption and electromagnetic emanations and these can play an important role in the choice of building blocks.

Round function design is only limited by the imagination of the designers. Still, when looking at actual round functions, we can distinguish a number of trends, each launched by some innovative or popular design.

1.6. A short history

In this section, we will discuss a number of ciphers that inspired interesting cryptanalysis and design.

1.6.1. *The data encryption standard*

In the early years of modern round function design, the dominant DES (NIST 1999) was a great source of inspiration. It has a Feistel structure with a round function that splits the (64-bit) plaintext into two equal parts, a *left* half and a *right* half. A function is applied to the right half that returns 32 bits and adds this bitwise to the left half. Then the left and right halves are swapped. This function is called the F-function.

The F-function consists of a number of simple steps. First, it expands the 32 input bits to 48 bits by duplicating half of them. Then it adds a 48-bit *round key* to this by means of bitwise addition. Subsequently, it splits the 48-bit vector into eight equal parts and applies to each a different function that converts 6 bits to 4 bits. These functions are called *S-boxes*. After this *S-box layer*, the 32 bits undergo a *bit shuffle* that permutes their positions. This is often called a (bit) permutation, but it is wise to call it a shuffle, as in symmetric cryptography the term permutation is more widely used with a different meaning.

The DES publication did not include its full design strategy but public cryptanalysis revealed peculiar properties of the components of the F-function. Over the years, the belief grew that the cryptographic strength of DES lies in its S-boxes. In particular, the S-boxes would be there to guarantee the *confusion* by their nonlinearity and *diffusion*, the two terms launched by the legendary Claude Shannon (Shannon 1949).

This belief led to research of (vectorial) Boolean functions with good nonlinearity and mixing properties in order to better understand the security of DES and possibly build better round functions. This research field grew out to a discipline of its own, with many sophisticated mathematical results (see Chapter 8). These were more and more seen as interesting in their own right rather than of actual relevance when building an actual round function. Still, it would give the world almost perfect nonlinear (APN) permutations and the near-APN power function $y = x^{2^8-2}$ over $\mathbb{F}_{2^8}$ (Nyberg 1993) that would become the single nonlinear component of the successor of DES and AES.

1.6.2. *The block cipher FEAL*

DES was really a hardware-oriented cipher not very well suited for efficient implementation in software due to the seemingly chaotic bit shuffle and eight different 6-to-4 bit S-boxes in its F-function. A software-oriented cipher inspired by DES was FEAL (Shimizu and Miyaguchi 1987), one of the first examples of primitives that get their alleged strength from the mixing of two representations and three types of operations. In this approach, the cipher operates on *words* that represent at the same time binary vectors and integers, or more correctly, as elements of $(\mathbb{Z}/2\mathbb{Z})^n$ and $\mathbb{Z}/2^n\mathbb{Z}$. The operations are addition modulo 2^n, rotation or shift and XOR (bitwise addition), and the approach is therefore called ARX (see Chapter 14 of volume 2). These operations interact in a way that is hard to analyze and they are all very efficient in software, provided the word length n matches the CPU word length or is a multiple thereof. In FEAL, the word length was 8, nicely matching the then common CPUs that operated on bytes. Remarkably, ARX ciphers have no S-boxes and lend themselves to much less theoreticizing. One could say that S-box based block ciphers are the favorites of the academic community and ARX primitives of the (free) software community.

1.6.3. *Differential and linear cryptanalysis*

Around 1990, both DES and FEAL were the victim of a true revolution in cryptanalysis. In a few years, time, the basis was laid for the two types of attacks that determine how ciphers are built up to this day: differential (Biham and Shamir 1990) and linear cryptanalysis (Tardy-Corfdir and Gilbert 1991; Matsui 1993). DES, and even more so FEAL, turned out to be surprisingly weak against these types of cryptanalysis and became outdated almost overnight.

1.6.4. *The block cipher* IDEA

As a response to differential cryptanalysis, a new block cipher was proposed called PES (Lai and Massey 1990), and in a slightly modified version, the proposed block cipher is called IDEA (Lai et al. 1991). It took the ARX idea of FEAL further by including multiplication modulo $2^n + 1$ in the operations and extending n from 8 to 16. IDEA has a very elegant description in terms of simple operations. Unlike DES, IDEA is not hardware-oriented as one of these operations, namely the multiplication modulo $2^{16} + 1$, has a high inherent computational cost. However, in software it becomes efficient on many platforms by the presence of instructions to multiply two 16-bit words.

IDEA is not a Feistel cipher but does make use of an involutive structure that partially helps with implementing its decryption, only partially, however, because the multiplications by a subkey in the data path require the computation of multiplicative inverses modulo $2^{16} + 1$ for determining decryption subkeys. IDEA grew to widespread use thanks to its inclusion as default block cipher in the secure email program PGP (Atkins et al. 1996). Still, DES, or rather its fix two-key 3DES (Tuchman 1979), continued to dominate symmetric crypto in industry and banking.

We had to wait for another standard to emerge in the early 21st century to break this dominance: the AES.

1.6.5. *The advanced encryption standard*

AES is a family of three block ciphers, each one with a block length of 16 bytes and key lengths 16, 24 and 32 bytes. These ciphers have a round function very different from both DES and IDEA:

– it does not have the Feistel structure but applies a sequence of steps that each treat the state in a *uniform* way;

– it operates on bytes rather than bits or 16-bit words;

– its round function has four distinct steps:

- an S-box layer with 16 identical 8-bit S-boxes,

- a byte shuffle,

- a round key addition,

- a dedicated *mixlayer*.

The mixlayer was an innovation in comparison with DES or IDEA and involves a so-called MDS mapping, where MDS stands for maximum-distance-separable, a term borrowed from coding theory (MacWilliams and Sloane 1978). An early incarnation of building blocks providing strong mixing were so-called *multipermutations*, as proposed by Schnorr and Vaudenay (1993). The first mixlayer equivalent to an MDS code, namely the extended binary Golay code, was that of the block cipher 3-WAY (Daemen et al. 1993). Follow-up work led to byte-oriented MDS mixlayers in the SHARK ciphers (Rijmen et al. 1996). The MDS mapping of AES appeared first as the mixlayer of our earlier design SQUARE (Daemen et al. 1997).

AES was the result of a public competition and represents a subset of the submission RIJNDAEL (Daemen and Rijmen 2020). RIJNDAEL is a family of 25 block ciphers supporting any combination of block and key lengths between 16 and 32 bytes that are multiples of 4 bytes. As stipulated by the competition organizer NIST (Nechvatal et al. 1999, 2001), the RIJNDAEL submission (Daemen and Rijmen 1998) came with a design rationale. In this rationale, there was a prominent place for resistance against differential and linear cryptanalysis, and the way AES achieves this is called the *wide trail strategy*. In a nutshell, this strategy says that the round function has been designed such that the cipher has no *differential or linear trails* with less than some (high) number of active S-boxes (Daemen 1995). In RIJNDAEL, the smart combination of the mixlayer with the byte shuffle allows an immediate proof that any trail over four rounds must have at least 25 active S-boxes (Daemen and Rijmen 2020). This proof is immediate because each of the step functions operate on bytes rather than bits, that is, that the round function is byte-aligned.

There are of course other attacks and it turns out that this byte-alignment is a double-edged sword. It does enable to prove resistance against basic differential and linear cryptanalysis, but it also introduces properties that allow mounting more specialized attacks such as truncated differentials, integral cryptanalysis and impossible differentials. Still, since its publication in 1998 the full-round versions of RIJNDAEL have withstood cryptanalysis very well, and AES has become one of the most trusted and used cryptographic algorithms in the world.

1.6.6. *Cache attacks*

Despite this, software implementations of AES were under serious attack in the beginning of this century. The attack was not cryptanalysis but a *side-channel* attack, in particular a timing attack. One of the main selling points of RIJNDAEL was its efficient implementation on 32-bit CPUs using table-lookups: one round can be executed in 16 table lookups and 16 bitwise word additions. We believed such table-lookups were constant-time operations but due to the presence of memory cache in quasi all modern CPUs, this is not the case: the lookup time depends on whether the table is in cache memory. This can be exploited to mount a key recovery attack. These attacks were thwarted with so-called table-less implementations such as bit-sliced software (Käsper and Schwabe 2009) and dedicated AES instructions.

1.6.7. KECCAK

In 2007/2008, NIST organized the SHA-3 competition to find a replacement of the SHA-2 standard, and we set out to build a candidate. Robbed of its table-lookup software advantage, the RIJNDAEL approach looked much less attractive. Conversion to bit-sliced software or dedicated hardware revealed the high computational cost, mainly of the S-box.

So, for the SHA-3 competition we turned to an older design thread: that of the PANAMA stream/hash module (Daemen and Clapp 1998). This traces back all the way to the stream/hash module SUBTERRANEAN (Daemen 1995) and the first wide-trail design: a submission to the RIPE hash function competition in 1991, CELLHASH (Daemen et al. 1991b).

Unlike RIJNDAEL, the round functions of these primitives have no alignment to bytes or any other identifiable bit groupings. Like RIJNDAEL, their round function consists of a nonlinear step, a mixlayer and a shuffle, in this case shuffling individual bits. These steps have a high degree of symmetry in the sense that they commute with state translation. To break this symmetry, we added round constants. In the case of the block ciphers in this design thread, 3-WAY or BASEKING, the asymmetry is ensured with the round keys.

All these primitives share the same nonlinear mapping, albeit in different configurations. This mapping has become known as χ (Daemen et al. 1991a; Daemen 1995). It considers the state bits arranged in circles and flips a bit if and only if its two right neighbors exhibit the pattern 01.

With our design team, we took as starting point PANAMA and our first attempt was RADIOGATÚN (Bertoni et al. 2009), an extendable output function (XOF) avant-la-lettre, 8 years before the term was launched (NIST 2015). Meanwhile, we were struggling to have a compact expression of the desired security properties of XOFs. This struggle led to the sponge construction (Bertoni et al. 2007). Instantiated with a random permutation or transformation the sponge construction could take the place of a random oracle as the ideal counterpart of a XOF.

After some analysis of RADIOGATÚN, for our submission to the NIST SHA-3 competition we decided to design a permutation that we would use in a sponge construction (Bertoni et al. 2014). The result of this design effort was the family of KECCAK-f permutations. These permutations do not come with immediate proofs for the lower bounds of its trails. However, with computer assistance very good bounds can be obtained (Mella et al. 2017).

1.6.8. *Lightweight cryptography*

Around the same time as the SHA-3 competition there was a general sentiment that it would be good to have lightweight block ciphers. This sentiment appeared to come mostly from the academic research community, in the search for a challenge. Initially, the focus was on building ciphers that can be implemented in low area, leading to such designs as PRESENT (Bogdanov et al. 2007), PRINTCIPHER (Knudsen et al. 2010) or KATAN and KTANTAN (Cannière et al. 2009). Later this trend also infected hash function design leading to low-area hash functions such as SPONGENT (Bogdanov et al. 2013) and stream ciphers such as GRAIN (Hell et al. 2008) and derived designs that are even smaller such as FRUIT (Aminghafari and Hu 2016). It also led to a new academic research thread: that of MDS mappings taking as few bitwise additions as possible. One could say that this trend replaced the S-box as the center of gravity of a cipher's security by the MDS mapping.

Of course, neither nonlinear layer or mixlayer determines the security of a cipher by itself. It is the smart combination of possibly simple and lightweight nonlinear layer, mixlayer and a shuffle that leads to a good trade-off between security and efficiency. This was already clear from the early 1990s when CELLHASH and SUBTERRANEAN were published and is illustrated by comparisons of hardware implementations of the candidates in the NIST lightweight competition in some previous studies (Aagaard and Zidaric 2021; Khairallah et al. 2020; Mohajerani et al. 2020), where SUBTERRANEAN 2.0 stands out despite its 30-year-old round function. In particular, ciphers that follow the non-aligned flavor of the wide trail design strategy seem to do best with respect to the metrics of energy consumption per bit or speed over resource usage.

1.7. Acknowledgments

I thank Bart Preneel for useful feedback and references.

1.8. References

Aagaard, M.D. and Zidaric, N. (2021). ASIC benchmarking of round 2 candidates in the NIST lightweight cryptography standardization process: (preliminary results). *IACR Cryptol. ePrint Arch.*, 2021, 49.

Aminghafari, V. and Hu, H. (2016). Fruit: Ultra-lightweight stream cipher with shorter internal state. *IACR Cryptol. ePrint Arch.*, 2016, 355.

Atkins, D., Stallings, W., Zimmermann, P. (1996). PGP message exchange formats. *RFC*, 1991, 1–21.

Bellare, M., Canetti, R., Krawczyk, H. (1996). Keying hash functions for message authentication. In *CRYPTO '96*, vol. 1109 of *Lecture Notes in Computer Science*, Koblitz, N. (ed.). Springer.

Bernstein, D.J. (2005). The Poly1305-AES message-authentication code. In *FSE 2005*, vol. 3557 of *Lecture Notes in Computer Science*, Gilbert, H., Handschuh, H. (eds). Springer.

Bernstein, D.J. (2008). The Salsa20 family of stream ciphers. In *New Stream Cipher Designs – The eSTREAM Finalists*, vol. 4986 of *Lecture Notes in Computer Science*, Robshaw, M.J.B., Billet, O. (eds). Springer.

Bertoni, G., Daemen, J., Peeters, M., Van Assche, G. (2006). Radiogatún, a belt-and-mill hash function. *IACR Cryptol. ePrint Arch.*, 2006, 369.

Bertoni, G., Daemen, J., Peeters, M., Van Assche, G. (2007). Sponge functions. *Ecrypt Hash Workshop 2007*, May 24–25, Barcelona, Spain.

Bertoni, G., Daemen, J., Peeters, M., Van Assche, G. (2008). On the indifferentiability of the sponge construction. In *EUROCRYPT 2008*, vol. 4965 of *Lecture Notes in Computer Science*, Smart, N.P. (ed.). Springer.

Bertoni, G., Daemen, J., Peeters, M., Van Assche, G. (2009). The road from Panama to Keccak via RadioGatún. In *Symmetric Cryptography, 11.01. – 16.01.2009*, vol. 09031 of *Dagstuhl Seminar Proceedings*, Handschuh, H., Lucks, S., Preneel, B., Rogaway, P. (eds). Schloss Dagstuhl – Leibniz-Zentrum für Informatik.

Bertoni, G., Daemen, J., Peeters, M., Van Assche, G. (2011a). Cryptographic sponge functions [Online]. Available at: https://keccak.team/files/SpongeFunctions.pdf.

Bertoni, G., Daemen, J., Peeters, M., Van Assche, G. (2011b). Duplexing the sponge: Single-pass authenticated encryption and other applications. In *SAC 2011*, vol. 7118 of *Lecture Notes in Computer Science*, Miri, A., Vaudenay, S. (eds). Springer.

Bertoni, G., Daemen, J., Peeters, M., Van Assche, G. (2014). The making of KECCAK. *Cryptologia*, 38(1), 26–60.

Bierbrauer, J., Johansson, T., Kabatianskii, G., Smeets, B. (1993). On families of hash functions via geometric codes and concatenation. In *CRYPTO '93*, vol. 773 of *Lecture Notes in Computer Science*, Stinson, D.R. (ed.). Springer.

Biham, E. and Shamir, A. (1990). Differential cryptanalysis of DES-like cryptosystems. In *CRYPTO '90*, vol. 537 of *Lecture Notes in Computer Science*, Menezes, A.K., Vanstone, S.A. (eds). Springer.

Biham, E., Anderson, R.J., Knudsen, L.R. (1998). Serpent: A new block cipher proposal. In *FSE '98*, vol. 1372 of *Lecture Notes in Computer Science*, Vaudenay, S. (ed.). Springer.

Biryukov, A. and Wagner, D.A. (1999). Slide attacks. In *FSE '99*, vol. 1636 of *Lecture Notes in Computer Science*, Knudsen, L.R. (ed.). Springer.

Bogdanov, A., Knudsen, L.R., Leander, G., Paar, C., Poschmann, A., Robshaw, M.J.B., Seurin, Y., Vikkelsoe, C. (2007). PRESENT: An ultra-lightweight block cipher. In *CHES 2007*, vol. 4727 of *Lecture Notes in Computer Science*, Paillier, P., Verbauwhede, I. (eds). Springer.

Bogdanov, A., Knezevic, M., Leander, G., Toz, D., Varici, K., Verbauwhede, I. (2013). SPONGENT: The design space of lightweight cryptographic hashing. *IEEE Trans. Computers*, 62(10), 2041–2053.

den Boer, B. (1993). A simple and key-economical unconditional authentication scheme. *J. Comput. Secur.*, 2, 65–72.

den Boer, B. and Bosselaers, A. (1993). Collisions for the compression function of MD5. In *EUROCRYPT '93*, vol. 765 of *Lecture Notes in Computer Science*, Helleseth, T. (ed.). Springer.

Boura, C. and Canteaut, A. (2010). Zero-sum distinguishers for iterated permutations and application to Keccak-*f* and Hamsi-256. In *SAC 2010*, vol. 6544 of *Lecture Notes in Computer Science*, Biryukov, A., Gong, G., Stinson, D.R. (eds). Springer.

Burwick, C., Coppersmith, D., D'Avignon, E., Gennaro, R., Halevi, S., Jutla, C., Matyas, S.M., O'Connor, L., Mohammad, P., Safford, D.R., Zunic, N. (1999). The MARS encryption algorithm. Paper, August 27 [Online]. Available at: https://shaih.github.io/pubs/mars/mars-short.pdf.

Cannière, C.D., Dunkelman, O., Knezevic, M. (2009). KATAN and KTANTAN – A family of small and efficient hardware-oriented block ciphers. In *CHES 2009*, vol. 5747 of *Lecture Notes in Computer Science*, Clavier, C., Gaj, K. (eds). Springer.

Canteaut, A., Duval, S., Leurent, G., Naya-Plasencia, M., Perrin, L., Pornin, T., Schrottenloher, A. (2020). Saturnin: A suite of lightweight symmetric algorithms for post-quantum security. *IACR Trans. Symmetric Cryptol.*, 2020(S1), 160–207.

Claesen, L.J.M., Daemen, J., Genoe, M., Peeters, G. (1993). Subterranean: A 600 mbit/sec cryptographic VLSI chip. In *ICCD '93: VLSI in Computers & Processors*. IEEE Computer Society.

Daemen, J. (1995). Cipher and hash function design, strategies based on linear and differential cryptanalysis. PhD Thesis, K.U.Leuven.

Daemen, J. and Clapp, C.S.K. (1998). Fast hashing and stream encryption with PANAMA. In *FSE '98*, vol. 1372 of *Lecture Notes in Computer Science*, Vaudenay, S. (ed.). Springer.

Daemen, J. and Rijmen, V. (1998). The Rijndael block cipher [Online]. Available at: https://csrc.nist.gov/CSRC/media/Projects/Cryptographic-Standards-and-Guidelines/documents/aes-development/Rijndael-ammended.pdf.

Daemen, J. and Rijmen, V. (2020). *The Design of Rijndael – The Advanced Encryption Standard (AES)*, 2nd edition. Information Security and Cryptography. Springer.

Daemen, J., Govaerts, R., Vandewalle, J. (1991a). Efficient pseudorandom sequence generation by cellular automata. In *Proceedings of the 12th Symposium on Information Theory in the Benelux*. Werkgemeenschap voor Informatie- en Communicatietheorie.

Daemen, J., Govaerts, R., Vandewalle, J. (1991b). A framework for the design of one-way hash functions including cryptanalysis of Damgård's one-way function based on a cellular automaton. In *ASIACRYPT '91*, vol. 739 of *Lecture Notes in Computer Science*, Imai, H., Rivest, R.L., Matsumoto, T. (eds). Springer.

Daemen, J., Govaerts, R., Vandewalle, J. (1993). A new approach to block cipher design. In *FSE '93*, vol. 809 of *Lecture Notes in Computer Science*, Anderson, R.J. (ed.). Springer.

Daemen, J., Knudsen, L.R., Rijmen, V. (1997). The block cipher square. In *FSE '97*, vol. 1267 of *Lecture Notes in Computer Science*, Biham, E. (ed.). Springer.

Daemen, J., Peeters, M., Van Assche, G., Rijmen, V. (2000). Nessie proposal: The block cipher Noekeon. Nessie Submission.

Daemen, J., Massolino, P.M.C., Mehrdad, A., Rotella, Y. (2020). The Subterranean 2.0 cipher suite. *IACR Trans. Symmetric Cryptol.*, 2020(S1), 262–294.

Even, S. and Mansour, Y. (1991). A construction of a cipher from a single pseudorandom permutation. In *ASIACRYPT '91*, vol. 739 of *Lecture Notes in Computer Science*, Imai, H., Rivest, R.L., Matsumoto, T. (eds). Springer.

Halevi, S., Hall, W.E., Jutla, C.S. (2014). The hash function "Fugue". *IACR Cryptol. ePrint Arch.*, 2014, 423.

Handschuh, H. and Preneel, B. (2008). Key-recovery attacks on universal hash function based MAC algorithms. In *CRYPTO 2008*, vol. 5157 of *Lecture Notes in Computer Science*, Wagner, D.A. (ed.). Springer.

Hell, M., Johansson, T., Maximov, A., Meier, W. (2008). The Grain family of stream ciphers. In *New Stream Cipher Designs – The eSTREAM Finalists*, vol. 4986 of *Lecture Notes in Computer Science*, Robshaw, M.J.B., Billet, O. (eds). Springer.

Jean, J., Nikolic, I., Peyrin, T. (2014). Tweaks and keys for block ciphers: The TWEAKEY framework. In *ASIACRYPT 2014, Part II*, vol. 8874 of *Lecture Notes in Computer Science*, Sarkar, P., Iwata, T. (eds). Springer.

Käsper, E. and Schwabe, P. (2009). Faster and timing-attack resistant AES-GCM. In *CHES 2009*, vol. 5747 of *Lecture Notes in Computer Science*, Clavier, C., Gaj, K. (eds). Springer.

Khairallah, M., Peyrin, T., Chattopadhyay, A. (2020). Preliminary hardware benchmarking of a group of round 2 NIST lightweight AEAD candidates. *IACR Cryptol. ePrint Arch.*, 2020, 1459.

Knudsen, L.R., Leander, G., Poschmann, A., Robshaw, M.J.B. (2010). PRINTcipher: A block cipher for IC-printing. In *CHES 2010*, vol. 6225 of *Lecture Notes in Computer Science*, Mangard, S., Standaert, F. (eds). Springer.

Lai, X. and Massey, J.L. (1990). A proposal for a new block encryption standard. In *EUROCRYPT '90*, vol. 473 of *Lecture Notes in Computer Science*, Damgård, I. (ed.). Springer.

Lai, X., Massey, J.L., Murphy, S. (1991). Markov ciphers and differential cryptanalysis. In *EUROCRYPT '91*, vol. 547 of *Lecture Notes in Computer Science*, Davies, D.W. (ed.). Springer.

MacWilliams, F. and Sloane, N. (1978). *The Theory of Error-Correcting Codes*. North-Holland Publishing Company.

Matsui, M. (1993). Linear cryptanalysis method for DES cipher. In *EUROCRYPT '93*, vol. 765 of *Lecture Notes in Computer Science*, Helleseth, T. (ed.). Springer.

McGrew, D.A. and Viega, J. (2004). The security and performance of the Galois/Counter Mode (GCM) of operation. In *INDOCRYPT 2004*, vol. 3348 of *Lecture Notes in Computer Science*, Canteaut, A., Viswanathan, K. (eds). Springer.

Mella, S., Daemen, J., Van Assche, G. (2017). New techniques for trail bounds and application to differential trails in Keccak. *IACR Trans. Symmetric Cryptol.*, 2017(1), 329–357.

Mohajerani, K., Haeussler, R., Nagpal, R., Farahmand, F., Abdulgadir, A., Kaps, J., Gaj, K. (2020). FPGA benchmarking of round 2 candidates in the NIST lightweight cryptography standardization process: Methodology, metrics, tools, and results. *IACR Cryptol. ePrint Arch.*, 2020, 1207.

Nechvatal, J., Barker, E., Dodson, D., Dworkin, M., Foti, J., Roback, E. (1999). Status report on the first round of the development of the advanced encryption standard. *Journal of Research of the National Institute of Standards and Technology*, 104(5), 435–459.

Nechvatal, J., Barker, E., Bassham, L., Burr, W., Dworkin, M., Foti, J., Roback, E. (2001). Report on the development of the advanced encryption standard (AES). *Journal of Research of the National Institute of Standards and Technology*, 106(3), 511–576.

NIST (1995). Federal information processing standard 180-1, Secure Hash Standard.

NIST (1999). Federal information processing standard 46-3, Data Encryption Standard (DES).

NIST (2001). Federal information processing standard 197, Advanced Encryption Standard (AES).

NIST (2002). Federal information processing standard 180-2, Secure Hash Standard.

NIST (2007). NIST special publication 800-38D, recommendation for block cipher modes of operation: Galois/Counter Mode (GCM) and GMAC.

NIST (2008). Federal information processing standard 198, The Keyed-Hash Message Authentication Code (HMAC).

NIST (2015). Federal information processing standard 202, SHA-3 standard: Permutation-based hash and extendable-output functions [Online]. Available at: http://dx.doi.org/10.6028/NIST.FIPS.202.

Nyberg, K. (1993). Differentially uniform mappings for cryptography. In *EUROCRYPT '93*, vol. 765 of *Lecture Notes in Computer Science*, Helleseth, T. (ed.). Springer.

Rijmen, V., Daemen, J., Preneel, B., Bosselaers, A., Win, E.D. (1996). The cipher SHARK. In *FSE '96*, vol. 1039 of *Lecture Notes in Computer Science*, Gollmann, D. (ed.). Springer.

Rivest, R.L. (1992). The MD5 message-digest algorithm. *RFC*, 1321 [Online]. Available at: https://doi.org/10.17487/RFC1321.

Schnorr, C. and Vaudenay, S. (1993). Parallel FFT-hashing. In *FSE '93*, vol. 809 of *Lecture Notes in Computer Science*, Anderson, R.J. (ed.). Springer.

Shannon, C.E. (1949). Communication theory of secrecy systems. *Bell Syst. Tech. J.*, 28(4), 656–715.

Shimizu, A. and Miyaguchi, S. (1987). Fast data encipherment algorithm FEAL. In *EUROCRYPT '87*, vol. 304 of *Lecture Notes in Computer Science*, Chaum, D., Price, W.L. (eds). Springer.

Stevens, M., Bursztein, E., Karpman, P., Albertini, A., Markov, Y. (2017). The first collision for full SHA-1. In *CRYPTO 2017, Part I*, vol. 10401 of *Lecture Notes in Computer Science*, Katz, J., Shacham, H. (eds). Springer.

Stinson, D.R. (1995). On the connections between universal hashing, combinatorial designs and error-correcting codes. *Electron. Colloquium Comput. Complex.*, 2(52) [Online]. Available at: https://dblp.org/rec/journals/eccc/ECCC-TR95-052.html?view=bibtex.

Tardy-Corfdir, A. and Gilbert, H. (1991). A known plaintext attack of FEAL-4 and FEAL-6. In *CRYPTO '91*, vol. 576 of *Lecture Notes in Computer Science*, Feigenbaum, J. (ed.). Springer.

Tuchman, W. (1979). Hellman presents no shortcut solutions to the des. *IEEE Spectrum*, 16, 40–41.

Wang, X. and Yu, H. (2005). How to break MD5 and other hash functions. In *EUROCRYPT 2005*, vol. 3494 of *Lecture Notes in Computer Science*, Cramer, R. (ed.). Springer.

2

The Design of Stream Ciphers

Chaoyun LI and Bart PRENEEL
imec-COSIC, Department of Electrical Engineering (ESAT),
KU Leuven, Belgium

This chapter presents an overview of the design approaches to stream ciphers. It starts with defining the scope and presenting generic constructions as well as attacks based on these constructions. Next, it presents an overview of stream cipher competitions and standards. The largest class of stream ciphers is based on feedback shift registers (FSRs): this part distinguishes linear and nonlinear FSRs. Subsequently, software-oriented constructions based on large tables are discussed. Stream ciphers that are constructed based on block ciphers and large permutations are presented. The chapter concludes with a discussion on authenticated encryption (AE) based on stream ciphers and with a treatment of low-complexity stream ciphers that are optimized for use in advanced cryptographic protocols.

2.1. Introduction

This chapter discusses the design principles of modern stream ciphers. The scope is restricted to *synchronous additive* stream ciphers, which are the only ones that are widely deployed. For simplicity, if the term stream cipher is used without any additional qualification, this refers to a synchronous additive stream cipher.

2.1.1. *What is a synchronous additive stream cipher?*

Synchronous additive stream ciphers provide data confidentiality between two users who share a common secret key K. Stream cipher designs are inspired by the *one-time pad*: in this scheme, plaintext P, ciphertext C and the key K are strings of the same length over a finite additive group. The ith ciphertext C_i is obtained from the ith plaintext P_i by adding the ith element of the secret key K_i using an additive group operation $+$ (the most common case is bitwise XOR or addition modulo 2): $C_i = P_i + K_i$; the decryption formula is $P_i = C_i - K_i$, where "$-$" denotes group subtraction (for bitwise XOR subtraction is equal to addition). Shannon (1949) proved that the one-time pad offers *perfect secrecy*, that is, the ciphertext does not provide any additional information on the plaintext, because ciphertext and plaintext are statistically independent. This property holds even for opponents with unlimited computational power, which is rare in cryptography. As indicated by the name, it is essential that each key element K_i is used only once: otherwise, we obtain the equations $C_i = P_i + K_i$ and $C_j = P_j + K_i$; subtracting both equations yields $C_i - C_j = P_i - P_j$, which leaks the difference between the plaintexts. This is known as "transmission in depth". The US Venona project[1] exploited the reuse of one-time pads by the Soviet Union in the 1940s.

Unfortunately, the one-time pad is not suitable for most applications since it requires a key that is at least as long as the plaintext. The idea is to stretch a short key K (say of 128 or 256 bits) to a much longer sequence κ that can subsequently be used for encryption; this sequence is called a keystream. For an opponent with limited computational power, this keystream seems random, which is why it is called a pseudo-random sequence. A generator that stretches a short key to a pseudo-random keystream is known as a *pseudo-random bit generator* (PRBG).

In practice, it is preferable to encrypt multiple packets or files with the same key. To avoid key reuse and to make these encryptions independent, an additional public parameter is introduced in the PRBG input, called the initialization vector IV. The IV is typically derived from the communication protocol (e.g. the frame counter) or from the filename in the case of file encryption. The receiver should know which IV value and which part of the keystream to use for a particular part of the ciphertext, which requires that sender and receiver are fully synchronized. The corresponding cryptographic primitive is called a *tweakable PRBG* or a synchronous additive stream cipher. In order to avoid "transmission in depth", it is essential for the security that the value of IV never repeats for the same value of K.

An important motivation to use additive synchronous stream ciphers is the *lack of error propagation* during transmission or storage: a single bit error in the ciphertext will only result in a single bit error in the plaintext. This makes stream ciphers the default solution for encryption at lower layers in wireless communications. This property was also important when plaintexts and ciphertexts were entered manually

---

1 Available at: https://en.wikipedia.org/wiki/Venona_project.

character by character in an encryption, respectively, decryption device resulting in frequent errors.

In contrast to block ciphers, stream ciphers operate on *small chunks* of plaintext, typically bits or words of 5–16 bits. This constraint was driven by the limitation of mechanical rotor machines and early hardware. Some recent stream ciphers operate on larger words in order to take advantage of the larger word lengths of modern processors.

A final characteristic of dedicated stream ciphers is that they tend to be *simpler* than block ciphers: block ciphers iterate a simple round function multiple times (8–32 is typical), which means they perform hundreds of operations before outputting 64 or 128 bits; stream ciphers only perform a few operations on a larger state before outputting one or a few bits. This results in a simpler implementation and a higher throughput per area than most block ciphers. This last distinction is not strict: low area block ciphers such as KATAN (Cannière et al. 2009) have a very simple round function similar to a stream cipher, and section 2.4 shows how larger primitives such as block ciphers and large permutations can be turned into efficient stream ciphers.

Section 2.5 explains how synchronous stream ciphers can be extended to offer AE or authenticated encryption with associated data (AEAD).

Note that *self-synchronizing* stream ciphers are not treated in this chapter: in these ciphers, the keystream is computed based on past ciphertexts and the secret key. This approach was useful for encryption at lower layers when complete chunks of the ciphertext could be lost, since self-synchronizing stream ciphers allow for automated recovery after such a loss. Today, loss of part of the ciphertext is typically dealt with by the communication protocol. The design of self-synchronizing stream ciphers turns out to be more difficult since a chosen ciphertext attack gives an attacker control over the internal state.

2.1.2. *Generic construction*

Most stream ciphers are *iterated* stream ciphers that can be modeled by a finite state machine. Such a stream cipher is characterized by three parameters that are typically measured in bits: the key length k, the IV length r and the size of the internal state S denoted by m.

An iterated stream cipher consists of three functions: (i) an initialization function f_I that expands a key K and an initial value IV into an initial internal state S; (ii) a state update function f_U that updates the state S, (iii) an output function f_O that takes the state S and produces an output κ_i, $1 \leq i \leq t$. The state update and output function may depend on the key K; they are iterated t times until the length of the concatenation of all the outputs κ_i is as least as long as the plaintext.

A pseudo-random function (PRF) family is a family of functions indexed by a key that is computationally indistinguishable from a randomly chosen function; in a PRF, the output size is typically equal to a small constant times the input size. Berbain and Gilbert (2007) show that the composition of a PRF that processes the key K and the initialization vector IV to obtain the initial state S with a PRBG that stretches a short key to a longer sequence yields a tweakable PRBG. In spite of this result, many stream ciphers use a very simple initialization function f_I, which has resulted in serious weaknesses.

For most stream ciphers, the state is updated in a serial way; some designs use a tree structure that allows for parallelism (see Goldreich et al. 1986).

2.1.3. *Generic attacks*

The security of a stream cipher requires defining an attacker model. It will be assumed that we are dealing with a tweakable PRBG.

First, we consider the *power* of an attacker. The weakest attacker has access only to the ciphertext, combined with some statistical information on the plaintext. In practice, we mostly assume that an attacker knows the plaintext and one or more IVs. A more powerful attacker knows the plaintext and can also choose the IVs. Typically, an upper bound is placed on the number of IVs and number of keystream bits the opponent has access to.

Second, we consider the *goal* of the attacker. The weakest goal is distinguishing the keystream from a random string: this shows that the tweakable PRBG does not achieve its design goal and results in leakage of plaintext information. A more powerful attack goal is for an attacker with known plaintext to obtain additional plaintext or to recover the key; the latter allows to recover the full plaintext. Note that one excludes a trivial attacker who recovers additional plaintext through IV reuse.

While distinguishers under chosen IV may seem to be of academic interest, attacks only get better: frequently distinguishers are the first step toward state and/or key recovery attacks. It is common to assume very strong attacker models to keep some security margin against more realistic attacks for the future.

There are several attacks that apply to any stream cipher; these attacks assume that the functions f_I, f_U and f_O are ideal. Attacks are characterized by the precomputation time P, the (on-line) time T, the memory M and the available known plaintext D (that also corresponds to known keystream). The unit of time is approximately the time for one initialization and the production of k keystream bits. The memory M and keystream D are measured in the size of the internal state (or sometimes the key size).

A first attack is *exhaustive key search*. This is a known plaintext attack that makes no assumptions on the internal structure of the stream cipher. This attack requires

$D = M = 1$ has expected cost $T = 2^{k-1}$ (note that $P = 0$). In 2021, $k = 80$ offers only limited protection; security for 15 years or more requires a 128-bit key. If one considers Grover's quantum search algorithm (Grover 1996), a key of at least 256 bits is needed for long-term security.

If one wants to recover multiple keys, the cost per key can be reduced. A precomputation attack requires $P = M = 2^k$ and recovers each key in time $T = 1$. With Hellman's time-memory tradeoff (Hellman 1980), one can obtain more attractive results: $P = 2^k$, $M = 2^{2k/3}$ and $T = 2^{2k/3}$ or variants with $T \cdot M^2 = 2^{2k}$.

An alternative attack applies to iterated stream ciphers for which the state update function f_U and the output function f_O do *not* depend on the secret key K. In this case, the tradeoff proposed by Babbage and Golic recovers the internal state with $D \approx T$ and $P = M$ in time T and with memory M if $T \cdot M = 2^m$. Biryukov and Shamir (2000) have extended this tradeoff to

$$T \cdot M^2 \cdot D^2 = 2^{2m} \text{ with } D^2 \leq T \leq 2^k \text{ and } P \cdot D = 2^m. \qquad [2.1]$$

One can also consider a setting in which an opponent wants to recover only one of t keys; an example is a broadcast application where the same session key is sent encrypted under t master keys. In this case, the cost of exhaustive key search is reduced to $2^k/(t+1)$. Biryukov et al. (2005) showed that in this case a similar tradeoff as in equation [2.1] is available with D replaced by t and m by k.

As a result of these tradeoffs, one should carefully choose the parameters to preclude generic attacks. One can put limitations on the number of plaintexts and initial values. If f_U and f_O do not depend on K, one should ensure $m \geq 2k$. If one chooses large enough random initial values, some of the precomputations become too expensive and the key size may be reduced. For more details, see Lano (2006).

2.1.4. *Open competitions*

During the last two decades, open competitions have played a central role in progressing research on stream ciphers. The EU NESSIE project (2000–2004) focused on a broad set of primitives and received several innovative stream cipher designs, but concluded that none of them was suitable.

The eSTREAM competition (2004–2008) was part of the ECRYPT Network of Excellence (Robshaw and Billet 2008). eSTREAM focused on stream ciphers only and searched for two profiles: the target of profile 1 was high throughput in software and the parameters were $k = 128$, and $r = 64$ or 128, while profile 2 was tuned toward low resource hardware and required $k = 80$ and $r = 32$ or 64. Adding data authentication was optional. The final portfolio contained four algorithms for each profile. Profile 1 consists of HC-128, RABBIT, SALSA20/12 and SOSEMANUK, and Profile 2 contains F-FCSR-H V2, GRAIN V1, MICKEY V2 and TRIVIUM; F-FCSR-H V2 was broken shortly after the portfolio was published.

The Competition for Authenticated Encryption: security, Applicability and Robustness (CAESAR) ran from 2013 to 2019 (CAESAR 2014). Its main goal was to improve over the AEAD block cipher modes GCM (McGrew and Viega 2004) and CCM (Whiting et al. 2003). The stream ciphers ACORN and AEGIS in the final portfolio are described in section 2.5.

In August 2018, NIST initiated a process to evaluate and standardize lightweight cryptographic algorithms that are suitable for use in constrained environments where the performance of current NIST cryptographic standards is not acceptable. The submissions should propose an algorithm, or a collection of algorithms, that implements the AEAD functionality; hence they go beyond synchronous stream ciphers by providing also data authentication (see section 2.5). In May 2021, 10 finalists were selected for the third round; they include the stream ciphers ASCON, ELEPHANT, ISAP, GRAIN-128-AEAD, TINYJAMBU and XOODYAK. More details can be found in Chapter 16 of volume 2 and in NIST Lightweight Cryptography Standardization (2019).

2.1.5. *Standards*

ISO/IEC JTC1 has published three stream cipher standards: ISO/IEC 18033-4: 2011 (ISO/IEC 2011) contains MUGI, SNOW 2.0, RABBIT, DECIM^{V2} and KCIPHER-2 (K2). ISO/IEC 29192-3:2012 (ISO/IEC 2012) specifies two lightweight stream ciphers, namely ENOCORO and TRIVIUM. Not all these ciphers were selected based on an open competition. ISO/IEC 29167-13 (ISO/IEC 2015) standardizes GRAIN-128A for RFID applications.

ETSI SAGE has standardized several stream ciphers for mobile communications. A5/1, A5/2 (Briceno et al. 1999) and A5/3 were designed for GSM; A5/2 was a deliberately weakened version for export; A5/3 is a block cipher in a special mode (ETSI/SAGE Specification TS 135 201 2001). For GPRS (packet data in 2G and 3G), the GEA-1 and GEA-2 stream ciphers were defined. These secret algorithms with 64-bit keys became public recently and were shown to offer only 40-bit (respectively, 45-bit) security (Beierle et al. 2021). For 3G, two AE schemes were proposed based on the stream ciphers SNOW 3G (ETSI/SAGE Specification 2006) and ZUC-128 (ETSI/SAGE Specification 2011). For 5G, extensions to 256-bit security are being developed called SNOW-V (Ekdahl et al. 2019) and ZUC-256 (Team 2015). More details are provided in section 2.2.

Bluetooth has standardized the E0 stream cipher (*Bluetooth Specification: version 1.2* (Bluetooth 2003)).

2.2. Constructions based on FSRs

Feedback shift registers (FSRs) are widely exploited in the design of stream ciphers. A natural stream cipher design considers the internal state as one or more shift registers that are updated at every clock cycle. We briefly recall the basics and then introduce two classes of constructions based on linear feedback shift registers (LFSRs) and nonlinear feedback shift registers (NFSRs), respectively.

Let f be an n-variable Boolean function. For an initial state $(a_0, \cdots, a_{n-1}) \in \mathbb{F}_2^n$, an n-stage FSR with feedback function f generates a binary *output sequence* $(a_0, a_1, a_2, \ldots)$ satisfying

$$a_{i+n} = f(a_i, a_{i+1}, \ldots, a_{i+n-1}) \quad \text{for} \quad i = 0, 1, 2, \ldots.$$

An n-stage FSR is illustrated in Figure 2.1.

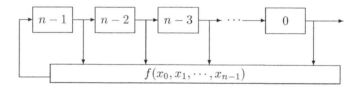

Figure 2.1. *An n-stage FSR*

The FSR is called an LFSR if f is a linear function, otherwise it is called an NFSR.

The periods and statistical properties of the LFSR sequences have been investigated for over 50 years (Selmer 1966; Golomb 1967). In contrast, not much is known about the periods and randomness properties of NFSR sequences. FSRs are common building blocks for stream ciphers since they can be implemented efficiently in both hardware and software. LFSRs can also be defined over any finite field $\mathbb{F}_q$ (Lidl and Niederreiter 1997).

2.2.1. *LFSR-based constructions*

LFSRs have been employed in stream cipher designs since the 1960s. While it is fine to use an LFSR as the state update function f_U, an LFSR needs to be combined with a nonlinear element to avoid trivial attacks. There are three main types of

LFSR-based stream ciphers (Menezes et al. 1996). The *filter generator* uses a long LFSR and employs a nonlinear filtering function f_O to generate keystream bits while the *combination generator* exploits several short LFSRs and uses a combining function f_O to generate keystream bits. The filtering or combining functions are designed to hide the linear weakness in the LFSR(s): various cryptanalytic results have led to the study of properties of Boolean functions, such as resilience, nonlinearity and algebraic immunity (Carlet 2010). SFINKS is a stream cipher based on a filter generator, which is dedicated to restricted hardware environments (Braeken et al. 2005). The GPRS algorithms GEA-1 and GEA-2 are combination generators (Beierle et al. 2021). The third type is to control the LFSRs by irregular clocks. A5/1 and A5/2 (Briceno et al. 1999) are two *irregular clocked* stream ciphers designed for GSM; as mentioned above, A5/2 was deliberately weakened, similar to GEA-1 and GEA-2. The shrinking (Coppersmith et al. 1993) and self-shrinking generators (Meier and Staffelbach 1994) are two simple and elegant irregular clocked generators.

Since the simple filter and combination generators are vulnerable to fast correlation attacks (Meier and Staffelbach 1989) and algebraic attacks (Courtois and Meier 2003), the stateless filtering/combing functions have been replaced by functions with memory (Rueppel 1986). A failed design is Bluetooth E0, which combined four LFSRs with a nonlinear memory (*Bluetooth Specification: version 1.2* (Bluetooth 2003)). More secure examples include the 3GPP standards SNOW 3G (ETSI/SAGE Specification 2006) and ZUC-128 (ETSI/SAGE Specification 2011). Both exploit finite state machines to filter the word-wise LFSRs, resulting in very fast software implementations. Recently, SNOW 3G and ZUC-128 have been updated to new versions SNOW-V (Ekdahl et al. 2019) and ZUC-256 (Team 2015), respectively, which have increased 256-bit keys and are suitable for 5G applications.

2.2.2. *NFSR-based constructions*

Despite the lack of theoretical foundation, NFSRs have been major components in the design of new stream ciphers, especially for hardware-oriented designs. As the state update function f_U is nonlinear, a simpler output function f_O can be used. Two representative ciphers in this category are the eSTREAM portfolio ciphers TRIVIUM (De Cannière and Preneel 2008) and the GRAIN family (Hell et al. n.d.).

TRIVIUM has a state consisting of 288-bit registers. At each round, the content of three registers is updated by applying three functions to the previous state bits, respectively, where each of the functions can be represented by three XOR gates and a single AND. The other state bits are updated by simply shifting the whole state one position. Then one keystream bit is produced by XORing six state bits. Remarkably, TRIVIUM uses extremely sparse update functions, which can be implemented with only 3 AND gates and 11 XOR gates.

GRAIN employs a hybrid structure by cascading an LFSR with an NFSR of equal length. At each clock cycle, the feedback bit of the NFSR is XORed with the output of the LFSR. The keystream bit is filtered by applying a sparse nonlinear Boolean function to the whole state. Similar to TRIVIUM, GRAIN has very efficient implementations in both hardware and software. Moreover, their structures also allow tradeoffs between throughput and area by exploiting internal parallelism.

Most stream ciphers, including TRIVIUM and GRAIN, require a large state size due to time/memory/data tradeoff attacks (see section 2.1.3). These tradeoffs can be avoided in so-called *small-state stream ciphers* by introducing a dependence on the key K in the state update function f_U. The stream cipher SPROUT (Armknecht and Mikhalev 2015), inspired by GRAIN, is of this type: its inner state size is less than twice the key size. This has inspired other designs (see, for example, Hamann et al. 2018).

2.3. Table-based constructions

In the late 1980s, software-oriented stream ciphers emerged: in software sufficient memory is available for a larger state and the update of the state uses simple processor instructions rather than FSRs.

The first known example is RC4 (Rivest 1992) with a 256-byte internal state. Lookup table operations are used in the initialization, state update and output function. Due to its remarkable simplicity and speed in software, RC4 has been widely used in cryptographic protocols such as SSL/TLS and WEP. Unfortunately, RC4 has serious statistical flaws. Moreover, RC4 is a PRBG and not a tweakable PRBG: no IV is defined. The designers of WEP inserted the public IV (under control of the attacker) in the entrance; this has resulted in key recovery attacks on WEP (Fluhrer et al. 2001).

There is very limited theory underlying the design or cryptanalysis of table-based stream ciphers. The recent designs include the software-oriented eSTREAM portfolio ciphers HC-128 (Wu 2008) and its extension HC-256 (Wu 2004). SPRITZ, a new variant of RC4 proposed in 2014, has a sponge-like construction (see section 2.4) and provides various cryptographic capabilities (Rivest and Schuldt 2016).

2.4. Block ciphers and permutations in stream cipher mode

The maturity of the theory of block ciphers and the emergence of low-cost block ciphers has inspired researchers to design stream ciphers from block ciphers. In 2007, research was started to redefine symmetric cryptology based on the simplest possible object: a fixed input size cryptographic permutation; this has inspired several new designs.

2.4.1. *Block cipher modes OFB and CTR*

As depicted in Figures 2.2 and 2.3, block ciphers can be used as keystream generators in output feedback (OFB) and CounTeR (CTR) modes, respectively. In both modes, the initialization function f_I sets the state equal to the IV. In OFB mode, the state update function f_U is the block cipher encryption and the output function f_O is the identity. In CTR mode, the state update function f_U is a simple counter, and the output function f_O is a block cipher encryption. The CTR mode has the advantage that it allows for parallel operation. The 3GPP standard uses the block cipher KASUMI in a combination of OFB and CTR mode called f8 (ETSI/SAGE Specification TS 135 201 2001).

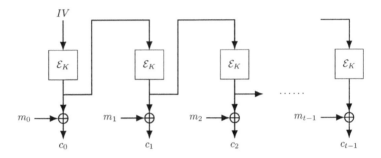

Figure 2.2. *OFB mode*

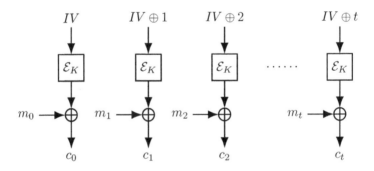

Figure 2.3. *Counter mode*

2.4.2. *Permutations in stream cipher mode*

The last decade has witnessed the rise of permutation-based cryptography: the idea is to build symmetric cryptography based on a fixed large permutation (input size $256 \ldots 1600$ bits), rather than on a block cipher. The most successful example is the SHA-3 competition winner KECCAK (Bertoni et al. 2011), which instantiates the sponge construction introduced in Bertoni et al. (2007).

To construct stream ciphers from a fixed permutation, the simplest approach is to create a variant of the counter mode where the input to a cryptographic permutation is the key K, the IV and a counter. Notable designs in this category are the SALSA and CHACHA families of stream ciphers (Bernstein 2008a,b). The other approach is to use the sponge construction in stream encryption mode, which is shown in Figure 2.4.

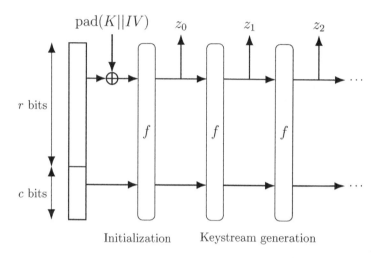

Figure 2.4. *Sponge in stream cipher mode*

2.5. Authenticated encryption (AE)

AE algorithms are symmetric cryptographic primitives that simultaneously ensure confidentiality and data authentication. Most existing AE schemes also allow to authenticate a public string, the associated data, along with the message and are called schemes for AE with associated data (AEAD) (Rogaway 2002). This section briefly summarizes the stream ciphers and related modes in AE designs.

The central problem of constructing AE based on stream ciphers and related modes is to integrate the authentication functionality into the encryption algorithm. One strategy is to combine a stream cipher with a MAC algorithm. In contrast, dedicated AE schemes use a single primitive which can be a stream cipher, a block cipher in stream cipher mode, or a permutation in a stream cipher mode.

The first approach is to combine a stream cipher with a MAC algorithm. A prominent example is the combination of the 3GPP confidentiality and integrity algorithms UEA2 & UIA2, which are based on SNOW 3G (ETSI/SAGE Specification 2006). The encryption algorithm UEA2 corresponds to SNOW 3G. UIA2 employs GMAC with a different key K and IV than for UEA2. For each packet, a new key is generated using SNOW 3G; the security is improved in comparison to AES-GCM (McGrew and Viega 2004), since UEA2 does not reuse part of the GMAC key material. Another examples are the 3GPP algorithms 128-EEA3 & 128-EIA3, which are based on ZUC-128 (ETSI/SAGE Specification 2011).

The second approach is to divide the keystream into two parts: one part for encryption and the other part for authentication. Typical ciphers in this category are GRAIN-128A (Ågren et al. 2011) and its new version GRAIN-128AEAD (Hell et al. 2021), which is a finalist in NIST-LWC competition. In GRAIN-128A and GRAIN-128-AEAD, for every two consecutive keystream bits, one bit is output for encryption, whereas the other bit is accumulated by a MAC algorithm for authentication. Compared to the first approach, this design has the advantage that encryption and data authentication are performed simultaneously, that is, it requires only one implementation of the stream cipher and a single $K/$IV pair.

The CAESAR portfolio contains the dedicated AE scheme ACORN (Wu 2016). Similar to GRAIN-128AEAD, the encryption and authentication are conducted by one primitive and a single $K/$IV pair. However, the authentication tag is computed by running the keystream generation after completing the message encryption. Compared to other dedicated AE algorithms, plaintext and keystream bits are not used to update the state during the encryption process. While SNOW 3G and ZUC-128 are efficient in software, ACORN exhibits excellent hardware performance and it is suitable for resource constrained environments.

AEGIS (Wu and Preneel 2013), another CAESAR competition winner, is a dedicated AE scheme based on AES round functions. Inspired by the stream cipher PHELIX (Whiting et al. 2005), at each step of the encryption, a 16-byte plaintext is encrypted with a 16-byte keystream and is also used to update the state of the cipher. Hence, message authentication can be achieved almost for free. AEGIS is very fast, and is suitable for high-performance applications such as network communications.

2.5.1. *Block ciphers and permutations in stream cipher modes*

The *Encrypt-then-MAC (EtM)* construction for AE, that is, applying a MAC algorithm to the ciphertext to obtain the tag, is the preferred option in terms of security and performance. In Bellare and Namprempre (2000), it is demonstrated that this composition is secure provided that the two component schemes are secure. AES-GCM (McGrew and Viega 2004) follows the EtM paradigm by combining a block cipher (e.g. AES) in counter mode with a Wegman-Carter MAC algorithm (Wegman and Carter 1981) (see Chapter 5). Two of the NIST-LWC finalists, ELEPHANT (Beyne et al. 2021) and ISAP (Dobraunig et al. 2021), are nonce-based EtM constructions, where the encryption is performed using permutations in stream cipher mode and message authentication using a MAC algorithm.

Ciphers	Construction	Primitive	Refs.
UEA2 & UIA2	Stream cipher & MAC algo.	SNOW 3G	(ETSI/SAGE Specification 2006)
128-EEA3 & 128-EIA3	Stream cipher & MAC algo.	ZUC-128	(ETSI/SAGE Specification 2011)
Grain-128A	Stream cipher & MAC algo.	GRAIN-128	(Ågren et al. 2011; Hell et al. 2021)
Grain-128AEAD	Dedicated AEAD	FSRs	(Wu 2016)
ACORN AEGIS	Dedicated AEAD	AES round	(Wu and Preneel 2013)

Table 2.1. *AE schemes based on stream ciphers*

Duplex constructions are closely related to the sponge construction. The duplex construction allows the alternation of input and output blocks at the same rate as the sponge construction without losing security. This allows implementing a stream cipher and an AE scheme with only one call to the permutation per input block. Several duplex constructions have been proposed including the NIST-LWC finalists ASCON (Dobraunig et al. 2016), TINYJAMBU (Wu and Huang 2021) and XOODYAK (Daemen et al. 2021).

2.6. Emerging low-complexity stream ciphers

Symmetric cryptographic primitives have been mainly employed to provide confidentiality and authenticity for communicated and stored data (Shannon 1949). Recently, they find new applications in advanced cryptographic protocols for computing on encrypted data, such as secure multi-party computation (MPC), zero-knowledge proofs (ZK) and fully homomorphic encryption (FHE). The adoption of dedicated symmetric key primitives turns out to be vital to improve the efficiency of these protocols. The main design goal is to minimize the multiplicative complexity (MC), that is, minimize the number of multiplications in a circuit and/or to minimize the multiplicative depth of the circuit. However, traditional block ciphers, stream ciphers and hash functions are typically not designed to minimize these parameters; on the contrary, having high multiplicative depth is seen as an important requirement to achieve strong security.

The block cipher LOWMC (Albrecht et al. 2015) is one of the earliest designs dedicated to FHE and MPC applications; it outperforms AES-128 in computation and communication complexity for these applications. However, due to its iterative structure, achieving low AND-depth seems challenging for LOWMC-like block ciphers.

FSR-based stream ciphers seem to be natural choices for low AND-depth primitives due to the lower algebraic degree of their outputs. Indeed, TRIVIUM turns out to have low MC, though it is inspired by other use cases. KREYVIUM (Canteaut et al. 2016), a variant of TRIVIUM with 128-bit key, further optimizes AND-related metrics for efficient homomorphic-ciphertext compression.

FLIP (Méaux et al. 2016) has been designed for efficient FHE with low-noise ciphertexts. This primitive generates a keystream by updating a key register by wire-cross permutations only, followed by applying a Boolean filtering function to the register. In this way, the AND-depth of the circuit can be as low as 4 at the cost of a large number of AND gates per bit.

RASTA (Dobraunig et al. 2018) intends to achieve both minimum AND-depth and minimum number of AND gates per encrypted bit. To produce the keystream, it applies a permutation with feed-forward to the key. The permutation adopts a new ASASA-like construction, where the substitution layer (S) is public and fixed, but the affine layers (A) are derived from a public nonce and a counter.

To sum up, there are some noticeable features of the low-complexity stream ciphers:

– the state update functions f_U are quadratic and extremely sparse; in the binary case, there can be only a single AND gate;

– a large number of rounds and/or a large state compared to traditional designs.

2.7. References

Ågren, M., Hell, M., Johansson, T., Meier, W. (2011). Grain-128a: A new version of Grain-128 with optional authentication. *IJWMC*, 5(1), 48–59.

Albrecht, M.R., Rechberger, C., Schneider, T., Tiessen, T., Zohner, M. (2015). Ciphers for MPC and FHE. In *EUROCRYPT 2015, Part I*, vol. 9056 of *Lecture Notes in Computer Science*, Oswald, E., Fischlin, M. (eds). Springer.

Armknecht, F. and Mikhalev, V. (2015). On lightweight stream ciphers with shorter internal states. In *FSE 2015*, vol. 9054 of *Lecture Notes in Computer Science*, Leander, G. (ed.). Springer.

Beierle, C., Derbez, P., Leander, G., Leurent, G., Raddum, H., Rotella, Y., Rupprecht, D., Stennes, L. (2021). Cryptanalysis of the GPRS encryption algorithms GEA-1 and GEA-2. In *EUROCRYPT 2021, Part II*, vol. 12697 of *Lecture Notes in Computer Science*, Canteaut, A., Standaert, F. (eds). Springer.

Bellare, M. and Namprempre, C. (2000). Authenticated encryption: Relations among notions and analysis of the generic composition paradigm. In *ASIACRYPT 2000*, vol. 1976 of *Lecture Notes in Computer Science*, Okamoto, T. (ed.). Springer.

Berbain, C. and Gilbert, H. (2007). On the security of IV dependent stream ciphers. In *FSE 2007*, vol. 4593 of *Lecture Notes in Computer Science*, Biryukov, A. (ed.). Springer.

Bernstein, D.J. (2008a). ChaCha, a variant of Salsa20 [Online]. Available at: http://cr.yp.to/chacha/chacha-20080128.pdf.

Bernstein, D.J. (2008b). The Salsa20 family of stream ciphers. In *New Stream Cipher Designs – The eSTREAM Finalists*, vol. 4986 of *Lecture Notes in Computer Science*, Robshaw, M.J.B., Billet, O. (eds). Springer.

Bertoni, G., Daemen, J., Peeters, M., Van Assche, G. (2007). Sponge functions. *ECRYPT Hash Workshop*, May 24-25, Barcelona, Spain.

Bertoni, G., Daemen, J., Peeters, M., Van Assche, G. (2011). The KECCAK reference version 3.0 [Online]. Available at: https://keccak.team/files/Keccak-reference-3.0.pdf.

Beyne, T., Chen, Y.L., Dobraunig, C., Mennink, B. (2021). Elephant v2 [Online]. Available at: https://csrc.nist.gov/Projects/lightweight-cryptography/finalists.

Biryukov, A. and Shamir, A. (2000). Cryptanalytic time/memory/data tradeoffs for stream ciphers. In *ASIACRYPT 2000*, vol. 1976 of *Lecture Notes in Computer Science*, Okamoto, T. (ed.). Springer.

Biryukov, A., Mukhopadhyay, S., Sarkar, P. (2005). Improved time-memory trade-offs with multiple data. In *SAC 2005*, vol. 3897 of *Lecture Notes in Computer Science*, Preneel, B., Tavares, S.E. (eds). Springer.

Bluetooth (2003). Bluetooth Specification: version 1.2 [Online]. Available at: http://www.bluetooth.org.

Braeken, A., Lano, J., Mentens, N., Preneel, B., Verbauwhede, I. (2005). SFINKS: A synchronous stream cipher for restricted hardware environments. Submission to ECRYPT Stream Cipher Project [Online]. Available at: http://www.ecrypt.eu.org/stream/sfinks.html.

Briceno, M., Goldberg, I., Wagner, D. (1999). A pedagogical implementation of the GSM A5/1 and A5/2 "voice privacy" encryption algorithms [Online]. Available at: http://cryptome.org/gsm-a512.htm.

CAESAR (2014). CAESAR: Competition for Authenticated Encryption: Security, Applicability, and Robustness [Online]. Available at: https://competitions.cr.yp.to/caesar.html.

Cannière, C.D., Dunkelman, O., Knezevic, M. (2009). KATAN and KTANTAN – A family of small and efficient hardware-oriented block ciphers. In *CHES 2009*, vol. 5747 of *Lecture Notes in Computer Science*, Clavier, C., Gaj, K. (eds). Springer.

Canteaut, A., Carpov, S., Fontaine, C., Lepoint, T., Naya-Plasencia, M., Paillier, P., Sirdey, R. (2016). Stream ciphers: A practical solution for efficient homomorphic-ciphertext compression. In *FSE 2016*, vol. 9783 of *Lecture Notes in Computer Science*, Peyrin, T. (ed.). Springer.

Carlet, C. (2010). Boolean functions for cryptography and error correcting codes. In *Boolean Models and Methods in Mathematics, Computer Science, and Engineeringd*, Crama, Y., Hammer, P.L. (eds). Cambridge University Press.

Coppersmith, D., Krawczyk, H., Mansour, Y. (1993). The shrinking generator. In *CRYPTO '93*, vol. 773 of *Lecture Notes in Computer Science*, Stinson, D.R. (ed.). Springer.

Courtois, N.T. and Meier, W. (2003). Algebraic attacks on stream ciphers with linear feedback. In *EUROCRYPT 2003*, vol. 2656 of *Lecture Notes in Computer Science*, Biham, E. (ed.). Springer.

Daemen, J., Hoffert, S., Peeters, M., Van Assche, G., Keer, R.V., Mella, S. (2021). XOODYAK, a lightweight cryptographic scheme [Online]. Available at: https://csrc.nist.gov/Projects/lightweight-cryptography/finalists.

De Cannière, C. and Preneel, B. (2008). Trivium. In *New Stream Cipher Designs – The eSTREAM Finalists*, vol. 4986 of *Lecture Notes in Computer Science*, Robshaw, M., Billet, O. (eds). Springer.

Dobraunig, C., Eichlseder, M., Mendel, F., Schläffer, M. (2016). Ascon v1.2. Submission to Round 3 of the CAESAR competition [Online]. Available at: https://competitions.cr.yp.to/round3/asconv12.pdf.

Dobraunig, C., Eichlseder, M., Grassi, L., Lallemand, V., Leander, G., List, E., Mendel, F., Rechberger, C. (2018). RASTA: A cipher with low AND-depth and few ANDs per bit. In *CRYPTO 2018, Part I*, vol. 10991 of *Lecture Notes in Computer Science*, Shacham, H., Boldyreva, A. (eds). Springer.

Dobraunig, C., Eichlseder, M., Mangard, S., Mendel, F., Mennink, B., Primas, R., Unterluggauer, T. (2021). ISAP [Online]. Available at: https://csrc.nist.gov/Projects/lightweight-cryptography/finalists.

Ekdahl, P., Johansson, T., Maximov, A., Yang, J. (2019). A new SNOW stream cipher called SNOW-V. *IACR Trans. Symmetric Cryptol.*, 2019(3), 1–42.

ETSI/SAGE Specification (2006). Specification of the 3GPP confidentiality and integrity algorithms UEA2 & UIA2. Document 2: SNOW 3G Specification Version 1.1.

ETSI/SAGE Specification (2011). Specification of the 3GPP confidentiality and integrity algorithms 128-EEA3 & 128-EIA3. Document 2: ZUC Specification Version 1.6.

ETSI/SAGE Specification TS 135 201 (2001). Specification of the 3GPP confidentiality and integrity algorithms. Document 1: f8 and f9 specification.

Fluhrer, S.R., Mantin, I., Shamir, A. (2001). Weaknesses in the key scheduling algorithm of RC4. In *SAC 2001*, vol. 2259 of *Lecture Notes in Computer Science*, Vaudenay, S., Youssef, A.M. (eds). Springer.

Goldreich, O., Goldwasser, S., Micali, S. (1986). How to construct random functions. *J. ACM*, 33(4), 792–807.

Golomb, S.W. (1967). *Shift Register Sequences*. Holden-Day Series in Information Systems. Holden-Day, San Francisco, USA.

Grover, L.K. (1996). A fast quantum mechanical algorithm for database search. In *ACM Symposium on the Theory of Computing 1996*, Miller, G.L. (ed.). ACM.

Hamann, M., Krause, M., Meier, W., Zhang, B. (2018). Design and analysis of small-state Grain-like stream ciphers. *Cryptogr. Commun.*, 10(5), 803–834.

Hell, M., Johansson, T., Maximov, A., Meier, W. (n.d.). The Grain family of stream ciphers. In *New Stream Cipher Designs – The eSTREAM Finalists* [Online]. Available at: https://dblp.org/rec/series/lncs/HellJMM08.html?view=bibtex.

Hell, M., Johansson, T., Maximov, A., Meier, W., Sönnerup, J., Yoshida, H. (2021). Grain-128AEADv2 – A lightweight AEAD stream cipher [Online]. Available at: https://csrc.nist.gov/Projects/lightweight-cryptography/finalists.

Hellman, M.E. (1980). A cryptanalytic time-memory trade-off. *IEEE Trans. Inf. Theory*, 26(4), 401–406.

ISO/IEC (2011). JTC1: IS 18033-4:2011(en) Information technology – Security techniques – Encryption algorithms – Part 4: Stream ciphers.

ISO/IEC (2012). JTC1: IS 291923-3:2012(en) Information technology – Security techniques – Lightweight cryptography – Part 3: Stream ciphers.

ISO/IEC (2015). JTC1: IS 29167-13: Information technology – Automatic identification and data capture techniques – Part 13: Crypto suite Grain-128A security services for air interface communications.

Lano, J. (2006). Cryptanalysis and design of synchronous stream ciphers. PhD Thesis, Katholieke Universiteit Leuven.

Lidl, R. and Niederreiter, H. (1997). *Finite Fields*, vol. 20. Cambridge University Press.

McGrew, D.A. and Viega, J. (2004). The security and performance of the Galois/counter mode (GCM) of operation. In *INDOCRYPT 2004*, vol. 3348 of *Lecture Notes in Computer Science*, Canteaut, A., Viswanathan, K. (eds). Springer.

Méaux, P., Journault, A., Standaert, F., Carlet, C. (2016). Towards stream ciphers for efficient FHE with low-noise ciphertexts. In *EUROCRYPT 2016, Part I*, vol. 9665 of *Lecture Notes in Computer Science*, Fischlin, M., Coron, J. (eds). Springer.

Meier, W. and Staffelbach, O. (1989). Fast correlation attacks on certain stream ciphers. *J. Cryptology*, 1(3), 159–176.

Meier, W. and Staffelbach, O. (1994). The self-shrinking generator. In *EUROCRYPT '94*, vol. 950 of *Lecture Notes in Computer Science*, Santis, A.D. (ed.). Springer.

Menezes, A.J., Van Oorschot, P.C., Vanstone, S.A. (1996). *Handbook of Applied Cryptography*. CRC Press.

NIST Lightweight Cryptography Standardization (2019). Lightweight cryptography: Project overview [Online]. Available at: https://csrc.nist.gov/Projects/Lightweight-Cryptography.

Rivest, R.L. (1992). The RC4 encryption algorithm [Online]. Available at: https://doi.org/10.17487/RFC1320.

Rivest, R.L. and Schuldt, J.C.N. (2016). Spritz – A spongy RC4-like stream cipher and hash function. *IACR Cryptol. ePrint Arch.*, 2016, 856.

Robshaw, M.J.B. and Billet, O. (eds) (2008). *New Stream Cipher Designs – The eSTREAM Finalists*, vol. 4986 of *Lecture Notes in Computer Science*. Springer.

Rogaway, P. (2002). Authenticated-encryption with associated-data. In *CCS 2002*, Atluri, V. (ed.). ACM.

Rueppel, R.A. (1986). *Analysis and Design of Stream Ciphers*. Communications and Control Engineering Series, Springer.

Selmer, E. (1966). *Linear Recurrence Relations over Finite Fields*. Department of Mathematics, University of Bergen [Online]. Available at: https://books.google.be/books?id=-gPvAAAAMAAJ.

Shannon, C.E. (1949). Communication theory of secrecy systems. *Bell Systems Technical Journal*, 28(4), 656–715.

Team, Z.D. (2015). The ZUC-256 Stream Cipher [Online]. Available at: http://www.is.cas.cn/ztzl2016/zouchongzhi/201801/W020180126529970733243.pdf.

Wegman, M.N. and Carter, L. (1981). New hash functions and their use in authentication and set equality. *J. Comput. Syst. Sci.*, 22(3), 265–279.

Whiting, D., Housley, R., Ferguson, N. (2003). Counter with CBC-MAC (CCM). RFC 3610 [Online]. Available at: https://rfc-editor.org/rfc/rfc3610.txt.

Whiting, D., Schneier, B., Lucks, S., Muller, F. (2005). Fast encryption and authentication in a single cryptographic primitive. Submission to ECRYPT Stream Cipher Project [Online]. Available at: http://www.ecrypt.eu.org/stream/sfinks.html.

Wu, H. (2004). A new stream cipher HC-256. In *FSE 2004*, vol. 3017 of *Lecture Notes in Computer Science*, Roy, B.K., Meier, W. (eds). Springer.

Wu, H. (2008). The stream cipher HC-128. In *New Stream Cipher Designs – The eSTREAM Finalists*, vol. 4986 of *Lecture Notes in Computer Science*, Robshaw, M.J.B., Billet, O. (eds). Springer.

Wu, H. (2016). Acorn v3. Submission to Round 3 of the CAESAR competition [Online]. Available at: https://competitions.cr.yp.to/round3/acornv3.pdf.

Wu, H. and Huang, T. (2021). TinyJAMBU: A family of lightweight authenticated encryption algorithms [Online]. Available at: https://csrc.nist.gov/Projects/ lightweight-cryptography/finalists.

Wu, H. and Preneel, B. (2013). AEGIS: A fast authenticated encryption algorithm. In *SAC 2013*, vol. 8282 of *Lecture Notes in Computer Science*, Lange, T., Lauter, K.E., Lisonek, P. (eds). Springer.

3

Block Ciphers

Orr DUNKELMAN

Computer Science Department, University of Haifa, Israel

A block cipher is a family of permutations. Indexed by a key K, the block cipher E_K accepts a plaintext m of n bits and produces a ciphertext of n bits, that is, it offers a permutation over the strings $\{0,1\}^n$. Ideally, we would like those 2^k different permutations to be randomly selected. However, each permutation over n bits requires $\log_2((2^n)!) = O(n \cdot 2^n)$ bits to describe. Hence, this ideal block cipher would require a huge memory that even for relatively small values of k and n would not be feasible.

Block cipher designers are thus tackled with the following problem – how to design a scheme as close to the ideal case in an efficient matter. However, meeting the "close to ideal case" aim is a bit hard – without using vast amounts of memory, any scheme will be very far from ideal. Hence, the problem that most designers tackle is – how to design a scheme as secure as possible in an efficient manner.

One possible solution to the problem of encrypting a block is to operate in *rounds*. Namely, instead of constructing a permutation from n bits to n bits which achieve security in one invocation, it is common to construct ciphers based on repeated invocations of *a round function*. This round function accepts a subkey derived from the key (sometimes called master key), and it "builds" security after a sufficient number of invocations. In many cases, these round functions are implementing Shannon's original ideas of "confusion" and "diffusion" (Shannon 1949), which suggest that each such round includes some confusion (that makes cryptanalysis harder) and some diffusion (that "spreads" the hardness).

Symmetric Cryptography 1,
coordinated by Christina BOURA and María NAYA-PLASENCIA. © ISTE Ltd 2023.

The two main common constructions are Feistel block ciphers and substitution permutation networks. We describe them later, but note that there are other structures which are used; for example, the IDEA block cipher uses a structure that is sometimes referred to as the Lai–Massey scheme. Other ciphers use generalizations of Feistel block ciphers (of different types). Even though we present these rounds only later, we note that each round should increase the security (and has efficiency cost). This transforms our basic questions into the question of how many rounds are needed to satisfy the requirement of a secure cipher, which is at the same time efficient.

To answer this question, we need to define two metrics, one for security and one for efficiency. While it seems like efficiency is easy to measure, it actually depends on the target platform (software implementation on the latest CPU or a specific hardware device produced in the 1990s) and on the use case (memory encryption is usually more affected by the latency of the cipher, whereas RFID devices have a huge constraint on their energy consumption).

While the problem of defining efficiency is hard, in most cases it has a very clear evaluation metric – how many cycles does the cipher take to encrypt a block of data, or how many LUTs are needed on an FPGA. Furthermore, it is usually easy to understand what is the cost of each additional round.

The problem of defining security is more involved. The majority of our discussion revolves around algorithmic security (also called *black-box security*), when the adversary can only access input/output of the block cipher. There are other security metrics to cover adversaries who may observe information about the execution of the cipher (side channel attacks, or *gray-box security*) or even control the encryption machine (e.g. in ransomware scenarios) where one should consider the *white-box security* model.

This leaves us with the problem of assessing the security of a given cipher. Unfortunately, in almost all cases, one cannot prove a lower bound on the amount of work an adversary needs to break a block cipher (and to date there are no ciphers that are both efficient and enjoy a security reduction to a well known and understood cryptographic hardness assumption). This calls for a different approach toward "proving" the security of a cipher. After years of academic effort, this approach can be summarized as "prove that known attacks fail".

In other words, a modern block cipher design is expected to come with a series of security claims that suggest that the cipher cannot be broken by existing attacks (such as reported in this book). The proofs of mitigation of specific attacks depend on the attack. For example, for the case of differential and linear cryptanalysis, it is usual to use the approach suggested by Nyberg and Knudsen of showing that such attacks against the scheme require more data than available to the adversary. For example, in the case of differential cryptanalysis (see Chapter 1 of volume 2), the data complexity of the attack is $O(1/p)$, where p is the probability of the differential. Hence, upper bounding the probability of any differential through the cipher suggests a lower bound on the amount of data needed for the attack.

In addition to such proofs, designers are expected to offer their best attacks, that is, show how far existing attacks can be used against their scheme. This serves one important goal of understanding the security margins offered by the scheme. For example, if the best known attack on r rounds of the scheme can still break it[1] and the scheme has s rounds, then the $s - r$ additional rounds serve as a security margin – either if the attacks are improved or new attacks developed, then the scheme would remain secure.

To summarize the above discussion, block cipher design is composed of defining a good round function (security-wise/performance-wise), repeating it a sufficient number of times to offer adequate security margins, as long as the performance is acceptable. The reminder of the chapter offers some more discussions of this process. We then mention a few methods to argue the resistance of a scheme to attacks.

Finally, we discuss the recent emerging need for special environment ciphers: secure multiparty computation (MPC) protocols or as part of succinct non-interactive argument of knowledge (SNARKs). These environments are very different than "encrypting data in bulk" we usually associate with block ciphers, as they have very different performance/security trade-offs and considerations.

3.1. General purpose block ciphers

Most block ciphers fall under the definition of general purpose block ciphers. Even if they are meant for a specific application or environment, block ciphers are used to encrypt multiple blocks of data (using an appropriate mode of operation, preferably, an authenticated one). Hence, from a security perspective the basic requirement is that an adversary, even with access to many plaintext/ciphertext pairs, cannot break the system.

There are several adversarial settings in which the adversary may obtain those plaintext/ciphertext pairs. When estimating the security of a block cipher, it is worthwhile to assume the strongest model, that is, adaptive chosen plaintext and ciphertext, in which the adversary is allowed to probe the block cipher directly with any input of its liking, either in the encryption direction or the decryption direction. This ensures that an adversary without such access is still incapable of breaking the block cipher.

---

1 The observant reader may recognize the fact that we have not defined when a cipher is broken. We will address this issue later.

However, we are yet to define what breaking of a cipher means. Obviously, finding the key constitutes a break of the cipher. We can again demand stronger requirements from the block cipher. For example, it is common in the theory of cryptography (and especially in the context of security proofs for modes of operation) to discuss the probability of distinguishing a block cipher from the ideal case. Obviously, once the key is found, the task of distinguishing is trivial, but we can construct cases in which distinguishing is indeed possible without the key being revealed.

3.1.1. *Feistel block ciphers*

As mentioned above, there are two common structures for block ciphers. The first is the Feistel block cipher, which was adopted by the designers of the *data encryption standard* (DES) (National Bureau of Standards 1977). In a Feistel block cipher, the n-bit input P is divided into two halves L and R, each of $n/2$ bits, that is, $P = (L, R)$. The round function of a Feistel cipher, depicted in Figure 3.1(a), is as follows:

$$R_k(L, R) = (R, L \oplus f_k(R)).$$

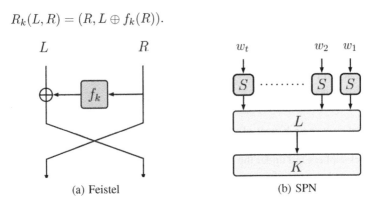

(a) Feistel   (b) SPN

Figure 3.1. *Feistel and SPN round functions*

In other words, the round function takes one half, and applies a keyed function $f_k(\cdot)$ to it. The output is then XORed (in some cases other group operations such as modular addition are used) to the second half, and the two halves are swapped.

It is interesting to note that $f_k(\cdot)$ itself does not have to be invertible to offer decryption. For example, in the case of DES, this is indeed the case. Decryption is thus achieved by calling the same structure, but with a reverse order of subkeys, that is, if encryption is done with the subkeys $k_1, k_2, \ldots, k_r$, decryption is performed with the subkeys $k_r, k_{r-1}, \ldots, k_1$.

After the introduction of DES (which together with the introduction of public-key cryptography mark the beginning of the era of "modern civilian cryptography"), the theoretical foundations of the security of Feistel ciphers were studied. The first who studied the security of such constructions were Luby and Rackoff who showed that at least a 3-round Feistel construction is needed to achieve security better than a polynomial one if the adversary is given access just to an encryption oracle, or 4-round if access to the decryption oracle is also given (Luby and Rackoff 1988). Over the years, many other works have studied the security of Feistel ciphers (e.g. studying many Feistel rounds in Nachef et al. (2017) or in the context of quantum attacks).

3.1.2. Substitution permutation networks

The second common structure of the block cipher is *substitution permutation networks (SPNs)*. In such structures, the n-bit input P is treated as t words of s bits each (i.e. $n = s \cdot t$). The round function is usually composed of three main components: the S-box layer, diffusion layer and subkey addition. A well-known example of this design is the *advanced encryption standard* (AES).

The S-box layer, S, is composed of r invertible nonlinear transformations, each from s bits to s bits. While S-boxes are also widely used in Feistel ciphers, for SPNs the S-boxes are almost mandatory as the source of nonlinearity in the cipher (or confusion). The S-boxes can be thought as a (set of) lookup table(s), that is, the input to the S-box layer $(w_1, w_2, \ldots, w_t)$ where each w_i is of s bits, is transformed into $(S(w_1), S(w_2), \ldots, S(w_t))$. While usually (due to performance) these S-boxes are the same, there are cases where this is not the same S-box. It is worth noting that it is common to have a full layer of S-boxes applied to the state, but in some cases (e.g. the block cipher ZORRO (Gérard et al. 2013) or in some new designs such as HADES (Grassi et al. 2020), targeting MPC use cases) the S-box is applied only to parts of the state.

The diffusion layer, L, mixes the different words. Some diffusion layers operate in a linear manner (e.g. can be considered as multiplying the input words by invertible matrix like in AES), whereas other layers operate in the bit-level and mix the different bits of the different words (like in PRESENT). Obviously, the diffusion layer and the S-box layer interact in determining the security (and the efficiency) of the scheme.

Finally, the third layer is the key addition, K. This layer injects the subkey into the state, for example, by XORing the key into the state. Again, we need to define a key schedule algorithm that transforms the key into the subkeys.

The result is a round function (depicted in Figure 3.1(b)) of the form:

$$R_k((w_1, w_2, \ldots, w_t)) = K(L((S(w_1), S(w_2), \ldots, S(w_t)))).$$

It is important to note that the order of the operations may change (we report here the common representation that follows the AES), but essentially for most cases, one can "swap" the order of the operations by making adjustments to the diffusion layer and/or key scheduling algorithm.

It is important to add one key addition before the first round function. This follows the fact that otherwise the first S and L layers operate on values known to (or even worse, directly controlled by) the adversary. Moreover, in some cases, where AES is the most well known, the last round does not have a diffusion layer. While this stems from the linear nature of the AES diffusion layer, many designs do forgo the last round linear layer.

Decryption of SPNs is actually done by calling the inverse operations (in the inverse order). If for example the key addition is done by XOR, then one calls the XOR again (with the inverse sequence of subkeys). The linear layer is also inverted, as well as the S-boxes. In most cases, the inverse S-boxes are needed for this operation, but in some cases, such as KHAZAD and ANUBIS, the S-boxes were chosen to be their own self inverse (i.e. $S(x) = y \Rightarrow S(y) = x$). This reduces the overall implementation complexity (when encryption and decryption may be performed using the same circuit), but may have impact on security.

It is worth noting that with the increased popularity of SPNs and the additional cost incurred by decryption, there are more and more modes of operation that allow decryption without relying on the decryption operation of the block cipher.

Finally, the theoretical treatment of SPNs is somewhat more limited than that of Feistels. The most common approach is to treat them as *iterated Even-Mansour* schemes (or *key alternating ciphers*). However, both approaches need to assume that the round function is quite strong to offer any meaningful security guarantee. However, if the round function is in itself quite strong, there is no need for many rounds.

3.2. Key schedule algorithms

Most block ciphers employ a key schedule algorithm, which expands the (master) key into subkeys. In some ciphers, the key schedule is composed of repeated uses of the same key, whereas in most ciphers some expansion of the key is used.

The first public example is the one by DES, in which each round has a 48-bit subkey, selected as a permuted subset of the 56-bit key of DES. Other ciphers also employ this selection idea, that is, in the IDEA block cipher.

Some other ciphers employ a more complex scheme. One can consider SERPENT's key schedule, which is a combination of an LFSR, on whose output a layer of S-boxes is applied. Another example is the AES key schedule that generates the next key(s) based on the current one using a transformation which is mostly linear, but contains some nonlinearity (as well as some round constants).

Another class of ciphers, such as BLOWFISH and TWOFISH, offer a more complex key schedule algorithm, as the key is used to derive S-boxes. Such *key-dependent S-boxes* have some advantages against cryptanalysis (as the S-boxes are unknown to the adversary, and thus, it is usually difficult to apply statistical attacks such as differential or linear attack). On the other hand, such key-dependent S-boxes are both more time consuming to generate, make hardware implementations (slightly) harder and more complicated, and finally, from security perspective, there is a chance that for some keys, the resulting S-boxes are weak.

Weak keys are keys for which the encryption algorithm is weaker than expected. Many ciphers have those, where DES ones are the most known. DES has four keys k, for which $DES_k(DES_k(P)) = P$ for all plaintexts P. The chance for a random permutation $\sigma : \{0,1\}^n \rightarrow \{0,1\}^n$ to satisfy this condition is negligible. DES also has six pairs of semi-weak keys (pairs of keys k_1, k_2 such that $DES_{k_1}(DES_{k_2}(P)) = P$ for all plaintexts). Again the chances of such pairs in a random permutation is negligible. Of course, other ciphers have weak keys, where the common definition is as follows: a set of keys is considered "weak keys" if there is an attack that identifies that the secret key is from this set (or recovers the key) faster than trying all possible keys in the set.

From an efficiency perspective, the comparison is thus between a relatively simple and efficient key schedule, or a more complex (and thus, time consuming) key schedule algorithm. We can argue that as the key schedule is run only once for each stream of encrypted data, we can perform the computation of the key schedule once, and thus its "computational cost" can be amortized over many invocations of the block cipher. While this is true for a user performing a single encryption/decryption at a time, for a server with multiple streams, or in cases that involve tweaks (which we discuss later), re-keying may happen every block. Finally, we must consider hash functions, which exploit the block cipher as the building block of their compression function, as they usually perform one key schedule operation per block (thus incurring the cost of the key schedule algorithm every block).

From a security perspective, we must indeed make sure that no weak keys can be found. Unfortunately, we usually cannot prove that all the keys indeed induce the same security level. At the same time, we can usually give sound reasoning why such keys, or pairs of semi-weak keys are not plausible in the design.

Finally, there is an issue of related-key attacks. In related-key attacks, the adversary is given access to encryption under two (or more) related-keys. While the original attack of Biham[2] (Biham 1994) did not require such access (as it just used the fact that encryption under keys that satisfied some relation was somewhat related), it is now common to allow the adversary to know the relation or even choose the relation. There are several justifications for this approach – starting from the obvious (ciphers secure against stronger adversaries have more security margins compared with ciphers which are susceptible to such attacks) through the fact that some real-life protocols allow such related-key access, to the case of hash functions, where the adversary usually controls the key as it is related to the message. It is worth noting that some attacks, such as the attack on WEP by Mantin et al., is at the end of a related-key attack. One can even view the famous complementation property of DES as a related-key differential property.

It is important to note that the ability to consider encryption under different keys offers the adversary stronger capabilities. As discussed in Chapter 1 of volume 2, there are no four-round differential characteristics with probability higher than 2^{-150} in AES. At the same time, it is possible to build an eight-round related-key differential characteristic for AES-256 with a probability of 2^{-54}! This gap is the outcome of the ability of the adversary to control key differences to their benefit.

3.3. Generic attacks

Any block cipher can be "broken" given enough resources. Namely, by using 2^k computations,[3] the adversary can try all possible keys of the cipher in an *exhaustive search* attack, until the correct key is found. If the key is sufficiently short, then this attack becomes practical. This fact was first observed by Diffie and Hellman (1977) who suggested a design that would have cost US\$20 million to find a DES key (56 bits) in a day. Later, a series of DES challenges set the record at about US\$220,000 for the DES Cracker machine that finds a DES key in 56 h. The computation power of course improves all the time (and more precisely, the computational power per US\$ is getting much better as time progress).

While it is impossible to know what the adversary's capabilities are, *today* it is considered sufficient to demand that $k \geq 128$ to offer security against such attacks. With the introduction of faster computing devices, this requirement may need to be updated. For example, in case quantum computers ever become realizable, one should expect that exhaustive search attacks could benefit from Grover's algorithm. Hence, one should expect an adversary that spends $O(2^{k/2})$ effort to find the secret key. Hence, in the case of realizable quantum computers, it is better to demand $k \geq 256$.

---

2 Related-key attacks were also introduced independently by Knudsen (1993).

3 We use here 2^k as the worst case measure. On average, 2^{k-1} computation is needed.

Another type of generic attack is the dictionary attack. The adversary may precompute a huge table of 2^k entries, each containing the encryption of a (few) plaintext(s) under some key, for all possible keys. Then, given the real ciphertexts of those plaintexts, it is easy to find the corresponding key with little computational effort. While this attack requires a lot of memory (2^k to be precise) and a lot of precomputation (again of 2^k operations), this is done once. Hence, the cost of the precomputation can be amortized over many applications of the attack (each taking a very short time).

The two approaches offer two distinct types of attacks. The first takes time 2^k and uses no memory, where the second takes 2^k memory and takes very little time (one memory search). This motivated Hellman to find a trade-off of the two approaches. Without describing in detail this seminal work (Hellman 1980) on time-memory trade-off attacks, we note that by building specially crafted tables, the adversary can offer an attack that has a running time of T encryptions using M memory blocks for any T, M values satisfying $TM^2 = 2^{2k}$. Obviously, with less memory than $2^{k/2}$, the running time of the attack is worse than exhaustive search, and when the memory is $M = 2^k$ one obtains the dictionary attack, but any value in between offers a valid attack whose time complexity is smaller than that of exhaustive search and its memory consumption is smaller than that of the dictionary attack.

Another variant of the problem is the time-memory-data trade-off attack. This is an extension of Hellman's original ideas to the case where the adversary is trying to find the key of one out of D encryptions. While exhaustive search for this case would take about $2^k/D$ time[4], it is possible to construct tables that allow finding one of the keys in running time T and memory M as long as $TM^2D^2 = 2^{2k}$ (and $T \geq D^2$). Hence, when picking the minimal key length needed for a given system, we should consider whether this attack scenario, in which a single key out of D is recovered, can collapse the full security of the system. If this is the case, it is better to pick a sufficiently long key, for which the above trade-off curve only yields parameter sets which are impractical for the adversary.

A completely different attack, again in the scenario in which multiple users use different keys, is the Biham's key collision attack (Biham 2002). Consider a case in which 2^t different keys are used. If in all these cases there is some known plaintext (e.g. a known header is encrypted in all communications), then the adversary can precompute a table of 2^{k-t} encryptions of this known plaintext under different random keys. With high enough probability, following the birthday paradox, we expect one of the keys in the table to correspond to one of the keys used in one of the communications.

---

4 We note that the average running time is $2^k/(D+1)$.

While the previous discussion addressed the key size, we note that the block size may also impact the security. If the block size n is sufficiently small, we can ask in a chosen plaintext scenario for the encryption of all plaintexts under the secret key, thus constructing a table of all (plaintext, ciphertext) pairs. In such a case, the adversary can instantly decrypt any message using only 2^n memory.

Furthermore, it is important to note that many modes of operation offer security as long as a limited amount of (plaintext, ciphertext) pairs is given to the adversary. For example, the widely used counter mode of operation is proved to be secure as long as the number of blocks q available to the adversary satisfies[5] $q^2 < 2^n$. This bound, called the *birthday bound*, exists for many modes. For example, a similar bound exists for CBC, and the security may completely collapse once $q > 2^{n/2}$, evident, for example, by the Sweet32 attack, which recovered messages encrypted under DES in CBC mode (Bhargavan and Leurent 2016). We note that while many modes offer beyond birthday bound security, their security may erode when the number of queries exceeds some $2^{\alpha \cdot n}$ queries for some $\alpha > 1/2$.

To conclude, block cipher designers must pick parameters for the block size n and the key size k such that the above generic attacks are mitigated.

3.4. Tweakable block ciphers

Tweakable block ciphers were introduced by Liskov et al. (2011). Such block ciphers accept three parameters: a secret key K, a public tweak t and a plaintext block P to produce the ciphertext block C. Formally, a tweakable block cipher E is a family of $\{0,1\}^k \times \{0,1\}^t$ permutations over $\{0,1\}^n$.

The tweak thus "changes" the behavior of the block ciphers, for example, in some modes of operation. For example, the electronic code book (ECB) mode of operation, which is well known to be dangerous, can be easily used in a tweakable setting. Each call to the block cipher can use a different counter number as a tweak, and as these tweaks "diversify" the encryption, the encryption of two equal plaintext blocks generates two ciphertext blocks which are not correlated (unlike standard ECB). Other modes of operation, which rely on this *domain separation*, are also very common, and widely considered as better suited than regular modes for many cases.

From the point of view of the block cipher designer, there is one major question that needs to be addressed – how should the tweak affect the encryption process. Is the tweak a part of the key that happens to be made public (as in WEP, where the IV is indeed public), giving the adversary more knowledge (or even control) on parts of

---

5 Actually, the security proof for counter mode suggests than an adversary with access to q blocks may succeed in distinguishing the encryption from random with probability $O(q^2/2^n)$.

the key and requiring full key schedule every new block? Another option is to inject the tweak into the encryption, for example, $E_{k,T}(P) = E_k(T \oplus E_k(P))$ proposed originally by Liskov et al.

The trade-off between these approaches allows also midway solutions, for example, the tweak is XORed into the encryption rounds independent of the subkeys. In this way, the key schedule is computed once, whereas the tweak schedule is run for each block cipher call (and might be significantly "lighter").

A very popular method for handling tweaks and keys is the TWEAKEY framework (Jean et al. 2014). Initialized by the tweak and the key, the state of the tweakey schedule is updated (using a nonlinear function), where a subkey is extracted (possibly in a nonlinear manner) from the state of the tweakey schedule. If indeed the update and extraction functions are secure, one should expect a secure cipher. Of course, this requires additional hardware/software resources for the tweakey schedule but if done properly, the latency of the encryption scheme may not be affected.

Finally, we note that the fact that the cipher has tweaks opens up related-tweak attacks. Similarly to related-key attacks, and to some extent, even more than related-key attacks, as tweaks are available to the adversary, the attacks may use the different tweaks to offer new cryptanalytic capabilities. For example, in the context of differential cryptanalysis, tweak differences may be used to cancel state differences, again leading to better differential characteristics.

Another "capability" the tweaks may offer is to mount attacks that require more than 2^n plaintexts. For example, in the context of *format preserving encryption*, where tweaks are used to allow for small domain sizes, there are multiple attacks that go beyond the 2^n plaintexts that can be obtained for non-tweakable block ciphers.

3.5. Some positive results concerning security

At this point, the reader may feel demotivated to design block ciphers. Not only that they must compete with existing ones performance wise, it seems that one cannot guarantee security of new ciphers. Dante's words, "Abandon hope all ye who enter here," may echo in the reader's mind.

Luckily, not all is lost, and one could hope to gain confidence in new designs. The first approach, mentioned above is indeed an "engineering" one. We can test all existing attacks and show that they fail to break a given number of rounds. Hence, if the cipher has more rounds as a security margin, than there is a good chance (or at least hope) that there will be no attacks against the full scheme in the future.

A different approach is to show (and prove) that no attacks of possible type are feasible. First proposed by Nyberg and Knudsen (1993) seminal work, it was shown that one can upper bound the probability of all differential characteristics to be sufficiently low, such that the data complexity of a differential attack may be close to the entire code book. Similar arguments can be made with respect to other statistical attacks, for example, linear cryptanalysis, and even algebraic attacks are usually treated in similar frameworks (where the security is usually related to the degree and density of the system).

The wide trail strategy that was developed on the basis of Nyberg and Knudsen's work offers a concrete method to ensure that there are indeed no differential characteristics or linear approximations, which may be used to break the cipher. More information about the strategy is given in Chapter 1 of volume 2. However, one needs to note that the wide trail strategy, similarly to Nyberg and Knudsen's work, discusses the security against specific differential characteristics (or a specific linear approximation). Hence, if many differential characteristics have the same input/output pair (thus suggesting a high probability differential) or clustering of linear approximations takes place, there may be statistical properties that "contradict" these security claims. We do note that for the specific case of AES there is a line of research that proves that there are no differentials with probability higher than 2^{-110} for 4-round AES (and a similar result holds for linear cryptanalysis).

A different approach for security is based on reductions to hard problems. The theoretical foundations of cryptography show that one can construct a secure block cipher if and only if *one way functions* exist. However, the existence of such one way functions implies that $P \neq NP$. Moreover, the definitions of security and performance suggested by this approach tend to be using the polynomial/exponential language, which is not compatible with the fact that one can attack AES in time $O(1)$, though this constant is quite high. In other words, the treatment offered by the theoretical cryptography of block ciphers is not sufficiently delicate to tell us whether AES is better than SERPENT.

At the same time, one can try to construct block ciphers directly based on hard mathematical problems. For example, Patarin's 2R construction builds a block cipher which could be used in public-key settings, based on the SPN structure and the hardness of solving multivariate polynomials. While the scheme was later broken (using differential cryptanalysis, and later using a variant of the Square attack), one can try and use such problems to construct secure ciphers. The only problem is that the running times of such cases is usually several orders of magnitude slower than that of "direct" constructions such as the ones discussed before.

A slightly different approach to security reductions is to use pre-existing ciphers (or parts of them) as a building block. For example, there are many constructions (block ciphers and hash functions) that utilize a reduced-round version of AES (e.g. four-round or five-round AES) as a building block. As four-round AES is known to offer great resistance against differential and linear attacks, and at the same time being very efficient (especially on platforms that have an AES instruction set), this seems like a good building block. We just alert the reader that when using this (or similar reductions), one needs to consider the use of the primitive. For example, if no round constants appear in the "4-round AES" (e.g. if the key schedule part is omitted), then one could find some internal symmetries which can be used for attacking schemes relying on reduced round AES. Alternatively, if the adversary can control the inputs to these secure components, they may be able to "go around them" altogether.

Finally, we note that there are other approaches for provable security. Instead of relying on "discarding" existing attacks, or reducing the security of the scheme to the hardness of some problem, *decorrelation theory* aims to show that the distribution of plaintext/ciphertext pairs is statistically close to the ideal case (Vaudenay 2003). For example, a scheme which has two-wise D-decorrelation suggests that all pairs of plaintexts (P_1, P_2) and their corresponding ciphertexts (C_1, C_2) have (almost) the same probability whether they were sampled in the ideal case or from the cipher.

The security assurance of the decorrelation theory stems from the fact that if the distributions are close, then an adversary should learn nothing from observing the plaintext/ciphertext pairs. Furthermore, a cipher that is d-wise decorrelated imitates (possibly perfectly) a random permutation. Hence, any attack procedure which studies d values at a time (e.g. pairs in differential cryptanalysis, or a plaintext in the case of linear cryptanalysis) is expected to fail.

While "local issues" in the theory were spotted and addressed, we need to take the security guarantee offered by the theory with a grain of a salt. This follows from two issues. First, it is very hard to efficiently provide full d-wise decorrelation for large values of d. Hence, attacks which consider such sets (e.g. the Square attack on AES which takes 2^{32} plaintexts in a specially crafted set) can still break the scheme. Second, the statistical distance is guaranteed between averages. For example, the probabilities considered are the average probabilities taken over all random permutations/keys. However, for a given key, the actual behavior might be very different than security guarantee (which is for the average case).

3.6. The case of algebraic ciphers

Block ciphers are usually associated with the encryption of data (usually in bulk). Recent advances in the fields of secure multiparty computation, of zero knowledge proofs (e.g. the introduction of SNARKs), and fully homomorphic encryption, raised a need for a new type of block ciphers (and hash functions). These schemes target very different performance metrics than the usual ones. For example, in the case of MPC schemes, it seems that the main cost metric is the number of AND gates, whereas XOR gates are mostly free (due to the fact that AND gates require communications in MPC protocols), suggesting a different "need". Furthermore, some of these scenarios are better with ciphers that handle inputs which are field elements, for example, from $GF(p)$ for some 64-bit or 128-bit prime number p.

Obviously, these ciphers are very different in nature to the ones discussed above. Not only do many of them use a different field than the binary field, and their performance metric is very different, but their security requirements are also far from the ones considered above. For some of these use cases, we should expect the adversary to obtain very limited amount of inputs (and sometimes even in a known plaintext scenario). For example, when using LowMC in an MPC protocol, we should expect the adversary to obtain just a single pair of known plaintext/ciphertext encrypted under the secret key. Hence, this further allows reducing the safety margins, as it is not necessary to withstand many statistical attacks.

At the same time, many of these ciphers rely on operations which are less understood. For example, in the case of LowMC, which relies on the complexity of solving low-degree polynomial equations over $GF(2)$, recent advances in algorithms for the task allow attacking more rounds than previously known. This problem magnifies when considering the ciphers working over $GF(p)$, where new statistical attacks (or algebraic ones) may be developed or when taking into consideration the special algebraic nature of many of these recent constructions.

The new set of requirements led to the introduction of several design methodologies, for example, HADES (Grassi et al. 2020) that mixes rounds of full S-box layers and rounds of partial S-box layers. At the same time, it seems that some internal parameters (namely, the MDS matrix used to offer diffusion) have a much greater impact on the security of ciphers designed in this methodology than expected. Namely, for some choices, the security of the cipher is significantly larger than claimed, whereas for some others there may be very large invariant subspaces.

At the moment, there is no well-established and fully understood design methodology for such ciphers, it seems that it may be better to "err" toward the higher security margins. This recommendation is supported by years of research in cryptography (that usually prefers one additional round to defend against unknown attacks), which is even more appealing when considering the fact that these block ciphers are going to be used inside higher level cryptographic protocols. For some of them, it is unclear how easy it would be to change ciphers (the fact that mobile communications still use ciphers designed in the 1980s, broken repeatedly since the 1990s, suggests that mitigating a bad cryptographic solution may not be trivial). For others, the total damage might not be just the ability of an adversary to read confidential information, but something of a larger severity.

3.7. References

Bhargavan, K. and Leurent, G. (2016). On the practical (in-)security of 64-bit block ciphers: Collision attacks on HTTP over TLS and OpenVPN. In *CCS 2016*, Weippl, E.R., Katzenbeisser, S., Kruegel, C., Myers, A.C., Halevi, S. (eds). ACM.

Biham, E. (1994). New types of cryptanalytic attacks using related keys. *J. Cryptol.*, 7(4), 229–246.

Biham, E. (2002). How to decrypt or even substitute DES-encrypted messages in 2^{28} steps. *Inf. Process. Lett.*, 84(3), 117–124.

Gérard, B., Grosso, V., Naya-Plasencia, M., Standaert, F. (2013). Block ciphers that are easier to mask: How far can we go? In *CHES 2013*, vol. 8086 of *Lecture Notes in Computer Science*, Bertoni, G., Coron, J. (eds). Springer.

Grassi, L., Lüftenegger, R., Rechberger, C., Rotaru, D., Schofnegger, M. (2020). On a generalization of substitution-permutation networks: The HADES design strategy. In *EUROCRYPT 2020, Part II*, vol. 12106 of *Lecture Notes in Computer Science*, Canteaut, A., Ishai, Y. (eds). Springer.

Hellman, M.E. (1980). A cryptanalytic time-memory trade-off. *IEEE Transactions on Information Theory*, 26(4), 401–406.

Jean, J., Nikolic, I., Peyrin, T. (2014). Tweaks and keys for block ciphers: The TWEAKEY framework. In *ASIACRYPT 2014, Part II*, vol. 8874 of *Lecture Notes in Computer Science*, Sarkar, P., Iwata, T. (eds). Springer.

Knudsen, L.R. (1993). Cryptanalysis of LOKI91. In *AUSCRYPT '92*, vol. 718 of *Lecture Notes in Computer Science*, Seberry, J., Zheng, Y. (eds). Springer.

Liskov, M.D., Rivest, R.L., Wagner, D.A. (2011). Tweakable block ciphers. *J. Cryptol.*, 24(3), 588–613.

Luby, M. and Rackoff, C. (1988). How to construct pseudorandom permutations from pseudorandom functions. *SIAM J. Comput.*, 17(2), 373–386.

Nachef, V., Patarin, J., Volte, E. (2017). *Feistel Ciphers – Security Proofs and Cryptanalysis*. Springer.

National Bureau of Standards (1977). Data encryption standard (DES). Technical Report. Federal Information Processing Standards Publication 46.

Nyberg, K. and Knudsen, L.R. (1993). Provable security against differential cryptanalysis. In *CRYPTO '92*, vol. 740 of *Lecture Notes in Computer Science*, Brickell, E.F. (ed.). Springer.

Shannon, C.E. (1949). Communication theory of secrecy systems. *Bell System Technical Journal*, 28(4), 656–715.

Vaudenay, S. (2003). Decorrelation: A theory for block cipher security. *J. Cryptol.*, 16(4), 249–286.

4

Hash Functions

Gilles VAN ASSCHE
STMicroelectronics, Belgium

Traditionally, cryptographic techniques are primarily divided according to the nature of the keys involved, namely, symmetric cryptography with secret keys and asymmetric cryptography with public-private key pairs. Under such a classification, hash functions would belong to a third category, namely, *keyless cryptography*. Yet, the design and cryptanalysis of hash functions and extendable output functions (XOFs), their generalization, share so much with symmetric cryptography that they are in practice assimilated to it. Also, hash functions can be transformed into symmetric cryptographic objects with a secret key, coming from a higher level layer, included in their input.

In this chapter, we focus on the specifically keyless nature of hash functions and XOFs, we review what is expected from them, and we dive into their design.

4.1. Definitions and requirements

DEFINITION 4.1.– A *hash function* H is a deterministic function that maps a *message*, a bit string of any length, to a *digest* of fixed length, say n bits, where n is a property of the hash function

$$H \; : \; \mathbb{F}_2^* \to \mathbb{F}_2^n \; : \; x \mapsto H(x).$$

The purpose of the digest is to act as a fingerprint, a unique representative of the message. One important application of hash functions is in digital signatures, where instead of signing a message directly, the signature scheme depends on the message only through its digest. This immediately highlights a security property of hash functions: collision resistance. A *collision* is a pair of distinct messages $x_1 \neq x_2$ such that $H(x_1) = H(x_2)$. We say that a hash function is *collision-resistant* if it is infeasible to find a collision. Without collision resistance, a signature scheme would not be able to give assurance that it signs a particular message, as a signature could also correctly verify with another message with the same digest (Yuval 1979).

Since the digest space is much smaller than the message space, collisions inevitably exist, but nevertheless collision resistance requires that they are computationally difficult to find. This leads to definitional issues. If the definition of collision resistance is based on the (non-)existence of an efficient algorithm (or adversary) that outputs a collision, then a hash function cannot be collision-resistant: even if we cannot find it, there does exist an algorithm that simply outputs $x_1 \neq x_2$ such that $H(x_1) = H(x_2)$. Alternatively, there exist formal definitions in which one adds an extra input parameter, which we shall call an index[1], to the hash function, and we require that the adversary can efficiently output a collision for a random index value. For more details, we refer to Rogaway and Shrimpton (2004). However, practical hash functions do not make use of such an extra input parameter, nor is it convenient to handle: for instance, the signature verifier would not be able to check whether the index used in the hash function was randomly chosen.

The usual security properties that a hash function should satisfy also include *preimage resistance* and *second preimage resistance*. Informally, in preimage resistance, given a challenge $z \in \mathbb{F}_2^n$, it is infeasible to find a message $x \in \mathbb{F}_2^*$ such that $H(x) = z$. Second preimage resistance works similarly, but the adversary is given an example of preimage instead: given $x \in \mathbb{F}_2^*$, the adversary has to find $x' \neq x$ such that $H(x) = H(x')$. These two security notions face similar, yet less striking, definitional issues, and we again refer to Rogaway and Shrimpton (2004) for more details. A second preimage is a particular kind of collision, so collision resistance implies second preimage resistance.

Hash functions have a fixed output length, while the applications may require a digest of a size not supported by the hash functions at hand. For instance, full domain hashing is a signature scheme used in conjunction on RSA where the digest needs to have the same size as that of the public modulus (Bellare and Rogaway 1993). The natural generalization of a hash function is an XOF.

---

1 The index is often called a key in the literature, but we think this can create confusion with the secret key in keyed applications.

DEFINITION 4.2.– An *extendable output function* H is a deterministic function that maps a message to an output of potentially infinite length, only truncated by the user,

$$H : \mathbb{F}_2^* \rightarrow \mathbb{F}_2^\infty : x \mapsto H(x).$$

In practice, an XOF is implemented to give a user-chosen amount of bits. We denote as $\lfloor H(x) \rfloor_n$ the first n bits of $H(x)$. The name XOF comes from the feature that, if the implementation allows it, the user can incrementally request more output bits.

Hash functions and XOFs can also play in the arena of keyed applications, as they can become keystream generators or MAC functions when a secret key is integrated in their input (see Chapter 5).

In terms of efficiency, keyed hash functions may be heavier to implement than dedicated keyed functions. However, in symmetric cryptography, keyed functions usually assume a uniformly distributed key, or at least a key with sufficient min-entropy. Hash functions fill in the gap as they can process secret values whose distribution is not uniform, such as a shared secret obtained from a Diffie-Hellman key exchange.

4.1.1. *An ideal model: the random oracle*

We define the random oracle as the model that hash functions and XOFs should follow. It outputs a potentially infinite number of bits like an XOF, and it can be truncated to the first n output bits to model a n-bit hash function.

DEFINITION 4.3 (Bellare and Rogaway (1993)).– A *random oracle* $\mathcal{RO}$ is a map from $\mathbb{F}_2^*$ to $\mathbb{F}_2^\infty$, chosen by selecting each output bit of $\mathcal{RO}(x)$ uniformly and independently, for every $x \in \mathbb{F}_2^*$.

Qualitatively, a hash function and a random oracle are quite different objects: the former is a deterministic algorithm and therefore can be computed by anyone at any moment, while the latter is a random object that centralizes queries. Yet, this highlights what we expect from a hash function or an XOF, namely that we cannot predict what value $H(x)$ will take before we explicitly evaluate it.

Quantitatively, the model allows us to estimate how much security we can ever expect from a hash function or an XOF. So far, we have expressed the security properties using only the word "infeasible". Now, we can test attacks on the random oracle and derive complexities or success probabilities as a function of the number of queries. For instance, it is well known as documented in literature (see, e.g. Menezes et al. (1996)) that a random oracle truncated to n bits has the following security properties:

– Collision resistance: due to the birthday paradox, it takes typically around $2^{n/2}$ queries before the random oracle exhibits a collision.

– Preimage and second preimage resistance: it takes typically 2^n attempts before we can find an input for which the random oracle outputs the desired digest.

Traditionally, it is expected from a hash function that it resists collisions up to complexity $2^{n/2}$ and (second) preimage attacks up to 2^n like the random oracle. However, requiring that these attacks are computationally difficult on a concrete hash function does not necessarily imply that these specific complexities are needed, and it turns out they may not always be appropriate, as discussed in the following.

4.1.2. *Expressing security claims*

The *security claim* of a given cryptographic function is a specification of its intended security strength against some attacks. This claim acts as a kind of "contract" between the designers of the function and its potential users, as well as a challenge for cryptanalysts. It is a claim rather than a specification because in general the security of cryptographic functions cannot be proven, and only the failure of cryptanalysts to refute the security claim, despite best efforts, is the main source of assurance.

Formulating a security claim can be done exhaustively by listing potential attacks and their claimed resistance, like for collision resistance, preimage resistance and second preimage resistance. However, some applications require more security properties, for instance, correlation-freeness (Anderson 1993) or chosen target forced prefix preimage resistance (Kelsey and Kohno 2006). There is no reason to assume that no new criteria will appear, so the design of a hash function seems like a moving target.

A way out of this is to express the security of a concrete function with respect to a model, that is, to claim that in all circumstances, the concrete function shall behave no worse than a random oracle. This approach, however, has some limitations.

First, there is a separation between a random oracle and any construction operating on a finite state. Iterative functions use a finite memory to store their state and process the input, block per block. At any point in time, the state of an iterated function summarizes the input blocks received so far. Because of its finite size, the processing of two different (partial) inputs may lead to identical states; this is called an *internal collision*. For a state of b bits, the birthday paradox says that collisions are likely to happen after about $2^{b/2}$ trials. Random oracles, on the other hand, do not have collisions in their state as their state contains the full input. We therefore cannot expect a hash function to be as strong as a random oracle in all cases, for example, as for multi-collisions (Joux 2004), second preimages (Kelsey and Schneier 2005), herding hash functions and the Nostradamus attack (Kelsey and Kohno 2006). These attacks exploit internal collisions and stress the importance of the state size b in iterated hash functions, as it is unwise to expect a security strength above $b/2$.

Concretely, this separation is an obstacle when claiming the security of an XOF: it does not make sense for a concrete XOF to resist collisions up to $2^{n/2}$ and (second) preimage attacks up to 2^n where n is the output length and n is unbounded!

Second, iterative functions cannot offer the same security as a random oracle against attacks that are modeled by so-called *multi-stage games*. Concretely, it has been shown in Ristenpart et al. (2011) that there are use cases where a random oracle offers security, whereas an iterated hash function or XOF construction cannot. An example proposed by Ristenpart et al. (2011) is hash-based storage auditing, in which a server has to prove to the client that it really stores the file uploaded by the client.

Ristenpart et al. (2011) define the concepts of single-stage games and multi-stage games to address these issues, where the hash-based storage auditing security implies a multi-stage game. Fortunately, single-state games still model many attacks, such as collision attacks, (second) preimage attacks and their variants, as well as generic attacks against keyed modes (Andreeva et al. 2010, Section B).

Finally, random oracles do not have an efficiently computable and finite algorithm, unlike concrete functions. This is the implementation impossibility property, of which a simple proof is given in Maurer et al. (2004, Section 2). It shows an (artificial) example where a signature scheme is secure with a random oracle and insecure with an efficiently computable function.

The following definition gives a generic claim that circumvents these limitations. It is parameterized by the *claimed capacity*, denoted c^*, that the designer has to choose. Informally, the flat sponge claim reads *to resist against any attack up to complexity $2^{c^*/2}$ unless easier on a random oracle*. The word "sponge" in its name comes from the inspiration from the random sponge model (Bertoni et al. 2011a), but the claim can be attached to any concrete hash function or XOF.

DEFINITION 4.4 (Flat sponge claim; Bertoni et al. 2011a).– A hash function or an XOF H is said to satisfy the *flat sponge claim with claimed capacity c^** if the success probability of any attack is not higher than the sum of that on a random oracle and $N^2/2^{c^*+1}$, with N the attack complexity in units that must be specified. We exclude from the claim weaknesses due to the mere fact that the function can be described compactly and can be efficiently executed, for example, the so-called random oracle implementation impossibility (Maurer et al. 2004), as well as properties that cannot be modeled as a single-stage game (Ristenpart et al. 2011). For a hash function or XOF that calls an underlying permutation or block cipher f, the attack complexity unit of N is a call to f or its inverse.

Attached to an XOF, the flat sponge claim implies collision resistance up to $2^{\min(c^\star/2,n/2)}$ and (second) preimage resistance up to $2^{\min(c^\star/2,n)}$ where n is the output length. If $c^\star$ is large enough, say $c^\star \geq 256$, the cap at $c^\star/2$ bits of security has no practical impact.

4.2. Design of hash functions

Hash functions, like many other symmetric cryptographic schemes, are typically specified in a modular, layered, fashion. At the lowest level lies a primitive like a block cipher or a permutation. Then, the designer defines a mode or a construction, that is, an algorithm that uses the primitive in a black box way to reach more advanced functionality like a hash function. The primitive processes a fixed number of bits, so the construction specifies, among other things, how to cut the input message into blocks and how to deal with the end of the message.

There can actually be more layers, so that the higher level constructions can build on the intermediate functionality provided by the lower levels. For instance, standard hash functions like those in the SHA-2 family use specific block ciphers, then the Davies-Meyer construction transforms them into compression functions, and finally, the Merkle-Damgård construction tells how to use the compression functions to do hashing (NIST 2015a). As another example, SHAKE128 and SHAKE256 start from a permutation, then the sponge construction uses it to deliver an XOF (NIST 2015b).

In this section, we show how concrete hash functions and XOFs are designed. We focus on the construction layers, as the design of block ciphers and permutations is covered in other chapters. Note that designs specifically dedicated to hash functions, without a layered approach, do exist but are rare.

4.2.1. *The Merkle-Damgård construction*

The first hash function construction was independently developed by Ralph Merkle and Ivan Damgård in 1989 (Merkle 1989; Damgård 1989). It relies on a compression function h, that is, a hash function whose input space is restricted to strings of $m + n$ bits, where m, the block length, is a property of the compression function

$$h : \mathbb{F}_2^m \times \mathbb{F}_2^n \to \mathbb{F}_2^n : (x, y) \mapsto h(x, y).$$

The Merkle-Damgård construction works on a state of n bits (sometimes also called the chaining value), whose initial value (IV) is fixed to some arbitrary constant s_0. The input message M is first padded according to some specified rule $M' = \mathrm{pad}(M)$ such that M' has a length that is a multiple of m bits and such that M can be unambiguously recovered from M'. For instance, one appends a bit 1 followed by the minimum number of bits 0 for $|M'|$ to be a multiple of m. In addition, the padding rule ensures that the length of M is encoded in binary and stored in the last block of M' – this process is known as Merkle-Damgård strengthening. The padded message M' is then cut into blocks of m bits $M' = M_1\|M_2\|\dots\|M_k$. As depicted in Figure 4.1, the processing consists of sequentially updating the state with the compression function applied to the current message block and state values. Once all blocks have been processed, the last state value is returned as the digest, that is,

$$H(M) = s_k \quad \text{with} \quad s_i = h(M_i, s_{i-1}).$$

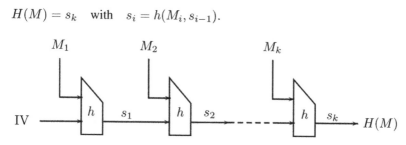

Figure 4.1. *The Merkle-Damgård construction*

The Merkle-Damgård construction has been widely used, among others, in the line of hash functions MD4, MD5, SHA-1 and the SHA-2 family (Rivest 1990, 1992; NIST 2015a). Its success is, among other reasons, due to its simple reduction; it is relatively easy to prove that if the compression function h is collision-resistant, then so is the entire hash function H (Merkle 1989; Damgård 1989).

4.2.2. Fixing the Merkle-Damgård construction

Unfortunately, the Merkle-Damgård construction is known to have the so-called *length-extension weakness* that permits to compute, knowing only the hash $H(M)$ of some message M, the hash for a second message M' of which M is a prefix. While it does not seem to be a problem in unkeyed hashing, this weakness becomes an attack if one attempts to build a message authentication code (MAC) by simply concatenating the secret key and the message to authenticate $\mathrm{MAC}_K(M) = H(K\|M)$, as this would allow easy forgeries.

Nevertheless, the length-extension weakness can be avoided in a number of ways, for example, by adding a non-invertible finalization function so that the digest $H(M)$ becomes a non-invertible function of s_k, by using a prefix-free encoding rule or by using the HMAC mode (Bellare et al. 1996; Coron et al. 2005).

Also, with the Merkle-Damgård construction, the output size is bound to its chaining value size, and there can be disappointing consequences such as multi-collisions (Joux 2004). In order to avoid the length-extension weakness, multi-collisions and other issues, Stefan Lucks proposed in 2005 the *wide-pipe construction* (Lucks 2005). His construction addresses the problem of the chaining value size explicitly by extending it to b bits, with b larger than the digest size n, and he suggested to treat b as a security parameter of its own right. In this construction, the compression function takes as input strings of $m + b$ bits, with m the block length,

$$h : \mathbb{F}_2^m \times \mathbb{F}_2^b \to \mathbb{F}_2^b : x, y \mapsto h(x, y).$$

In addition, a second compression function $g : \mathbb{F}_2^b \to \mathbb{F}_2^n$ is then applied to the last state value in order to produce a digest of size n, that is,

$$H(M) = g(s_k) \quad \text{with} \quad s_i = h(M_i, s_{i-1}).$$

There exist different instantiations of the *wide-pipe* construction, like *Chop-MD*, where the function g simply truncates a b-bit string to n bits, and the *double-pipe* construction, that does the same with $b = 2n$.

By contrast, the hash functions with $b = n$, as in the original Merkle-Damgård construction, are often tagged *narrow-pipe*. There exist other ways to fix the Merkle-Damgård construction that do not extend the size of the chaining value. One of them is called the *enveloped Merkle-Damgård transform* (EMD) (Bellare and Ristenpart 2006). Given two fixed constants $s_0 \neq s_0'$, it pads and cuts the message into blocks of m bits $M' = M_1 \| M_2 \| \dots \| M_k$, except that $|M_k| = m - n$ bits. Then it computes the digest as follows:

$$H(M) = h(s_{k-1} \| M_k, s_0') \quad \text{with} \quad s_i = h(M_i, s_{i-1}).$$

Finally, we would like to mention the *HAsh Iterative FrAmework* (HAIFA) (Biham and Dunkelman 2007). This framework generalizes many of the variants and extensions of the Merkle-Damgård construction. At its center, it iterates a compression function $h(x, y, z, t)$, where the input is extended with z to indicate the number of bits hashed so far and with t as a salt value for randomized hashing. It supports both narrow-pipe and wide-pipe state sizes and can be used to recast EMD and other variants. For instance, HAIFA is used by the BLAKE hash function family (Aumasson et al. 2014).

4.2.3. *Building a compression function*

If we zoom further inside the MD4-to-SHA-2 family, we see that the compression function is itself a construction on top of a block cipher. These functions in particular use the Davies-Meyer construction (see Quisquater and Girault 1989). In this construction, the compression function's input block is mapped to the block cipher's key, the current state value to the block cipher's input data block, and the next state value is obtained by XORing (or adding) the previous state value with the block cipher's output data block:

$$h(M_i, s_{i-1}) = E_{M_i}(s_{i-1}) \oplus s_{i-1}.$$

Similar constructions exist, such as Matyas-Meyer-Oseas (Matyas et al. 1985). Compared to Davies-Meyer, the compression function's input block is moved to the block cipher's input data block, while the next state value is obtained by XORing the input block with the block cipher's output data block. The current state value goes to the block cipher's key input after going through a simple public function g to map it to the block cipher's key space:

$$h(M_i, s_{i-1}) = E_{g(s_{i-1})}(M_i) \oplus M_i.$$

This construction can be found in the SKEIN hash function (Ferguson et al. 2011).

As a last example of block-cipher based construction, Miyaguchi-Preneel resembles Matyas-Meyer-Oseas, with the exception that the current state value is also XORed with the block cipher's output data block (Miyaguchi et al. 1990; Preneel et al. 1993):

$$h(M_i, s_{i-1}) = E_{g(s_{i-1})}(M_i) \oplus M_i \oplus s_{i-1}.$$

For instance, the Miyaguchi-Preneel construction is used by the WHIRLPOOL hash function (Barreto and Rijmen 2000). The properties of these block-cipher based constructions and many others can be found in details in Preneel et al. (1993).

Finally, a compression function can be built from a cryptographic permutation f, that is, a bijective function on $\mathbb{F}_2^b$. For instance, in the JH hash function, the compression function takes as input a message block whose size is half of the state (Wu 2011). It works by adding the input block to the first half of the state, applying the permutation to the state, and adding again the input block but this time to the second half of the state:

$$h(M_i, s_{i-1}) = f(s_{i-1} \oplus (M_i \| 0^{b/2})) \oplus (0^{b/2} \| M_i).$$

And in GRØSTL, the compression function makes use of two cryptographic permutations f and g, with both state and block sizes of b bits (Gauravaram et al. 2011):

$$h(M_i, s_{i-1}) = f(s_{i-1} \oplus M_i) \oplus g(M_i) \oplus s_{i-1}.$$

4.2.4. *Indifferentiability*

In the scope of hash functions and XOFs, the indifferentiability framework has imposed itself as a way to prove that a construction is secure against generic attacks. Developed by Maurer et al. (2004), this framework was then applied specifically to iterated hash functions by Coron et al. (2005). In this framework, we are interested in proving an upper bound on the advantage in distinguishing two systems: the real-world system, which contains an instance of the construction $\mathcal{H}$ calling an idealized underlying primitive $\mathcal{F}$, and the ideal-world system, which is in our case a random oracle $\mathcal{RO}$. We consider an adversary $\mathcal{D}$, which is presented with a system that is either the real-world system or the ideal-world system. It does not know which one and both have a priori probability $\frac{1}{2}$. It may send queries, even adaptively, and then has to guess which system it is. When interacting with the real-world system, the adversary is given access to the idealized primitive $\mathcal{F}$ since, in a concrete hash function, the specifications of the underlying primitive are public and no keys are involved. To ensure identical interfaces in both systems, the ideal-world system provides a simulator $\mathcal{S}$ to mimic $\mathcal{F}$. In order for it to be able to act consistently, $\mathcal{S}$ can access $\mathcal{RO}$. This is illustrated in Figure 4.2.

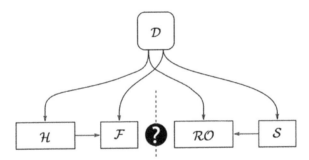

Figure 4.2. *The indifferentiability setting for a hash function or XOF construction*

The $\mathcal{RO}$-differentiating bound in general depends on the resources of the adversary, such as the number of queries to the construction interface (i.e. $\mathcal{H}$ or $\mathcal{RO}$) and to the primitive interface (i.e. $\mathcal{F}$ or $\mathcal{S}$). This aims at modeling the complexity of an attack on a concrete function, under the assumption that there is no known shortcut way of evaluating the primitive on a given input.

The benefit of the indifferentiability framework is that a $\mathcal{RO}$-differentiating bound automatically translates to a bound on the resistance of the construction against generic attacks. Intuitively, if an attack can succeed faster on a given construction than on a random oracle, this attack shows a way to distinguish the construction from a random oracle. This is captured by the following theorem.

THEOREM 4.1 (Andreeva et al. 2010).– Let $\mathcal{H}$ be a hash function construction, built on an underlying primitive $\mathcal{F}$, and $\mathcal{RO}$ be a random oracle, where $\mathcal{H}$ and $\mathcal{RO}$ have the same domain and range space. Denote by $\mathbf{Adv}_{\mathcal{H}}^{\text{pro}}(q)$ the advantage of distinguishing $(\mathcal{H}, \mathcal{F})$ from $(\mathcal{RO}, \mathcal{S})$, for some simulator $\mathcal{S}$, maximized over all distinguishers $\mathcal{D}$ making at most q queries. Let atk be a security property of $\mathcal{H}$. Denote by $\mathbf{Adv}_{\mathcal{H}}^{\text{atk}}(q)$ the advantage of breaking $\mathcal{H}$ under atk, maximized over all adversaries making at most q queries. Then:

$$\mathbf{Adv}_{\mathcal{H}}^{\text{atk}}(q) \leq \mathbf{Pr}_{\mathcal{RO}}^{\text{atk}}(q) + \mathbf{Adv}_{\mathcal{H}}^{\text{pro}}(q),$$

where $\mathbf{Pr}_{\mathcal{RO}}^{\text{atk}}(q)$ denotes the success probability of a generic attack against $\mathcal{RO}$ under atk, after at most q queries.

We make two important remarks. First, the indifferentiability framework captures as security properties only single-stage games, as discussed in section 4.1.2. Second, the indifferentiability framework deals only with the construction level, hence it provides assurance only against generic attacks. After ruling out generic attacks below a certain complexity, this rather obviously stresses the need of cryptanalyzing the underlying concrete primitive.

Due to the length-extension weakness, the Merkle-Damgård construction offers no security whatsoever in the indifferentiability setting. However, the generic security of many of the more recent constructions could be proved thanks to the indifferentiability framework (e.g. Coron et al. 2005), and this has become a standard requirement.

4.2.5. The sponge construction

Introduced in 2007 by Bertoni et al. (2007), the *sponge construction* builds an XOF on top of a cryptographic permutation (or a transformation). The sponge construction is parameterized by two integers, the *rate* r and the *capacity* c, where $r + c$ must be equal to the width b of the permutation. A *sponge function* is an instance of the sponge construction with a concrete permutation, a padding rule and fixed values for (r, c).

The sponge construction operates on a state of b bits that is initialized to $s_0 = 0^b$. Hashing a message M works as follows. First, the message is padded with a reversible padding rule to reach a multiple of r bits. This step is similar to what is done for the Merkle-Damgård construction, with the only requirement that the padding rule is injective. The padded message M' is cut into blocks of r bits $M' = M_1 \| M_2 \| \ldots \| M_k$. Then, as depicted in Figure 4.3, the process is split into two phases, one to input M and the other to produce an output of arbitrary length.

– In the *absorbing phase*, the message blocks are bitwise added to the first r bits, that is, the *outer part*, of the state, interleaved with applications of the permutation f

$$s_i = f(s_{i-1} \oplus (M_i \| 0^c)) \text{ for } i \leq k.$$

When all message blocks are processed, the sponge construction switches to the squeezing phase.

– In the *squeezing phase*, the outer part of the state is iteratively returned as output blocks, interleaved with applications of f. The number of iterations is determined by the requested number of bits:

$$\lfloor H(M) \rfloor_{mr} = \lfloor s_k \rfloor_r \| \cdots \| \lfloor s_{k+m-1} \rfloor_r \,, \quad \text{with} \quad s_i = f(s_{i-1}) \text{ for } i > k.$$

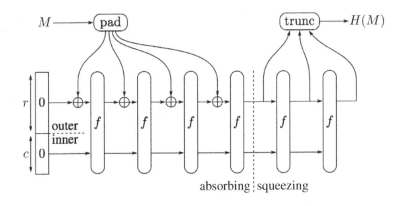

Figure 4.3. *The sponge construction*

Tuning the rate and the capacity allows for security-performance trade-offs. While increasing the rate speeds up the function, the capacity determines the security level. More precisely, the security of the sponge construction is bound to the ability to produce collisions in the last c bits, that is, the *inner part*, of the state. When two sequences of blocks lead to the same inner part value, the next message block can immediately compensate for any differences in the outer part. It turns out that this is the most powerful generic attack on the sponge construction, as captured in the following theorem.

THEOREM 4.2 (Bertoni et al. 2008).– The $\mathcal{RO}$-differentiating advantage of the sponge construction when calling a random permutation π is upper bounded as

$$\mathbf{Adv}^{\text{pro}}_{\text{sponge}^\pi}(N) \leq \frac{N(N+1)}{2^{c+1}},$$

where N denotes the number of queries to π or $\mathcal{S}$ plus the number of blocks input to and obtained from sponge$^\pi$ or $\mathcal{RO}$.

Combined with theorem 4.1, this means that a sponge function has the generic security of a random oracle up to a complexity of $2^{c/2}$, and up to the limits of the indifferentiability framework discussed in section 4.1.2. In other words, with f a strong cryptographic permutation, a sponge function can claim security as in definition 4.4 with claimed capacity equal to the construction capacity $c^\star = c$.

The most notable example of sponge function is KECCAK, but there are many others: for instance, it is the construction of choice for the hash functions submitted to the NIST lightweight cryptography standardization process (see Chapter 16 of volume 2).

Finally, the sponge construction has a security-equivalent sister construction called the *duplex construction*, which hashes messages incrementally (Bertoni et al. 2011b). When keyed, the duplex construction is the basis for many permutation-based authenticated encryption schemes.

4.2.6. KECCAK, SHA-3 *and beyond*

Designed by Guido Bertoni, Joan Daemen, Michaël Peeters and Gilles Van Assche, KECCAK is a family of sponge functions that relies on the seven KECCAK-f permutations (Bertoni et al. 2013). It was selected in 2012 by NIST to become the basis of the SHA-3 standard after an open, yet fierce, competition. Next to the SHA-3 hash functions, NIST standardized the SHAKE128 and SHAKE256 XOFs as well as several other functions such as CSHAKE, KMAC and TUPLEHASH (NIST 2015b, 2016).

The round function of KECCAK-f is described as operating on a three-dimensional state of $5 \times 5 \times w$ bits, with w a power of 2 between 1 and 64. It consists of the following step mappings:

– θ, a column-parity mixer, which adds a pattern that depends solely on the parity of the columns of the state, as studied in its generality in Stoffelen and Daemen (2018);

– ρ and π that displace bits without altering their value;

– χ, a degree-2 nonlinear mapping that processes each row independently and that can be seen as the application of a translation-invariant 5-bit S-box;

– ι, the addition of a round constant to break symmetry properties.

KECCAK and all the instances standardized by NIST have several distinctive properties that set them apart from their predecessors SHA-1 and SHA-2. For instance, KECCAK does not instantiate the Merkle-Damgård construction and instead uses a cryptographic permutation. Also, SHA-3 is the first hash standard that includes XOFs in addition to the traditional fixed output-size functions. Finally, the round function is non-aligned, as defined in Bordes et al. (2021), and has interesting implementation properties, notably a short critical path when implemented in hardware.

Despite these distinctive properties, and perhaps also thanks to them, KECCAK has undergone extensive third-party cryptanalysis, with a record number of cryptanalysis papers published on an unbroken hash function. This is a valuable asset, which allows one to propose alternate performance-security trade-offs knowingly (Bertoni et al. 2018).

For a more complete description of KECCAK, the reader can also refer to Appendix 4.

4.3. Tree hashing

Like the Merkle-Damgård and sponge constructions, most hash functions are iterated, that is, the message blocks are processed sequentially, and the processing of a block requires all previous blocks to be processed. This limits the efficient use of multi-processors and single-instruction multiple-data (SIMD) units, when hashing a single (long) message.

We view tree hashing as a mode of operation on top of a compression function or another hash function, in both cases dubbed the *inner hash function*. Tree hashing consists of cutting the message in parts, or *chunks*, hashing them independently and then recursively hashing together the resulting digests. The process can be depicted as a tree, where a node contains a chunk and/or the digests of other nodes, and an edge represents the application of the inner hash function. The digest is taken as the output of the inner hash function applied to the root of the tree. With tree hashing, several parts of the message can be processed simultaneously, and parallel architectures are used more efficiently.

Ralph Merkle introduced tree hashing in 1979 (Merkle 1979), and Damgård (1989) proposed a tree hash mode that is provably collision-resistant if the underlying compression function is collision-resistant. Using the indifferentiability framework, Daemen et al. (2018) analyzed tree hash modes in the most general way and derived a series of conditions for a mode to be secure if the inner hash function is secure. The conditions can be summarized as follows:

– *subtree-freeness*, which mandates that subtrees and complete trees can be distinguished, and therefore prevents length-extension attacks;

– *radical-decodability*, which requires that chaining value bits, that is, bits that come from hashing another node, can be identified in a node;

– *message-decodability*, which requires that chunk bits can be identified in a node, and that the entire message is processed.

Such conditions are fairly easy to satisfy, and we point out the Sakura encoding as a systematic way to do so (Bertoni et al. 2014). Note that these conditions also apply to sequential modes, which means that this provides yet another way of fixing the Merkle-Damgård construction (see section 4.2.2).

We conclude with examples of hash functions and XOFs that exploit tree hashing on top of a sequential hash function. These include different instances of PARALLELHASH, on top of CSHAKE (NIST 2016), KANGAROOTWELVE, on top of a reduced-round SHAKE128 (Bertoni et al. 2018), and BLAKE3 (O'Connor et al. 2020). The possible tree topologies are numerous (e.g. Atighehchi and Bonnecaze 2017).

4.4. References

Anderson, R. (1993). The classification of hash functions. In *Proceedings of the IMA Conference in Cryptography and Coding*.

Andreeva, E., Mennink, B., Preneel, B. (2010). Security reductions of the second round SHA-3 candidates. In *ISC 2010*, vol. 6531 of *Lecture Notes in Computer Science*, Burmester, M., Tsudik, G., Magliveras, S.S., Ilic, I. (eds). Springer.

Atighehchi, K. and Bonnecaze, A. (2017). Asymptotic analysis of plausible tree hash modes for SHA-3. *IACR Trans. Symmetric Cryptol.*, 2017(4), 212–239.

Aumasson, J., Meier, W., Phan, R.C., Henzen, L. (2014). *The Hash Function BLAKE*. Information Security and Cryptography. Springer.

Barreto, P.S.L.M. and Rijmen, V. (2000). The Whirlpool hashing function. *Proceedings of the 1st NESSIE Workshop*, Leuven.

Bellare, M. and Ristenpart, T. (2006). Multi-property-preserving hash domain extension and the EMD transform. In *ASIACRYPT 2006*, vol. 4284 of *Lecture Notes in Computer Science*, Lai, X., Chen, K. (eds). Springer.

Bellare, M. and Rogaway, P. (1993). Random oracles are practical: A paradigm for designing efficient protocols. In *CCS '93, Proceedings of the 1st ACM Conference on Computer and Communications Security*, Denning, D.E., Pyle, R., Ganesan, R., Sandhu, R.S., Ashby, V. (eds). ACM.

Bellare, M., Canetti, R., Krawczyk, H. (1996). Keying hash functions for message authentication. In *CRYPTO '96*, vol. 1109 of *Lecture Notes in Computer Science*, Koblitz, N. (ed.). Springer.

Bertoni, G., Daemen, J., Peeters, M., Van Assche, G. (2007). Sponge functions. Ecrypt Hash Workshop 2007.

Bertoni, G., Daemen, J., Peeters, M., Van Assche, G. (2008). On the indifferentiability of the sponge construction. In *EUROCRYPT 2008*, vol. 4965 of *Lecture Notes in Computer Science*, Smart, N.P. (ed.). Springer.

Bertoni, G., Daemen, J., Peeters, M., Van Assche, G. (2011a). Cryptographic sponge functions [Online]. Available at: https://keccak.team/sponge_duplex.html.

Bertoni, G., Daemen, J., Peeters, M., Van Assche, G. (2011b). Duplexing the sponge: Single-pass authenticated encryption and other applications. In *SAC 2011*, vol. 7118 of *Lecture Notes in Computer Science*, Miri, A., Vaudenay, S. (eds). Springer.

Bertoni, G., Daemen, J., Peeters, M., Van Assche, G. (2013). Keccak. In *EUROCRYPT 2013*, vol. 7881 of *Lecture Notes in Computer Science*, Johansson, T., Nguyen, P.Q. (eds). Springer.

Bertoni, G., Daemen, J., Peeters, M., Van Assche, G. (2014). Sakura: A flexible coding for tree hashing. In *ACNS 2014*, vol. 8479 of *Lecture Notes in Computer Science*, Boureanu, I., Owesarski, P., Vaudenay, S. (eds). Springer.

Bertoni, G., Daemen, J., Peeters, M., Van Assche, G., Van Keer, R., Viguier, B. (2018). KangarooTwelve: Fast hashing based on Keccak-p. In *ACNS 2018*, vol. 10892 of *Lecture Notes in Computer Science*, Preneel, B., Vercauteren, F. (eds). Springer.

Biham, E. and Dunkelman, O. (2007). A framework for iterative hash functions – HAIFA. *IACR Cryptol. ePrint Arch.*, 2007, 278.

Bordes, N., Daemen, J., Kuijsters, D., Van Assche, G. (2021). Thinking outside the Superbox. In *CRYPTO 2021, Part III*, vol. 12827 of *Lecture Notes in Computer Science*, Malkin, T., Peikert, C. (eds). Springer.

Coron, J., Dodis, Y., Malinaud, C., Puniya, P. (2005). Merkle-Damgård revisited: How to construct a hash function. In *CRYPTO 2005*, vol. 3621 of *Lecture Notes in Computer Science*, Shoup, V. (ed.). Springer.

Daemen, J., Mennink, B., Van Assche, G. (2018). Sound hashing modes of arbitrary functions, permutations, and block ciphers. *IACR Trans. Symmetric Cryptol.*, 2018(4), 197–228.

Damgård, I. (1989). A design principle for hash functions. In *CRYPTO '89*, vol. 435 of *Lecture Notes in Computer Science*, Brassard, G. (ed.). Springer.

Ferguson, N., Lucks, S., Schneier, B., Whiting, D., Bellare, M., Kohno, T., Callas, J., Walker, J. (2011). The Skein hash function family. Submission to NIST SHA-3 competition (Round 3).

Gauravaram, P., Knudsen, L.R., Matusiewicz, K., Mendel, F., Rechberger, C., Schläffer, M., Thomsen, S.S. (2011). Grøstl – a SHA-3 candidate. Submission to NIST SHA-3 competition (Round 3).

Joux, A. (2004). Multicollisions in iterated hash functions. Application to cascaded constructions. In *CRYPTO 2004*, vol. 3152 of *Lecture Notes in Computer Science*, Franklin, M.K. (ed.). Springer.

Kelsey, J. and Kohno, T. (2006). Herding hash functions and the Nostradamus attack. In *EUROCRYPT 2006*, vol. 4004 of *Lecture Notes in Computer Science*, Vaudenay, S. (ed.). Springer.

Kelsey, J. and Schneier, B. (2005). Second preimages on n-bit hash functions for much less than 2^n work. In *EUROCRYPT 2005*, vol. 3494 of *Lecture Notes in Computer Science*, Cramer, R. (ed.). Springer.

Lucks, S. (2005). A failure-friendly design principle for hash functions. In *ASIACRYPT 2005*, vol. 3788 of *Lecture Notes in Computer Science*, Roy, B.K. (ed.). Springer.

Matyas, S., Meyer, C., Oseas, J. (1985). Generating strong one-way functions with cryptographic algorithm. *IBM Techn. Disclosure Bull.*, 27(10A), 5658–5659.

Maurer, U.M., Renner, R., Holenstein, C. (2004). Indifferentiability, impossibility results on reductions, and applications to the random oracle methodology. In *TCC 2004*, vol. 2951 of *Lecture Notes in Computer Science*, Naor, M. (ed.). Springer.

Menezes, A., van Oorschot, P.C., Vanstone, S.A. (1996). *Handbook of Applied Cryptography*. CRC Press.

Merkle, R.C. (1979). Secrecy, authentication, and public key systems. PhD Thesis, Electrical Engineering, Stanford.

Merkle, R.C. (1989). One way hash functions and DES. In *CRYPTO '89*, vol. 435 of *Lecture Notes in Computer Science*, Brassard, G. (ed.). Springer.

Miyaguchi, S., Ohta, K., Iwata, M. (1990). 128-Bit hash function (N-hash). In *Proc. Securicom*, 127–137.

NIST (2015a). Federal information processing standard 180-4, secure hash standard [Online]. Available at: https://doi.org/10.6028/NIST.FIPS.180-4.

NIST (2015b). Federal information processing standard 202, SHA-3 standard: Permutation-based hash and extendable-output functions [Online]. Available at: https://doi.org/10.6028/NIST.FIPS.202.

NIST (2016). Special publication 800-185, SHA-3 derived functions: cSHAKE, KMAC, TupleHash and ParallelHash [Online]. Available at: https://doi.org/10.6028/NIST.SP.800-185.

O'Connor, J., Aumasson, J.-P., Neves, S., Wilcox-O'Hearn, Z. (2020). BLAKE3 [Online]. Available at: https://blake3.io.

Preneel, B., Govaerts, R., Vandewalle, J. (1993). Hash functions based on block ciphers: A synthetic approach. In *CRYPTO '93*, vol. 773 of *Lecture Notes in Computer Science*, Stinson, D.R. (ed.). Springer.

Quisquater, J. and Girault, M. (1989). 2n-bit hash-functions using n-bit symmetric block cipher algorithms. In *EUROCRYPT '89*, vol. 434 of *Lecture Notes in Computer Science*, Quisquater, J., Vandewalle, J. (eds). Springer.

Ristenpart, T., Shacham, H., Shrimpton, T. (2011). Careful with composition: Limitations of the indifferentiability framework. In *EUROCRYPT 2011*, vol. 6632 of *Lecture Notes in Computer Science*, Paterson, K.G. (ed.). Springer.

Rivest, R.L. (1990). The MD4 message digest algorithm. In *CRYPTO '90*, vol. 537 of *Lecture Notes in Computer Science*, Menezes, A., Vanstone, S.A. (eds). Springer.

Rivest, R.L. (1992). The MD5 message-digest algorithm. *RFC*, 1321, 1–21.

Rogaway, P. and Shrimpton, T. (2004). Cryptographic hash-function basics: Definitions, implications, and separations for preimage resistance, second-preimage resistance, and collision resistance. In *FSE 2004*, vol. 3017 of *Lecture Notes in Computer Science*, Roy, B.K., Meier, W. (eds). Springer.

Stoffelen, K. and Daemen, J. (2018). Column parity mixers. *IACR Trans. Symmetric Cryptol.*, 2018(1), 126–159.

Wu, H. (2011). The hash function JH. Submission to NIST SHA-3 competition (Round 3).

Yuval, G. (1979). How to swindle Rabin. *Cryptologia*, 3(3), 187–191.

5

Modes of Operation

Gaëtan LEURENT
Inria, Paris, France

Cryptographic schemes are usually designed with a bottom-up approach. We start from primitives that operate on small message blocks (of n bits) and achieve a well-defined security notion (such as a block cipher), and use them inside a mode of operation (or mode) to deal with arbitrary-length messages. A mode divides the message M into n-bit blocks m_i, and processes the blocks one by one through the primitive, with a chaining rule to produce output blocks.

In this chapter, we describe the main modes for encryption and authentication and discuss their security.

5.1. Encryption schemes

The goal of an encryption scheme is to keep the content of a message secret, so that an adversary seeing the ciphertext does not learn anything about the message (apart from metadata such as its length). Moreover, we usually require the stronger property that the ciphertext is indistinguishable from a random string. The most common encryption schemes are based on stream ciphers, or block ciphers with a mode of operation such as cipher block chaining (CBC) or counter mode (CTR).

An encryption scheme is an efficiently computable function

$$\mathcal{E} : \begin{cases} \mathbb{F}_2^k \times \mathbb{F}_2^\nu \times \mathbb{F}_2^* \to \mathbb{F}_2^* \\ (K, N, M) \mapsto C \end{cases}$$

Symmetric Cryptography 1,
coordinated by Christina BOURA and María NAYA-PLASENCIA. © ISTE Ltd 2023.

called the encryption function, which maps a k-bit key K, ν-bit nonce N and plaintext M of arbitrary length m to a ciphertext C of length $c = c(m)$ such that $\mathcal{E}_K^N = \mathcal{E}(K, N, \cdot)$ is a family of injective functions. Its inverse $(\mathcal{E}_K^N)^{-1} = \mathcal{D}_K^N = \mathcal{D}(K, N, \cdot)$ for each K, N defines the corresponding decryption function such that $\mathcal{D}_K^N(\mathcal{E}_K^N(M)) = M$ for all plaintexts M. The nonce N is a value that must be unique for each usage of the encryption scheme with a given key, so that encrypting the same message twice results in distinct ciphertexts. It must be known by the sender and receiver, but does not have to be secret. Some modes have stronger requirements on the nonce, and call it an initialization value (IV). In practice, it is usually implemented by a counter or generated as a random value and sent alongside the ciphertext.

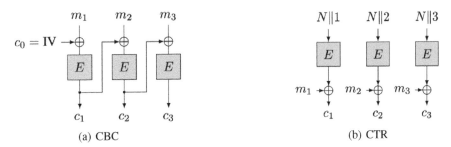

(a) CBC   (b) CTR

Figure 5.1. *CBC and CTR modes*

5.1.1. *Cipher block chaining*

The CBC mode is one of the oldest encryption modes (NIST 1980), and is still widely used. The message M is divided into n-bit blocks m_i, $1 \leq i \leq \ell$ and encrypted with a random IV c_0 using the chaining rule shown in Figure 5.1(a):

$$c_i = E_K(m_i \oplus c_{i-1}).$$

The ciphertext chaining ensures that the encryption of each block depends on the IV and the previous blocks. When encrypting several messages, each one should be encrypted with a fresh random IV. CBC decryption reverses the encryption steps: $m_i = E_K^{-1}(c_i) \oplus c_{i-1}$.

In order to accommodate messages with a length that is not a multiple of the block size n, a padding rule is used to encode the message before encryption. Two simple methods are commonly used:

– 10* *padding*: can handle messages with an arbitrary bit length. A message of length $\ell n + p$ bits ($0 \leq p < n$) is padded by appending a single "1" bit, and $n - p - 1$ "0" bits. This is defined as padding method 2 in ISO/IEC 9797-1.

– PKCS#7 padding: can handle messages with an arbitrary byte length. A message of length $\ell n/8 + p$ bytes ($0 \le p < n/8$) is padded by appending $n/8 - p$ bytes, all set to the value $n/8 - p$. This is defined in RFC 5652.

Both methods are injective, so that the padding can be removed unambiguously after decryption (all messages are padded, even if the length is a multiple of n). However, they generate a ciphertext that is longer than the plaintext, with up to n extra bits.

Alternatively, CBC can be modified to handle a final partial block with *ciphertext stealing* (Dworkin 2010). During encryption, the partial plaintext block is padded with zeroes, and the previous ciphertext block is truncated to the length of the partial plaintext block (resulting in a ciphertext with the same length as the plaintext). During decryption, the last block must be decrypted first to recover the missing bits of the previous ciphertext block from the padding of the partial block.

5.1.2. *Counter mode*

The CTR mode (Dworkin 2001) is a simple way to turn a block cipher into a stream cipher by encrypting a counter. Each message block is therefore encrypted as $c_i = m_i \oplus E_K(n_i)$, with n_i a non-repeating counter. In order to encrypt several messages with the same key, the counter is usually constructed as the concatenation of a nonce N and a block counter ($n_i = N\|i$), as seen in Figure 5.1(b):

$$c_i = m_i \oplus E_K(N\|i).$$

The CTR mode has several advantages over CBC. Since each block can be encrypted independently of the others, the encryption (and decryption) process can be parallelized easily, enabling high-speed implementation in software or hardware. Since CTR is effectively a stream cipher, there is no need for a padding scheme (the ciphertext length is the same as the plaintext length). The decryption process is the same as the encryption: $m_i = c_i \oplus E_K(n_i)$; in particular, neither encryption nor decryption use the inverse block cipher, reducing the implementation size in hardware. CTR has been standardized more recently than CBC and is slowly replacing it in new versions of internet protocols.

5.2. Message authentication codes

A message authentication code (MAC) protects the authenticity of a message. It is a short tag computed by the sender from the message and a key, sent together with the (plaintext) message. To confirm the authenticity of the message, the receiver recomputes the tag using his copy of the key, and verifies that it matches the received tag. The main security requirement of a MAC is to resist forgery attacks: it should be hard to predict the tag of any message without knowing the key, even when the attacker is given access to the tag of known or chosen messages. MAC algorithms can be built in many ways, from block ciphers, from hash functions, or from scratch.

Formally, a MAC is an efficiently computable function $\mathcal{H}$ which maps a k-bit key K and a message M of arbitrary length m to a t-bit tag T

$$\mathcal{H} : \begin{cases} \mathbb{F}_2^k \times \mathbb{F}_2^* \to \mathbb{F}_2^t \\ (K, M) \mapsto T \end{cases}$$

Some MACs also use a nonce N, in the same way as encryption schemes.

5.2.1. *CBC-MAC*

One of the first MAC proposals was CBC-MAC, a block-cipher-based algorithm (NIST 1985). CBC-MAC follows the same structure as CBC, but does not use an IV (the MAC is deterministic) and uses only the last block cipher output as MAC. The CBC-MAC construction requires a finalization function to avoid simple attacks with messages of different lengths.[1] A popular option is to encrypt the final block again with a different key, known as encrypt-last-block CBC-MAC ECBC-MAC) (Figure 5.2(a)):

$$ECBC - MAC(M) = E_{K'}\Big(E_K\Big(m_\ell \oplus \cdots E_K\big(m_2 \oplus E_K(m_1)\big) \cdots \Big)\Big)$$

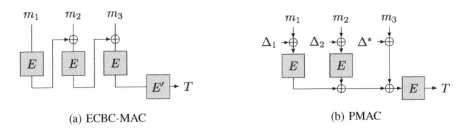

(a) ECBC-MAC   (b) PMAC

Figure 5.2. *ECBC-MAC and PMAC*

More recent variants such as OMAC (Iwata and Kurosawa 2003) modify the finalization function to use a single key. CBC-MAC requires a padding scheme to authenticate messages of arbitrary length; OMAC separates messages whose last block is full and partial, and uses 10* padding if the last block is partial.

---

1 A naive CBC-MAC satisfies $MAC(m_1 \| m_2) = MAC(m_2 \oplus MAC(m_1))$.

5.2.2. *PMAC*

Alternatively, PMAC (Black and Rogaway 2002) is a parallelizable block-cipher-based MAC. In order to prevent reordering of message blocks, PMAC uses secret offsets Δ_i and Δ^* that are different for each block cipher call (the offsets are computed from $E_K(0)$ with a few elementary operations). With full message blocks, PMAC is defined as follows (Figure 5.2(b)):

$$PMAC(M) = E_K\left(\bigoplus_{i=1}^{\ell-1} E_K(\Delta_i \oplus m_i) \oplus \Delta^* \oplus m_\ell \right).$$

If the last block is partial, PMAC uses 10^* padding and a different value of Δ^*. PMAC is not widely used by itself, but it is integrated into many authentication encryption schemes.

5.2.3. *Hash-based MACs*

MAC algorithms can also be built from hash functions. If the hash function is indifferentiable from a random oracle, very simple constructions can be used such as the secret-prefix MAC $H(K\|M)$. For efficiency reasons, the key is often padded to a full block $\bar{K}$. Unfortunately, common hash functions such as the SHA-1 and SHA-2 family give out the raw internal state as output. Therefore, it is possible to compute $H(K\|M\|S)$ from $H(K\|M)$ without knowing K for some suffixes S (S has to include the padding of M). This corresponds to a simple forgery attack against the secret-prefix MAC. Consequently, more complex MAC constructions are used, with some finalization operation to avoid this length-extension attack, such as:

$$Envelope - MAC(M) = H(K\|M\|K)$$
$$Sandwich - MAC(M) = H(\bar{K}\|pad(M)\|\bar{K})$$
$$HMAC(M) = H\big((\bar{K} \oplus opad)\|H((\bar{K} \oplus ipad)\|M)\big),$$

where *pad* is a padding scheme, and *ipad* and *opad* are constant values.

In particular, HMAC (Bellare et al. 1996) is more robust than earlier variants such as envelope-MAC, and it is widely used in internet standards. Hash-based MACs are not parallelizable, but the hash functions used at the time of standardization (MD5, SHA-1) were significantly faster than the available block ciphers (in particular DES).

5.2.4. *Wegman-Carter MACs and GMAC*

The Wegman-Carter construction (Wegman and Carter 1981) authenticates a message M with a nonce N using two keys K and K'

$$WC - MAC(M, N) = H_K(M) \oplus F_{K'}(N),$$

where H is a family of ε-almost XOR universal hash functions (ε-AXU) and F is a pseudo-random function (PRF). The nonce must be unique and known by both parties, but does not need to be secret or random. Instead of using a function with cryptographic properties to compress the message (as in hash-based MACs), the function H has combinatorial properties. More precisely, a family of ε-AXU hash functions $H_K : \mathbb{F}_2^* \to \mathbb{F}_2^n, K \in \mathbb{F}_2^k$ is defined thus:

$$\forall M \neq M' \in \mathbb{F}_2^*, \forall \Delta \in \mathbb{F}_2^n, |\{K \in \mathbb{F}_2^k : H_K(M) \oplus H_K(M') = \Delta\}| \leq \varepsilon 2^k.$$

An important example of ε-AXU function is polynomial hashing, in which the input message is interpreted as a polynomial with coefficients in $\mathbb{F}_{2^n}$, and evaluated on the secret key (with $k = n$): $\sum_{i=1}^{\ell} m_i \times K^i$. In order to maintain security with messages of different lengths, the length must be included in the computation, leading to:

$$H_K(M) = \sum_{i=1}^{\ell} m_i \times K^i \oplus \mathrm{len}(M) \times K^{\ell+1},$$

where $\mathrm{len}(M)$ this length of the message in bits. The last block is padded with zeros if it is incomplete. The family H is $\ell/2^n$-AXU with messages of at most ℓ blocks. When evaluated using Horner's rule, polynomial hashing requires a single multiplication and addition per message block.

GMAC is a Wegman-Carter-style MAC using polynomial hashing for H and a block cipher encryption for F:

$$GMAC(M, N) = \sum_{i=1}^{\ell} m_i \times K^i \oplus \mathrm{len}(M) \times K^{\ell+1} \oplus E_{K'}(N).$$

GMAC is more efficient to implement than CBC-MAC because the polynomial hashing can be parallelized, and multiplication in the finite field $\mathbb{F}_{2^n}$ is typically more efficient than a block cipher call. It is widely used in internet standards, as part of the GCM authenticated encryption mode.

5.3. Security of modes: generic attacks

The security of modes of operation is typically studied with a proof-based approach, starting from a security assumption on the primitive in order to bound the success probability (or advantage) of an adversary to break the scheme. For a concrete example, the proof of the CTR mode given in Chapter 11 states:

$$\text{Adv}^{\text{prf}}_{\text{CTR[AES]}}(\mathcal{A}) \leq \frac{\binom{|Q_d|}{2}}{2^{128}} + \text{Adv}^{\text{prp}}_{\text{AES}}(\mathcal{A}').$$

In particular, when the number of encrypted blocks $|Q_d|$ satisfies $|Q_d| \ll 2^{64}$, and the block cipher is a secure pseudo-random permutation (PRP) ($\text{Adv}^{\text{prp}}_{\text{AES}} \ll 1$), this proves the security of the CTR mode as a family of PRFs ($\text{Adv}^{\text{prf}}_{\text{CTR[AES]}} \ll 1$).

In this section, we focus instead on generic attacks, that is, attacks that are independent of the choice of the primitive and only exploit properties of the mode. Security proofs give lower bounds on the security of modes, and generic attacks give upper bounds; when the two bounds match, the proof is tight and we understand the precise security level of the mode in a given model. Still, more precise study of generic attacks provides a better view of what goes wrong when the hypotheses of the proof are not satisfied, and informs the design of better modes.

5.3.1. *The birthday bound*

The security of the vast majority of cryptosystems is affected by the presence of collisions. This is a well-known issue for hash functions: due to the birthday paradox we expect to find collisions in an n-bit hash function with roughly $2^{n/2}$ queries.

The birthday bound also appears in block-cipher based modes because of the PRF-PRP switching lemma. Indeed, an n-bit block cipher should behave like a PRP, but it can be considered as a PRF when the number of queries is significantly below $2^{n/2}$. However, when approaching $2^{n/2}$ queries, a PRF should start having collisions, while a block cipher called with different inputs always has non-colliding outputs. Most modes of operations can be distinguished from random after roughly $2^{n/2}$ queries, either by detecting special collisions, or by detecting the lack of some collisions.

5.3.2. *Generic attack against iterated MACs*

Preneel and van Oorschot described a generic attack against all deterministic iterated MACs with a state size of n bits (Preneel and van Oorschot 1995). After $2^{n/2}$ queries with small messages of the same length, we expect that two messages reach the same internal state. The internal collision can be detected because it implies a collision in the tag (for some MACs there are also false-positive pairs colliding on the tag but not on the internal state). If we have an internal collision M_i, M_j, we also have a collision $MAC(M_i\|S) = MAC(M_j\|S)$ for any suffix S; we can create a forgery by asking for the tag of $MAC(M_i\|S)$ and using it to predict the tag of $MAC(M_j\|S)$.

Even though all deterministic iterated MACs have essentially the same security bound, the impact of the attacks can be quite different. For instance, the envelope MAC and the sandwich MAC are very similar hash-based MACs, but the best known attack against the sandwich MAC is a forgery attack, while there is a more complex key-recovery attack against the envelope MAC with birthday complexity (Preneel and van Oorschot 1996). The generic attack also motivates the design of MAC algorithms with security beyond the birthday bound: they must either be non-deterministic (like the Wegman-Carter MAC using a nonce), or use a larger internal state (like SUM-ECBC (Yasuda 2010) or 3kf9 (Zhang et al. 2012)).

5.3.3. *Generic attack against Wegman-Carter MACs*

Wegman-Carter MACs are not susceptible to the generic attack of Preneel and van Oorschot thanks to the use of a nonce; they can be secure up to $|Q_d| \ll 2^n$ queries. Nonetheless, GMAC is only secure up to the birthday bound, because it uses a block cipher to instantiate the PRF. In particular, when authenticating the same message multiple times, an attacker can observe that all the tags are different, while random tags should have collisions after roughly $2^{n/2}$ queries. This observation can be turned into an attack recovering the hash key with $2^{n/2}$ queries and time roughly 2^n, or with $2^{2n/3}$ queries and time roughly $2^{2n/3}$, using techniques from attacks against the CTR mode (Leurent and Sibleyras 2018).

5.3.4. *Generic attack against CBC*

After encrypting $2^{n/2}$ blocks with CBC (either as one long message, or several shorter messages), we expect a collision $c_i = c_j$. Following the definition of CBC, this reveals the XOR of two plaintext blocks: $c_i = c_j \iff E(m_i \oplus c_{i-1}) = E(m_j \oplus c_{j-1}) \iff m_i \oplus m_j = c_{i-1} \oplus c_{j-1}$. This is only a small amount of information about the plaintext, but it breaks the definition of secure encryption, and shows that the security proof is tight. In practice, the Sweet32 attack (Bhargavan and Leurent 2016) has shown that this information is sufficient to break the security of concrete applications, such as secure websites. The attack is based on the model of the BEAST attack (Duong and Rizzo 2011): a malicious website can force the browser to generate a large number of encrypted messages containing both known information and a repeated secret cookie. Eventually, a collision reveals the XOR difference between some known information and the cookie, leaking the secret value.

5.3.5. *Generic attack against CTR*

On the other hand, when using CTR, each block cipher call has a unique input, and there are no collisions to exploit. Interestingly, this also leads to a distinguisher with birthday complexity. If an adversary has access to $2^{n/2}$ blocks of known plaintext and ciphertext, he can recover the corresponding keystream $E(n_i) = c_i \oplus m_i$ and detect that the values are unique (because E is a permutation), while collisions would be expected with a random ciphertext. This distinguisher has the same complexity as the CBC generic attack and shows that the CTR proof is also tight. However, the loss of security seems quite different: the attack against CBC lets an attacker recover message blocks from collisions, but the attack against the counter mode does not directly reveal information about the message.

Actually, this distinguisher can also be used to recover plaintext information. Every pair of blocks reveals an inequality involving the plaintext: $i \neq j \implies c_i \oplus m_i \neq c_j \oplus m_j$. When repeatedly encrypting a low entropy message, this is sufficient to recover the message with roughly $2^{n/2}$ blocks of data, after eliminating each possible value of the message (McGrew 2013). In practice, in the BEAST setting the attacker can manipulate the message so that a target block contains known bytes together with a single secret byte, and recover a cookie byte by byte. More advanced attacks are applicable to high entropy message blocks with complexity $2^{2n/3}$ (Leurent and Sibleyras 2018).

5.3.6. *Small block sizes*

The attacks on CTR and CBC show that block ciphers with a small block size of $n = 64$ bits (such as DES, 3DES, BLOWFISH, or some lightweight block ciphers) should not be used in general-purpose cryptosystems. They can be attacked in practice when the amount of encrypted data is around 2^{32} blocks, which corresponds to just 32 GB. In order to keep the probability of having a collision sufficiently small, each key must be used for significantly fewer than 2^{32} blocks ($|Q_d| \ll 2^{n/2}$). In particular, NIST now recommends that 3DES is only used with at most 2^{20} blocks of data per key or 8 MB (Barker and Mouha 2017).

Block ciphers with small block sizes can be used with dedicated modes with security beyond the birthday bound, like CENC (Iwata 2006). Indeed, CENC is secure up to $|Q_d| \ll 2^n$ blocks of data (Iwata et al. 2016).

5.3.7. *Misuse*

More generally, modes of operation fail if nonces or IVs are not used properly. Even when security requirements are well understood, there is a risk that users do not implement them properly, leading to catastrophic security failures. This has been observed repeatedly in practice, starting with the reuse of one-time-pad material by the soviets during the Cold War. When keystream is reused, the difference between two encrypted messages is recovered as the difference between the corresponding ciphertexts: $C \oplus C' = M \oplus M'$. Cryptanalysts working on the Venona project managed to reconstruct the plaintexts using redundancy in the messages.

Modern cryptosystems also fail when misused:

– The CTR mode requires the block cipher input (the counter) to be unique. If the counter can be reset without changing the key, this leads to keystream reuse. Unfortunately, this type of weakness is present in several protocols, such as WPA (Vanhoef and Piessens 2017) and VoLTE (Rupprecht et al. 2020).

– The CBC mode requires random IVs. It is important that the IV cannot be predicted by an adversary who can encrypt chosen messages. Otherwise, attacks are possible, as first observed by Rogaway (1995), and demonstrated in practice by the BEAST attack (Duong and Rizzo 2011).

– The Wegman-Carter MAC requires a unique nonce, and the construction fails badly when nonces are repeated (Joux 2006). Let us consider a Wegman-Carter MAC with polynomial hashing, like GMAC. If two different messages $M \neq M'$ are authenticated with the same nonce (resulting in tags T and T'), the hash key K can be extracted by solving a polynomial equation in the field:

$$\sum_{i=1}^{\ell} m_i \times K^i \oplus \sum_{i=1}^{\ell'} m_i' \times K^i = T \oplus T'.$$

Nonce repetition has been observed in practice in TLS (Böck et al. 2016). To mitigate this issue, variants of the Wegman-Carter construction have been proposed with better resistance against nonce repetition, such as WMAC (Black and Cochran 2009) and EWCDM (Cogliati and Seurin 2016).

5.3.8. *Limitations of encryption*

Secure encryption prevents third parties from learning anything about the content of the message, but there are important limitations. In particular, encryption schemes are usually malleable: modifications of the ciphertext are not detected and some well-chosen modifications have a predictable effect on the decrypted plaintext. This is particularly true with stream ciphers and the CTR mode: without knowing the secret key, if an attacker flips a bit of the ciphertext, it will flip the corresponding bit of plaintext. This type of attack is considered out of scope for an encryption scheme, and authenticated encryption (described in the next chapter) should be used to provide security against an active adversary. In practice, the malleability of stream ciphers has been used to break the WEP protocol with "IP redirection" (Borisov et al.

2001): an attacker can modify the encrypted IP address encoded in WEP packets such that the decrypted packets are sent to self instead of the legitimate receiver.

Encryption schemes that require padding (such as CBC) also leak information if the decryption fails with a specific error message when the padding is invalid (Vaudenay 2002). An adversary that can modify the ciphertext and observe the error messages can use the "padding oracle" to recover information about the plaintext. Again, authenticated encryption should be used to avoid this issue.

Finally, encryption schemes do not protect the metadata. An adversary monitoring the communication channel can learn the timing and length of messages, as well as the identity of the parties (e.g. IP addresses). Metadata by itself reveals a lot of information, and we know that it is collected by intelligence agencies. The message length can also reveal the message content when there are only a few possible messages, as demonstrated with the Tinder app (Checkmarx 2018). Protecting this metadata is considered out of the scope of cryptography, but can be achieved with privacy-enhancing technologies such as the Tor network.

5.4. References

Barker, E. and Mouha, N. (2017). Recommendation for the triple data encryption algorithm (TDEA) block cipher. NIST Special Publication 800-67 revision 2, National Institute for Standards and Technology.

Bellare, M., Canetti, R., Krawczyk, H. (1996). Keying hash functions for message authentication. In *CRYPTO'96*, vol. 1109 of *Lecture Notes in Computer Science*, Koblitz, N. (ed.). Springer.

Bhargavan, K. and Leurent, G. (2016). On the practical (in-)security of 64-bit block ciphers: Collision attacks on HTTP over TLS and OpenVPN. In *ACM CCS 2016*, Weippl, E.R., Katzenbeisser, S., Kruegel, C., Myers, A.C., Halevi, S. (eds). ACM Press.

Black, J. and Cochran, M. (2009). MAC reforgeability. In *FSE 2009*, vol. 5665 of *Lecture Notes in Computer Science*, Dunkelman, O. (ed.). Springer.

Black, J. and Rogaway, P. (2002). A block-cipher mode of operation for parallelizable message authentication. In *EUROCRYPT 2002*, vol. 2332 of *Lecture Notes in Computer Science*, Knudsen, L.R. (ed.). Springer.

Böck, H., Zauner, A., Devlin, S., Somorovsky, J., Jovanovic, P. (2016). Nonce-disrespecting adversaries: Practical forgery attacks on GCM in TLS. *WOOT '16*, Austin, TX, USA [Online]. Available at: https://dblp.org/rec/conf/woot/BockZDSJ16.html?view=bibtex.

Borisov, N., Goldberg, I., Wagner, D. (2001). Intercepting mobile communications: The insecurity of 802.11. In *MobiCom '01*, Rose, C. (ed.), ACM [Online]. Available at: https://dblp.org/rec/conf/mobicom/BorisovGW01.html?view=bibtex.

Checkmarx (2018). Are you on Tinder? Someone may be watching you swipe. Technical report [Online]. Available at: https://www.checkmarx.com/blog/tinder-someone-may-watching-swipe-2/.

Cogliati, B. and Seurin, Y. (2016). EWCDM: An efficient, beyond-birthday secure, nonce-misuse resistant MAC. In *CRYPTO 2016, Part I*, vol. 9814 of *Lecture Notes in Computer Science*, Robshaw, M., Katz, J. (eds). Springer.

Duong, T. and Rizzo, J. (2011). Here come the $\oplus$ ninjas [Online]. Available at: https://bugzilla.mozilla.org/attachment.cgi?id=540839.

Dworkin, M. (2001). *Recommendation for Block Cipher Modes of Operation: Methods and Techniques*. NIST Special Publication 800-38A, National Institute for Standards and Technology.

Dworkin, M. (2010). *Recommendation for Block Cipher Modes of Operation: Three Variants of Ciphertext Stealing for CBC Mode*. NIST Special Publication 800-38A (addendum), National Institute for Standards and Technology.

Iwata, T. (2006). New blockcipher modes of operation with beyond the birthday bound security. In *FSE 2006*, vol. 4047 of *Lecture Notes in Computer Science*, Robshaw, M.J.B. (ed.). Springer.

Iwata, T. and Kurosawa, K. (2003). OMAC: One-key CBC MAC. In *FSE 2003*, vol. 2887 of *Lecture Notes in Computer Science*, Johansson, T. (ed.). Springer.

Iwata, T., Mennink, B., Vizár, D. (2016). CENC is optimally secure. Cryptology ePrint Archive, Report 2016/1087.

Joux, A. (2006). Authentication failures in NIST version of GCM [Online]. Available at: https://csrc.nist.gov/csrc/media/projects/block-cipher-techniques/documents/bcm/jouxcomments.pdf.

Leurent, G. and Sibleyras, F. (2018). The missing difference problem, and its applications to counter mode encryption. In *EUROCRYPT 2018, Part II*, vol. 10821 of *Lecture Notes in Computer Science*, Nielsen, J.B., Rijmen, V. (eds). Springer.

McGrew, D. (2013). Impossible plaintext cryptanalysis and probable-plaintext collision attacks of 64-bit block cipher modes. In *FSE 2013*, Moriai, S. (ed.), Lecture Notes in Computer Science, Springer.

NIST (1980). DES modes of operation. NIST Special Publication 81, National Institute for Standards and Technology.

NIST (1985). Computer data authentication. NIST Special Publication 113, National Institute for Standards and Technology.

Preneel, B. and van Oorschot, P.C. (1995). MDx-MAC and building fast MACs from hash functions. In *CRYPTO'95*, vol. 963 of *Lecture Notes in Computer Science*, Coppersmith, D. (ed.). Springer.

Preneel, B. and van Oorschot, P.C. (1996). On the security of two MAC algorithms. In *EUROCRYPT'96*, vol. 1070 of *Lecture Notes in Computer Science*, Maurer, U.M. (ed.). Springer.

Rogaway, P. (1995). Problems with proposed IP cryptography [Online]. Available at: http://web.cs.ucdavis.edu/~rogaway/papers/draft-rogaway-ipsec-comments-00.txt.

Rupprecht, D., Kohls, K., Holz, T., Pöpper, C. (2020). Call me maybe: Eavesdropping encrypted LTE calls with ReVoLTE. In *USENIX Security 2020*, Capkun, S., Roesner, F. (eds). USENIX Association.

Vanhoef, M. and Piessens, F. (2017). Key reinstallation attacks: Forcing nonce reuse in WPA2. In *ACM CCS 2017*, Thuraisingham, B.M., Evans, D., Malkin, T., Xu, D. (eds). ACM Press.

Vaudenay, S. (2002). Security flaws induced by CBC padding – Applications to SSL, IPSEC, WTLS... In *EUROCRYPT 2002*, vol. 2332 of *Lecture Notes in Computer Science*, Knudsen, L.R. (ed.). Springer.

Wegman, M.N. and Carter, L. (1981). New hash functions and their use in authentication and set equality. *Journal of Computer and System Sciences*, 22, 265–279.

Yasuda, K. (2010). The sum of CBC MACs is a secure PRF. In *CT-RSA 2010*, vol. 5985 of *Lecture Notes in Computer Science*, Pieprzyk, J. (ed.). Springer.

Zhang, L., Wu, W., Sui, H., Wang, P. (2012). 3kf9: Enhancing 3GPP-MAC beyond the birthday bound. In *ASIACRYPT 2012*, vol. 7658 of *Lecture Notes in Computer Science*, Wang, X., Sako, K. (eds). Springer.

6

Authenticated Encryption Schemes

Maria EICHLSEDER

Graz University of Technology, Austria

6.1. Introduction

Authenticated encryption offers the combined security properties of an encryption scheme and a message authentication code (MAC): it protects both confidentiality and authenticity of data. For this reason, authenticated encryption is the preferred cryptographic solution for protecting data in transit as well as at rest. In many communication protocols like TLS, sender and receiver first agree on a shared secret key in a handshake phase and then use this key for an authenticated encryption scheme to protect the actual data to be transmitted. Authenticated encryption schemes are also referred to as authenticated ciphers or authenticated encryption with associated data (AEAD).

Only few applications still use only *non*-authenticated encryption. This is because whenever data are worth encrypting, it is usually also worth protecting against manipulation. Pure encryption schemes cannot provide this. For example, in a streaming-based encryption scheme, an adversary can cause any bit in the plaintext to flip by flipping the corresponding bit in the ciphertext. Assume the adversary suspects that a particular portion of the ciphertext corresponds to some important numeric value, like someone's bank balance or transaction cost: they can flip one of the most significant bits and thus likely produce a much larger value, without detection.

Even when only confidentiality of data is desired as a security goal, using authenticated encryption is often the most efficient way to provide a strong security notion. This facilitates more robust implementations in practice, for example, in the presence of adaptive adversaries, side channels, or when using error messages (Katz and Yung 2000; Black and Urtubia 2002; Degabriele and Paterson 2007).

An authenticated encryption scheme with associated data (AEAD) is a function,

$$\mathcal{AE}: \begin{cases} \mathbb{F}_2^k \times \mathbb{F}_2^\nu \times \mathbb{F}_2^* \times \mathbb{F}_2^* \to \mathbb{F}_2^* \times \mathbb{F}_2^t, \\ (K, N, A, M) \mapsto (C, T), \end{cases}$$

which maps a k-bit key K, ν-bit nonce N, associated data A of arbitrary length a and a message M of arbitrary length m to a ciphertext C of length $c = c(m)$ and a t-bit tag T. Here, $\mathcal{AE}_K^{N,A} = \mathcal{AE}(K, N, A, \cdot)$ is a family of efficiently computable, injective functions. Its inverse $(\mathcal{AE}_K^{N,A})^{-1} = \mathcal{AD}_K^{N,A} = \mathcal{AD}(K, N, A, \cdot, \cdot)$ for each K, N, A defines the corresponding verified decryption function such that $\mathcal{AD}_K^{N,A}(\mathcal{AE}_K^{N,A}(M)) = M$ for all plaintexts M, and $\mathcal{AD}_K^{N,A}(\cdot, \cdot) = \perp$ for all other inputs:

$$\mathcal{AD}: \begin{cases} \mathbb{F}_2^k \times \mathbb{F}_2^\nu \times \mathbb{F}_2^* \times \mathbb{F}_2^* \times \mathbb{F}_2^t \to \mathbb{F}_2^* \cup \{\perp\}, \\ (K, N, A, C, T) \mapsto M \text{ or } \perp. \end{cases}$$

If Alice wants to send a message to Bob, they need a shared secret key K. She generates a fresh nonce N that is different from all previously used nonces for the same key K. She encrypts the message M with $\mathcal{AE}_K^{N,A}$ under K, N and optional additional associated data A that is not confidential, such as routing information. The resulting output of $\mathcal{AE}$ is the ciphertext C and a tag T, which may be encoded as part of C. In some implementations, the nonce N is generated internally by $\mathcal{AE}$ and also encoded as part of C, that is, $\mathcal{AE}$ is a randomized function. Then, she can transmit N, A, C and T to Bob over an insecure channel. The scheme protects the confidentiality of M and K, as well as the authenticity of M (and (C, T)), A and N. Bob decrypts with $\mathcal{AD}_K^{N,A}(C, T)$ and either receives back the message M or an error symbol $\perp$. The latter case indicates that the received ciphertext was invalid, for example, because they were modified by an adversary in transit. If an error occurs, implementations must not return M together with the error symbol.

6.2. Security notions

The adversary's goal is to forge valid ciphertexts with tag, learn information about the plaintexts, or recover the key. Generically, for any authenticated cipher, an adversary can try to achieve this with an exhaustive search over all k-bit key candidates (expected to require close to 2^k offline trial encryptions) or by guessing the t-bit tag for a ciphertext (success probability 2^{-t} for each online verification attempt). Designs are expected to provide security against adversaries with lower resources than this generic complexity that can query the encryption and decryption, under some additional requirements: adversaries must never reuse a nonce in their encryption queries, and the design may specify limits on the number and size of queries. Attacks are quantified in terms of the number, type and size of queries, computational complexity and success probability, but also in terms of damage potential, with key recovery the worst case.

Like pure encryption schemes, authenticated encryption schemes and their security notions were originally formalized in terms of probabilistic algorithms (Bellare and Namprempre 2000; Katz and Yung 2000). The explicit, user-controlled nonce (Rogaway 2004b) and associated data (Rogaway 2002) are later additions. The CAESAR call proposes an additional optional input, the secret message number, but this has not found widespread adoption.

A succinct all-in-one security notion that covers both confidentiality (indistinguishability) and authenticity (unforgeability) was proposed by Rogaway and Shrimpton (2006): the adversary is given access either to a pair of authenticated encryption and verified decryption oracles $(\mathcal{AE}_K, \mathcal{AD}_K)$, or to a pair of oracles $(\$, \perp)$ with the same interfaces, where $\$(\cdot)$ returns a random string of the correct length, and $\perp(\cdot)$ returns $\perp$ on every input. Distinguishing these two cases should be negligible for any adversary with reasonable resources as long as the queries to the first oracle are nonce respecting and no outputs of the first oracle are forwarded to the second oracle.

6.3. Design strategies for authenticated encryption

The two security goals of authenticated encryption, confidentiality and authenticity, are also reflected in its design: an authenticated cipher needs to iterate a core processing step that, on the one hand, translates the plaintext to a ciphertext block by block and, on the other hand, updates an internal state to produce a final authentication tag for the entire message. There are different approaches to constructing such a design, using building blocks of different sizes and abstraction levels:

– **Generic compositions of other schemes**: combine existing schemes that already provide some security properties for data of arbitrary length, such as encryption schemes and MACs.

– **Dedicated designs iterating a primitive**: derive their security from an idealized building block with fixed input size, such as a block cipher.

– **Dedicated designs iterating simpler update functions**: these can achieve a higher performance by using state update functions that have no strong security claim in isolation, but provide security in the iterated context of the design.

These are not strictly separate: *composed* designs will internally still iterate primitives just like *dedicated* schemes, and the step from idealized primitives to more ad hoc designs is rather a continuum. Important properties of designs include the following:

– **Rate, calls**: primitive-based designs usually call the primitive once or twice per message block and may require additional calls for initialization and finalization. The rate is the number of message blocks encrypted per primitive call, for example, 1 or $\frac{1}{2}$. In *parallelizable* designs, the calls for consecutive blocks can be executed in parallel.

– **Online encryption**: a construction is online if it can start producing ciphertext blocks from incoming plaintext blocks on the fly, without waiting for the entire message to arrive first. In a similar vein, a *single-pass* scheme processes the message only once and does not require a second, separated pass over the data.

– **Performance characteristics**: depending on the target application area, desirable goals include *lightweight* designs (e.g. low hardware area, low power requirements, low overhead for short messages) and *high-performance* designs (e.g. high throughput in software on high-end CPUs). This is strongly influenced by the underlying primitive, but also by the mode. For example, a lightweight mode is often *inverse-free* (does not require the inverse of the block cipher).

– **Security**: the security level depends generically on the key size k and tag size t, as well as the cryptanalytic security of the primitive. Many designs are also limited by the *birthday bound*, that is, $b/2$ where b is the block size of the underlying primitive.

– **Misuse robustness**: generally, nonces must never be reused for the same key (nonce misuse), and decryption should not release the unverified plaintext in case the tag verification fails (decryption misuse, RUP). Designs differ in how much damage an attacker can cause if they violate these requirements in a *misuse setting*. Important notions include *full misuse resistance* (MRAE), where an attacker learns nothing in case of nonce misuse except whether two plaintexts encrypted under the same nonce are completely identical; *online misuse resistance*, where an attacker may additionally learn whether two such plaintexts start identically up to a certain block; and *integrity under RUP*, where decryption misuse does not give an attacker the power to forge additional messages. Some designs also impose additional requirements for the nonce, such as unpredictability, while others work with both random nonces and counters.

– **Implementation robustness**: when attackers target a real implementation rather the abstract algorithm, they may exploit physical side-channels such as power consumption or timing, or try to fault the computation. A few designs provide a level of inherent protection against such attacks, or use primitives where implementation countermeasures like masking can be added with a lower performance overhead.

6.3.1. *Generic composition*

Authenticated ciphers can be built by combining an encryption scheme $\mathcal{E}_K$ and a MAC $\mathcal{H}_K$. Figure 6.1 illustrates the classic generic compositions of these two schemes: encrypt-then-authenticate (EtA), encrypt-and-authenticate (E&A) and authenticate-then-encrypt (AtE). In this simplified view, the nonce N is implicit (i.e. $\mathcal{E}_K$ is a probabilistic algorithm), and associated data A can be included as an additional, properly domain-separated input to $\mathcal{H}_K$.

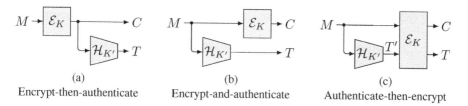

(a)   (b)   (c)

Encrypt-then-authenticate   Encrypt-and-authenticate   Authenticate-then-encrypt

Figure 6.1. *Generic compositions for authenticated encryption*

Krawczyk (2001) and Bellare and Namprempre (2000) analyzed the generic security of these constructions for probabilistic $\mathcal{E}_K$ and found that only EtA is generally secure for secure $\mathcal{H}_{K'}$ and $\mathcal{E}_K$ with independent keys K, K'. The security of AtE and E&A depends on details of $\mathcal{E}_K$ and $\mathcal{H}_{K'}$ beyond the usual security notions. Namprempre et al. (2014) revisited the question for nonce-based $\mathcal{E}_K$, with more differentiated results. Several popular authenticated ciphers instantiate such generic compositions:

– **Counter-with-CBC-MAC mode (CCM)** (Whiting et al. 2003) is an AtE design: we first compute a CBC-MAC tag of N and message length m, A and M. Then encrypt M and this tag with CTR encryption (Figure 6.2(b)). A downside is that it requires two block cipher calls per block and knowing m and N in advance. It is not well parallelizable.

– **Galois/counter mode (GCM)** (McGrew and Viega 2004) is an EtA design using CTR encryption of M and the polynomial GMAC of A and C (Figure 6.2(a)). Compared to CCM, it processes a, m, N after A, C, and replaces some block cipher calls with 128-bit finite-field multiplications, denoted as $\otimes$. On the downside, it is very fragile to nonce misuse attacks – if the nonce is reused only once, the adversary can easily recover the authentication key for the MAC, thus completely breaking authenticity.

– **SIV (synthetic IV/key wrap)** is a "nonce-free" scheme to encrypt high-entropy messages, such as keys. Instead of a fresh nonce, it computes $T = \mathcal{H}_K(A, M)$ and then uses this value as nonce to encrypt M in a second pass.

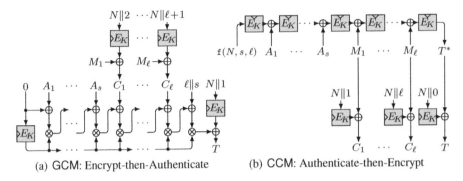

(a) GCM: Encrypt-then-Authenticate   (b) CCM: Authenticate-then-Encrypt

Figure 6.2. *Two AEAD modes based on generic composition*

Some protocols still require the separate selection of an encryption scheme (such as AES-CBC or AES-CTR) and a MAC (such as HMAC-SHA2), but it is generally preferable to directly use a predefined AEAD scheme for security, usability and performance. Unfortunately, it is easy to accidentally combine a secure encryption scheme and MAC, but still end up with an insecure AEAD from generic composition.

6.3.2. *Dedicated primitive-based designs*

More recent designs, such as the ciphers in the CAESAR portfolio, show that dedicated constructions can be very competitive both in terms of efficiency and in terms of simplicity. They can be based on different underlying primitives. Ideally, the scheme will provide a reduction proof to show the scheme's security under the assumption of the primitive's security. While most classical designs are built on block ciphers, other primitives also have their own advantages. In particular, block ciphers have a significant downside: their inputs are only a plaintext block and a key, but there is no dedicated place to encode the current *context* of the block, such as its index. Block cipher modes of operation have to jump through hoops to solve this issue. Tweakable block ciphers, on the other hand, offer such an extra input: the tweak. Permutations take a different approach and accommodate only a single, larger input: a current state that can implicitly accumulate this context.

– **Block ciphers (BC)**: the most widely known designs are based on the AES or other BCs. They usually require at least one BC call per data block for encryption, and often a second one to update the accumulated state for the tag.

- **Parallelizable modes** translate message blocks M_i one by one, but modify each block based on a current counter value. An example is OCB, which XORs a secret, nonce-dependent counter value Δ_i before and after the block cipher call (XE/XEX, Figure 6.3(a)) to ensure that identical message blocks are not detectable in the ciphertext. The tag is computed by simply encrypting the XOR of all message blocks. This has the advantage of being parallelizable, which is well suited for software implementations and low-latency designs.

- **Feedback-based modes** update an internal state with a linear function of block cipher outputs and message blocks, and the encryption of the next block depends on this state. An example is the CoFB combined feedback function (Figure 6.3(c)), which uses a linear function ρ for mixing. Another variant of this is the encrypt-mix-encrypt construction used by COLM to combine authentication and encryption: the output of the first BC call on the plaintext is mixed linearly with the current state and then encrypted a second time to produce the ciphertext block. In this way, designs can potentially achieve higher robustness against nonce misuse and reduce the state size, but they lose parallelizability.

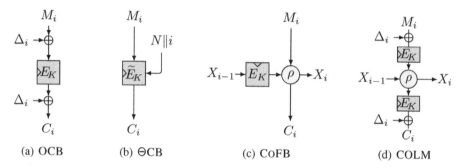

Figure 6.3. *Update functions for modes based on block ciphers E and TBCs $\tilde{E}$*

– **Tweakable block ciphers (TBC)**: parallelizable BC-based modes often implicitly create a tweakable block cipher from a block cipher. Unfortunately, generic constructions for TBCs from BCs like XE/XEX (Rogaway 2004a) either need more than one BC call, or provide only birthday-level security. These modes can be improved and simplified by instantiating them directly with a TBC. For example, ΘCB3 (Krovetz and Rogaway 2011) (Figure 6.3(b)) is the TBC variant of OCB and can provide beyond-birthday security. Dedicated TBC modes like SCT (Peyrin and Seurin 2016) provide additional features, such as an acceptable security level under nonce misuse.

– **Permutations**: in *sponge* constructions, a large state consisting of an inner and outer part is updated by applying an unkeyed, cryptographically strong permutation. Data blocks can be *absorbed into* and *squeezed from* the state by XO Ring to or copying from the outer part. Duplex schemes (Bertoni et al. 2011) achieve authenticated encryption with almost no overhead compared to encryption by squeezing the tag from the state after the final ciphertext block (Figure 6.4(a)). The approach can easily be adapted to provide intermediate tags.

Keyed sponges like the KEYEDSPONGE and keyed DUPLEX can process data more efficiently than unkeyed sponges and can achieve higher security levels than the birthday bound $2^{c/2}$ on the c-bit capacity, as long as the online data complexity is bounded. Additionally, keyed sponges can securely absorb more data per permutation call by using not just the outer part, but also the inner part to absorb, as in the Full-state SPONGEWRAP (FSW) (6.4(b)) (Mennink et al. 2015). This mode concurrently absorbs associated data blocks A_i in the inner part and message blocks M_i in the outer part, or, if the number of A_i blocks is larger than of M_i, absorbs A in both the inner and outer part.

The steps can also be tweaked to improve the resistance of sponges against side-channel and implementation attacks. For example, by adding the key before and after the initial and final P like in ASCON (Figure 6.4(c)) (Dobraunig et al. 2021), it becomes infeasible to extend state recovery attacks from data processing steps into key recovery or forgery attacks. Sponges can also be adapted to provide a level of inherent protection against side-channel attack, as in ISAP.

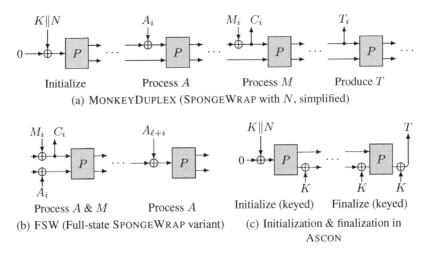

(a) MONKEYDUPLEX (SPONGEWRAP with N, simplified)

(b) FSW (Full-state SPONGEWRAP variant)

(c) Initialization & finalization in ASCON

Figure 6.4. *Authenticated encryption modes based on permutation P*

6.3.3. *Fully dedicated designs*

In some of the schemes discussed so far, the internal primitive is instantiated with a number of rounds that allows the function to be distinguished from its idealized description. For example, in duplex constructions with a small rate, the number of rounds of the permutation in the data processing steps is much lower than in the initialization and finalization. Such designs rely on the fact that an attacker has only limited options to control the input of the permutation: most of the state is unknown and depends on K and N. The attacker can try to gain more information by using multiple data blocks, but then they need to bridge multiple permutation calls in their cryptanalysis. This combined complexity of multiple calls is the first requirement for the security of such designs, for example against guess-and-determine state recovery attacks. The second requirement is the absence of exploitable properties for a single call, under the limited interface available to the attacker. For example, in duplex constructions, there must be no linear or differential characteristics with active bits only in the small outer part. Thus, these designs require dedicated cryptanalysis of the update function.

6.3.4. *Standards and competitions*

– **Internet Standards**: some of the most widely used authenticated ciphers are those standardized by the US National Institute of Standards and Technology (NIST): AES-CCM and AES-GCM are widely used in TLS and other protocols. For misuse resistance, SIV (Key Wrap) can be used. The Internet Engineering Task Force (IETF) provides several additional RFC specifications, including OCBv3 (RFC 7253) or specifications related to TLS, like CHACHA20-POLY1305 (RFC 7539). The current version, TLS v1.3, supports two AES-based designs, AES-CCM and AES-GCM, and one non-AES design, CHACHA20-POLY1305, which combines a stream cipher with a polynomial MAC similar to GCM.

– **CAESAR Competition**: the "CAESAR Competition for Authenticated Encryption: Security, Applicability, and Robustness" is a cryptographic competition launched by the academic community with the goal of identifying a portfolio of secure, efficient authenticated ciphers with advantages over AES-GCM. The competition started in 2014 with 57 first-round submissions. In 2019, the CAESAR committee announced the final portfolio of winners for three use-cases, which showcases several very different design approaches:

- **Lightweight applications**: (suitable for resource-constrained environments such as low area, low power, etc.): the first choice, ASCON, is a permutation-based duplex design with tweaks for increased robustness against implementation attacks. The second choice, ACORN, is an LFSR-based stream cipher.

- **High-performance applications** (in software): OCB is a dedicated design that turns AES into a tweakable block cipher to achieve high parallelizability with just one block cipher call per block. AEGIS-128 also uses the AES round function, but only as a building block for its fully dedicated design that works on a large state and thus provides high throughput, but is not parallelizable.

- **Defense in depth** (with higher robustness against nonce misuse): the first choice, DEOXYS-II, defines a tweakable block cipher from the AES round function to build a misuse-resistant (MRAE) mode that additionally maintains higher security levels when large amounts of data are processed. The second choice, COLM, uses the block cipher AES in a feedback-based construction that achieves online misuse resistance.

– **NIST LWC Project**: the "NIST LightWeight Cryptography (LWC) Standardization Process" is a cryptographic competition organized by NIST. Its goal is the standardization of a lightweight authenticated cipher suitable for resource-constrained environments, optionally together with a lightweight hash function. It started in 2019 with 56 first-round submissions. In 2021, NIST announced a list of 10 finalists: most are permutation-based (ASCON, ELEPHANT, ISAP, PHOTON-BEETLE, SPARKLE, XOODYAK), others use a block cipher (GIFT-COFB, TINYJAMBU), tweakable block cipher (ROMULUS), or fully dedicated NFSR stream cipher (GRAIN-128AEAD). The competition is still ongoing at the time of writing this chapter – the winner(s) will set new standards in AEAD. For more details, see Chapter 16 of volume 2.

6.4. References

Bellare, M. and Namprempre, C. (2000). Authenticated encryption: Relations among notions and analysis of the generic composition paradigm. In *ASIACRYPT 2000*, vol. 1976 of *Lecture Notes in Computer Science*, Okamoto, T. (ed.). Springer.

Bertoni, G., Daemen, J., Peeters, M., Van Assche, G. (2011). Duplexing the sponge: Single-pass authenticated encryption and other applications. In *SAC 2011*, vol. 7118 of *Lecture Notes in Computer Science*, Miri, A., Vaudenay, S. (eds). Springer.

Black, J. and Urtubia, H. (2002). Side-channel attacks on symmetric encryption schemes: The case for authenticated encryption. In *USENIX Security 2002*, Boneh, D. (ed.). USENIX.

Degabriele, J.P. and Paterson, K.G. (2007). Attacking the IPsec standards in encryption-only configurations. In *S&P 2007*. IEEE Computer Society.

Dobraunig, C., Eichlseder, M., Mendel, F., Schläffer, M. (2021). Ascon v1.2: Lightweight authenticated encryption and hashing. *Journal of Cryptology*, 34(3) [Online]. Available at: https://dblp.org/rec/journals/joc/DobraunigEMS21.html?view=bibtex.

Katz, J. and Yung, M. (2000). Unforgeable encryption and chosen ciphertext secure modes of operation. In *FSE 2000*, vol. 1978 of *Lecture Notes in Computer Science*, Schneier, B. (ed.). Springer.

Krawczyk, H. (2001). The order of encryption and authentication for protecting communications (or: How secure is SSL?). In *CRYPTO 2001*, vol. 2139 of *Lecture Notes in Computer Science*, Kilian, J. (ed.). Springer.

Krovetz, T. and Rogaway, P. (2011). The software performance of authenticated-encryption modes. In *FSE 2011*, vol. 6733 of *Lecture Notes in Computer Science*, Joux, A. (ed.). Springer.

McGrew, D.A. and Viega, J. (2004). The security and performance of the Galois/counter mode (GCM) of operation. In *INDOCRYPT 2004*, vol. 3348 of *Lecture Notes in Computer Science*, Canteaut, A., Viswanathan, K. (eds). Springer.

Mennink, B., Reyhanitabar, R., Vizár, D. (2015). Security of full-state keyed sponge and duplex: Applications to authenticated encryption. In *ASIACRYPT 2015*, vol. 9453 of *Lecture Notes in Computer Science*, Iwata, T., Cheon, J.H. (eds). Springer.

Namprempre, C., Rogaway, P., Shrimpton, T. (2014). Reconsidering generic composition. In *EUROCRYPT 2014*, vol. 8441 of *Lecture Notes in Computer Science*. Nguyen, P.Q., Oswald, E. (eds). Springer.

Peyrin, T. and Seurin, Y. (2016). Counter-in-tweak: Authenticated encryption modes for tweakable block ciphers. In *CRYPTO 2016*, vol. 9814 of *Lecture Notes in Computer Science*, Robshaw, M., Katz, J. (eds). Springer.

Rogaway, P. (2002). Authenticated-encryption with associated-data. In *CCS 2002*, Atluri, V. (ed.). ACM.

Rogaway, P. (2004a). Efficient instantiations of tweakable blockciphers and refinements to modes OCB and PMAC. In *ASIACRYPT 2004*, vol. 3329 of *Lecture Notes in Computer Science*, Lee, P.J. (ed.). Springer.

Rogaway, P. (2004b). Nonce-based symmetric encryption. In *FSE 2004*, vol. 3017 of *Lecture Notes in Computer Science*, Roy, B.K., Meier, W. (eds). Springer.

Rogaway, P. and Shrimpton, T. (2006). A provable-security treatment of the key-wrap problem. In *EUROCRYPT 2006*, vol. 4004 of *Lecture Notes in Computer Science*, Vaudenay, S. (ed.). Springer.

Whiting, D., Housley, R., Ferguson, N. (2003). IETF RFC 3610: Counter with CBC-MAC (CCM). Internet Engineering Task Force (IETF) Request for Comments.

7

MDS Matrices

Gaëtan LEURENT
Inria, Paris, France

MDS matrices are linear layers with optimal properties. They are used in many SPN block ciphers, and in particular in the AES standard (AES 2001). In recent years, there has been a lot of work on the construction of MDS matrices with a low implementation cost, in the context of lightweight cryptography.

7.1. Definition

The linear layer of a block cipher is a linear mapping over $\mathbb{F}_2^n$, which can be represented as an $n \times n$ matrix over $\mathbb{F}_2$. However, in this chapter we consider linear layers as used in SPN ciphers. If the cipher uses s-bit S-boxes, we consider that the linear layer operates on t words of s bits (with $n = st$). The state is an element of $(\mathbb{F}_2^s)^t$, and the linear layer is represented as a $t \times t$ matrix whose elements are linear mappings over $\mathbb{F}_2^s$ (or equivalently, elements are $s \times s$ matrices over $\mathbb{F}_2$). We define the Hamming weight w of a vector in $(\mathbb{F}_2^s)^t$ as the number of non-zero s-bit elements.

We measure the diffusion properties of a linear layer L by its *differential branch number* $\mathcal{B}_d$, defined as (Vaudenay 1995; Rijmen et al. 1996):

$$\mathcal{B}_d(L) = \min_{x \neq 0} \left\{ w(x) + w(L(x)) \right\}.$$

The maximal possible value of the branch number is $t + 1$, and this corresponds to linear layers with optimal diffusion properties: changing the value of u words of input affects at least $t + 1 - u$ words of output. If L has branch number $t + 1$, then the set of all $(x, L(x))$ is an error correcting code with minimal distance $t + 1$; this code reaches the Singleton bound and is called an MDS (maximum distance separable) code. Therefore, the matrix of an optimal linear layer is called an *MDS matrix*.

DEFINITION 7.1.– L is MDS if $\mathcal{B}_d(L) = t + 1$.

MDS matrices have a simple characterization based on the square submatrices formed from any i rows and any i columns[1], with $1 \leq i \leq t$.

LEMMA 7.1 (MacWilliams and Sloane 1977, page 321).– L is MDS if and only if every square submatrix is non-singular. While error correcting codes are typically studied over a field, this characterization also holds over a (non-commutative) ring.

Proof. Let $I, J \subseteq \{1, \ldots t\}$ with $|I| = |J| = i$ be such that the square submatrix $L_{|I,J}$ (with lines in I and columns in J) is singular. Then there exist $x_{|J}$ with support over J such that $L_{|I,J}(x_{|J}) = 0$; if we extend $x_{|J}$ with zeros, we obtain a vector x with $w(x) \leq i$ and $w(L(x)) \leq t - i$. Therefore, L is not MDS.

Conversely, let x be such that $w(x) + w(L(x)) \leq t$. We consider $I = \{i : L(x)[i] = 0\}$ and $J = \{j : x[j] \neq 0\}$. We have $|I| = t - w(L(x))$ and $|J| = w(x)$, therefore $|J| \leq |I|$. We can select a subset $I' \subseteq I$ with $|I'| = |J|$, and we obtain $L_{|I',J}$ a square submatrix of L that is singular (since $L_{|I',J}(x_{|J}) = 0$). $\square$

In particular, an MDS matrix is necessarily invertible, and all its coefficients must be invertible.

7.1.1. *Differential and linear properties*

The wide trail strategy (Daemen and Rijmen 2001) links the branch number with the differential and linear properties of the cipher. The number of non-zero elements in a state difference corresponds to the number of active S-boxes; therefore, the differential branch number corresponds to the minimum number of active S-boxes in two consecutive rounds of an SPN cipher for differential cryptanalysis.

Similarly, we define the *linear branch number*, following the propagation of linear masks explained in Chapter 2 of volume 2:

$$\mathcal{B}_l(L) = \min_{x \neq 0} \left\{ w(x) + w(L^\top(x)) \right\},$$

---

1 As a remainder, the linear layer is considered as a $t \times t$ matrix whose elements are themselves linear mappings over $\mathbb{F}_2^s$.

where $L^\top$ is the linear mapping whose binary matrix representation is the transposed of that of L. It corresponds to the minimum number of active S-boxes in two consecutive rounds of an SPN cipher for linear cryptanalysis. The maximal value of the linear branch number is also $t + 1$, and the differential branch number is maximal if and only if the linear branch number is maximal (this is a direct consequence of lemma 7.1):

$$\mathcal{B}_d(L) = t + 1 \iff \mathcal{B}_l(L) = t + 1.$$

7.1.2. *Near-MDS matrices*

Linear layers with branch number t are called *near-MDS*. Their diffusion properties are not as good as MDS matrices, but they can offer an interesting trade-off between implementation cost and diffusion properties. For instance, the following matrix with branch number 4 is used in the ciphers ARIA (Kwon et al. 2004), PRINCE (Borghoff et al. 2012), and MIDORI (Banik et al. 2015). It can be implemented with just 6 s-bit XORs.

$$M_{\text{Near-MDS}} = \begin{bmatrix} 0 & 1 & 1 & 1 \\ 1 & 0 & 1 & 1 \\ 1 & 1 & 0 & 1 \\ 1 & 1 & 1 & 0 \end{bmatrix}$$

7.2. Constructions

A $t \times t$ MDS matrix is equivalent to an error-correcting code with length $2t$, dimension t and minimal distance $t + 1$. If we write the generator matrix of such a code in the standard form $G = [I|M]$, then M is an MDS matrix. In particular, when $2t \leq 2^s$, we can use the Reed-Solomon construction over the field $\mathbb{F}_{2^s}$ to build an MDS matrix. This construction is used in the cipher SHARK (Rijmen et al. 1996) with $t = 8$ and in the MARVELLOUS family (Aly et al. 2020) with $4 \leq t \leq 14$.

However, many block ciphers use relatively small MDS matrices, and ad hoc constructions offer better implementation. Since we have an efficient way to test the MDS property, a simple method to build an MDS matrix is to search through a space of matrices with desirable properties (for instance: circulant matrices with low-weight coefficients, or matrices that are involutions) until finding one that is MDS. For small t's, the probability that a random matrix is MDS is high enough for this approach to be successful.

For a concrete example, let us study the AES MixColumns operation. It uses a 4×4 MDS matrix operating on 8-bit words, corresponding to $t = 4$ and $s = 8$. We use those parameters as a basis for comparison when discussing various MDS matrix constructions. The `MixColumns` matrix is usually written thus

$$M_{\text{AES}} = \begin{bmatrix} 2 & 3 & 1 & 1 \\ 1 & 2 & 3 & 1 \\ 1 & 1 & 2 & 3 \\ 3 & 1 & 1 & 2 \end{bmatrix},$$

where 1, 2 and 3 represent elements of the finite field $\mathbb{F}_{2^8}$, using a hexadecimal notation for the bitwise representation of finite fields elements. More precisely, 2 and 3 denote elements α and $\alpha \oplus 1$, respectively, with α a generator of the field. In the AES specification, the field is constructed as $\mathbb{F}_2[\alpha]/(\alpha^8 \oplus \alpha^4 \oplus \alpha^3 \oplus \alpha \oplus 1)$, so that multiplication by α can be evaluated by an 8-bit LFSR

$$\alpha : (x_7, x_6, \ldots, x_1, x_0) \mapsto (x_6, x_5, x_4, x_3 \oplus x_7, x_2 \oplus x_7, x_1, x_0 \oplus x_7, x_7)$$

Since all elements of the matrix correspond to a multiplication by a finite field element, we can check the MDS property by computing the determinants of all square submatrices using a few operations in the finite field.

7.3. Implementation cost

In a software implementation, MDS linear layers are usually implemented with tables, and the efficiency is independent of the choice of the MDS matrix. In a hardware implementation, the MDS matrix can be a significant part of the cipher, and there are different ways to optimize its implementation. Some ciphers also use a bitsliced implementation in software, which has properties similar to a hardware implementation.

In order to estimate the hardware cost of a linear operation, we count the number of gates (usually bitwise XORs) used in an implementation. In general, an implementation can be described as a sequence of operations $x_i \leftarrow x_{a_i} \oplus x_{b_i}$ with $a_i, b_i < i$, where $x_0, \ldots, x_n$ is the input, and the output is some subset of the x_i's. This corresponds to a linear straight line program. We define the *XOR count* of an implementation as the length of the corresponding straight line program.

Ideally, we would like to evaluate the minimal XOR count of any implementation of a given matrix, but there is no efficient way to do it. Therefore, the *direct* XOR count was introduced by Sim et al. (2015) as a more practical metric. It corresponds to counting the number of gates used in a naive implementation of the linear mapping. When considering the binary matrix representing the linear mapping, each line gives a formula to compute one output bit, and if there are u non-zero bits in a line, this formula is computed with $u-1$ XOR gates. Therefore, the direct XOR count is defined as the number of 1 bits in the binary matrix, minus n. With this metric, the cost of an MDS matrix is equal to the cost of the evaluation of each coefficient (an $s \times s$ matrix) plus the cost of $t \times (t - 1)$ XORs on s-bit words. There has been a long line of works optimizing MDS matrices for this metric, by optimizing the coefficients of the matrix. The best known result for a 4×4 matrix over 8-bit words requires 106 bitwise XORs (Li and Wang 2016), and there is a trivial lower bound of $t \times (t - 1) \times s = 96$ bitwise XORs. However, this form of local optimization is too limited, because global optimization often provides implementations with a XOR cost below the trivial lower bound of the direct XOR count.

For example, the direct XOR count of M_{AES} corresponds to 1 multiplication by 2, 1 multiplication by 3 and 3 s-bit XORs for each row (again, 2 and 3 are finite field elements). This leads to a XOR count of $4 \times (3 + 11 + 3 \times 8) = 152$. However, better implementations are possible by reusing some common terms that are required for distinct output bits. Indeed, an evaluation of M_{AES} can be written thus:

$$M_{\mathrm{AES}} \begin{bmatrix} a \\ b \\ c \\ d \end{bmatrix} = \begin{bmatrix} 2a \oplus 3b \oplus c \oplus d \\ a \oplus 2b \oplus 3c \oplus d \\ a \oplus b \oplus 2c \oplus 3d \\ 3a \oplus b \oplus c \oplus 2d \end{bmatrix} = \begin{bmatrix} 2a \oplus 2b \oplus b \oplus c \oplus d \\ a \oplus 2b \oplus 2c \oplus c \oplus d \\ a \oplus b \oplus 2c \oplus 2d \oplus d \\ 2a \oplus a \oplus b \oplus c \oplus 2d \end{bmatrix}.$$

With this expression, the evaluation of M_{AES} requires only 4 multiplications by 2 (the values $2a$, $2b$, $2c$, $2d$ are used twice) and 16 s-bit XORs; this translates to 140 bitwise XORs, which is lower than a naive implementation. Furthermore, some intermediate values can also be reused. In particular, each of the values $a \oplus b$, $b \oplus c$, $c \oplus d$ and $d \oplus a$ is used twice if we slightly rewrite the output, as shown by Satoh et al. (2001):

$$M_{\mathrm{AES}} \begin{bmatrix} a \\ b \\ c \\ d \end{bmatrix} = \begin{bmatrix} 2a \oplus 3b \oplus c \oplus d \\ a \oplus 2b \oplus 3c \oplus d \\ a \oplus b \oplus 2c \oplus 3d \\ 3a \oplus b \oplus c \oplus 2d \end{bmatrix} = \begin{bmatrix} 2(a \oplus b) \oplus b \oplus (c \oplus d) \\ 2(b \oplus c) \oplus c \oplus (d \oplus a) \\ 2(c \oplus d) \oplus d \oplus (a \oplus b) \\ 2(d \oplus a) \oplus a \oplus (b \oplus c) \end{bmatrix}.$$

With this formula, the matrix can be evaluated with just 12 s-bit XORs and 4 multiplications by 2, leading to a XOR count of only 108.

7.3.1. Optimizing the implementation of a matrix

When implementing a standardized cipher (such as the AES), we want to find an efficient implementation of the linear layer given in the specification. This problem is known to be NP-hard in general (Boyar et al. 2008), but some automatic tools find good implementations using heuristics. This was first applied to the implementation of cryptographic functions in Boyar et al. (2013), where the authors used linear straight line programs to globally optimize the implementation of a predefined linear function. More recently, those tools have been applied to various MDS matrices in the literature, leading to significant improvements over the state of the art (Kranz et al. 2017). In particular, they obtained an implementation of the AES MixColumns matrix with a XOR count of 97. Later works provided improved heuristics, and at the time of writing, the best known implementation of the AES MixColumns matrix uses only 92 bitwise XORs (Xiang et al. 2020). This strategy has also been applied to find good implementations of various MDS matrices proposed in the literature, resulting in an MDS matrix with the same parameters ($t = 4$ and $s = 8$) and a XOR count of only 72 (Kranz et al. 2017).

It should be noted that counting the number of XOR gates of a circuit is only an approximation of the true hardware cost of an implementation. In particular, small gains in the XOR count do not necessary lead to a better hardware implementation. Indeed, hardware design tools rewrite the circuit to optimize it, and can use other gates than two-input XORs. In particular, modern FPGAs have relatively large look-up tables, so that a multi-input XOR gate is not much more expensive than a two-input one. Moreover, another important criterion is the depth of the circuit, that is, the maximal number of gates on any path from input to output. This impacts the propagation delay of signals, which defines the maximum frequency at which a circuit can be run, and also impacts performances.

7.3.2. *Implementation of the inverse matrix*

When implementing the decryption algorithm of an SPN cipher, the inverse of the MDS matrix will be needed. Therefore, MDS matrices with an efficient inverse are preferred. If the direct MDS matrix and the inverse can share some parts of the circuit, this leads to an even more efficient implementation when both the encryption algorithm and the decryption algorithm are needed. In particular, a number of lightweight ciphers use an involutory matrix, so that the same implementation can be used for encryption and decryption.

7.4. Construction of lightweight MDS matrices

When designing a new cipher, we can select an MDS matrix that allows a more efficient implementation, by searching over a class of good implementations until an MDS matrix is found, instead of first searching an MDS matrix, and then searching a good implementation of the matrix. This strategy has been applied with a search by increasing order of implementation cost, so that the matrix was found to have an optimal cost within the search space (Duval and Leurent 2018).

Following previous works (Augot and Finiasz 2013), the search algorithm builds formal matrices whose coefficients are polynomials, and filters matrices when the determinant of one of the square submatrices is zero. This step is independent of the word size s. Next, the indeterminate of the polynomials is replaced by a linear mapping α over $\mathbb{F}_2^s$, so that the final coefficients are in the ring $\mathbb{F}_2[\alpha]$ of polynomials in α. This ensures that the coefficients commute, and the ring is a field if the minimal polynomial of α is irreducible. The resulting matrix is MDS if and only if the minimal polynomial of α is relatively prime with all the determinants of the square submatrices of the formal matrix (computed as polynomials).

7.4.1. *Choice of the field or ring*

The choice of the ring plays an important role in the implementation cost of an MDS matrix. For instance, the AES MixColumns matrix is defined over the field $\mathbb{F}_{2^8}$, but better results can be achieved over commutative rings.

In particular, the sub-field construction used in ECHO (Benadjila et al. 2009) corresponds to using a product ring. It can be applied to M_{AES} as follows: the inputs are considered as elements of the ring $\mathbb{F}_{2^4} \times \mathbb{F}_{2^4}$, and the coefficients 1 in the matrix are interpreted as $(1,1)$, 2 as (α, α) and 3 as $(\alpha \oplus 1, \alpha \oplus 1)$, with α a generator of the field $\mathbb{F}_{2^4}$. This actually corresponds to applying two copies of M_{AES} defined over $\mathbb{F}_{2^4}$, independently on each nibble of the input[2]. It is interesting because multiplication by α in $\mathbb{F}_{2^4}$ requires a single bitwise XOR (there exist irreducible trinomials of degree 4 in $\mathbb{F}_2[X]$), while multiplication by 2 in $\mathbb{F}_{2^8}$ requires three bitwise XORs (there are no irreducible trinomials of degree 8 in $\mathbb{F}_2[X]$). Therefore, multiplication by 2 in the ring $\mathbb{F}_{2^4} \times \mathbb{F}_{2^4}$ requires only 2 bitwise XORs rather than 3 in the field $\mathbb{F}_{2^8}$.

We can even replace α by a linear operation on 8 bits with a single bitwise XOR. Following Beierle et al. (2016), the minimal polynomial of α must be a trinomial of degree 8, and an easy choice for α is to take the companion matrix of such a trinomial. For instance, using $x^8 \oplus x^2 \oplus 1$, we obtain the following α, and the corresponding variant of M_{AES} is still an MDS matrix, with coefficients in the ring $\mathbb{F}_2[\alpha]$:

$$\alpha : (x_7, x_6, \ldots, x_1, x_0) \mapsto (x_6, x_5, x_4, x_3, x_2, x_1 \oplus x_7, x_0, x_7).$$

7.4.2. *MDS matrices with the lowest XOR count*

The best results given by Duval and Leurent (2018) require only 67 bitwise XORs with $t = 4$ and $s = 8$ (and 35 bitwise XORs with $t = 4$ and $s = 4$). The search

---

2 Alternatively, we can see $\mathbb{F}_{2^8}$ as an extension of $\mathbb{F}_{2^4}$, so that elements of $\mathbb{F}_{2^8}$ correspond to degree-1 polynomials with coefficients in $\mathbb{F}_{2^4}$. Taking a generator of the subfield $\mathbb{F}_{2^4}$ as α, multiplication by α in $\mathbb{F}_{2^8}$ corresponds to multiplying each coefficient in $\mathbb{F}_{2^4}$.

algorithm returns several matrices and their implementation with this cost, with depth 5 or 6, such as the example given in Figure 7.1.

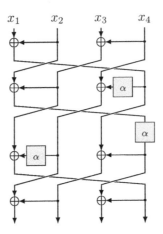

Figure 7.1. *Implementation of a* 4×4 *MDS matrix* $M = \begin{bmatrix} 3 & 1 & 4 & 4 \\ 1 & 3 & 6 & 4 \\ 2 & 2 & 3 & 1 \\ 3 & 2 & 1 & 3 \end{bmatrix}$.

With $s = 8$, *this matrix is MDS with a XOR count of 67 using*
$\alpha : (x_7, x_6, \ldots, x_1, x_0) \mapsto (x_6, x_5, x_4, x_3, x_2, x_1 \oplus x_7, x_0, x_7)$

However, different ciphers have different optimization goals, and it can be beneficial to select an MDS matrix tailored to the cipher. For instance, the lightweight cipher SATURNIN uses the results of Duval and Leurent (2018), but chooses a matrix with better symmetry properties (the chosen matrix has a XOR count of 38 with $t = 4$ and $s = 4$). We note that several of the results follow a generalized Feistel structure, which implies that the inverse also has an efficient implementation. This type of matrix has also been studied in several related works, including Li et al. (2019b).

7.4.3. Iterative MDS matrices

Instead of implementing the full MDS matrix, different types of implementation are possible for some MDS matrices, with trade-offs between the circuit size and the number of cycles required. For instance, we can take advantage of the fact that M_{AES} is a circulant matrix. Instead of building a circuit for the full MDS matrix, we can build a circuit for the function:

$$f : a, b, c, d \mapsto 2a \oplus 3b \oplus c \oplus d,$$

and evaluate $M_{\text{AES}}(a, b, c, d)$ as $\big(f(a, b, c, d), f(b, c, d, a), f(c, d, b, a), f(d, a, b, c)\big)$. The circuit is roughly four times smaller, but we need to evaluate it four times to compute one MDS matrix.

An alternative approach to reduce the implementation footprint of MDS matrices was introduced by Guo et al. (2011) in the lightweight hash function PHOTON. They proposed to design an MDS matrix M that can be written as $M = A^k$ for some efficiently implementable matrix A (and some integer k, typically $k = t$). This allows to trade some implementation speed against implementation size: instead of implementing directly M, one can implement the lighter matrix A, and iterate it over k clock cycles. In particular, companion matrices are good candidates for this construction and can be found by exhaustive search in small dimensions. The PHOTON paper proposes an example over $\mathbb{F}_{2^8}$ with the same parameters as the AES MixColumns matrix ($t = 4$ and $s = 8$) that can be implemented with 33 bitwise XORs:

$$M_{\text{Serial}} = \begin{bmatrix} 0 & 1 & 0 & 0 \\ 0 & 0 & 1 & 0 \\ 0 & 0 & 0 & 1 \\ 1 & 2 & 1 & 4 \end{bmatrix}^4.$$

This is comparable to a circuit for the function f for the first output byte of M_{AES}, but there is a smaller memory overhead because the matrix can be iterated in place. For larger dimensions, a direct construction from BCH codes is given by Augot and Finiasz (2015).

This approach has been revisited recently with matrices that do not correspond to companion matrices, but follow different types of Feistel structure (Li et al. 2019b). They obtain several trade-offs between the XOR count and the number of cycles k with circuits significantly smaller than achievable with companion matrices. For instance with $t = 4$ and $s = 8$, they found a matrix with a XOR count of 6 using $k = 451$ cycles and a matrix with a XOR count of 18 using $k = 4$ cycles.

7.4.4. Involutory MDS matrices

There are many proposals of involutory MDS matrices optimized for the direct XOR count metric, but few constructions that can take advantage of global optimizations. Indeed, the best known involutory MDS matrix with $t = 4$ and $s = 8$ has a XOR count of 78. It was obtained by building a large set of involutory matrices and applying automatic tools to find a good implementation (Li et al. 2019a). Better results might be achievable using a method that starts from the circuit rather than starting from the matrix.

7.5. References

AES (2001). Advanced encryption standard (AES). National Institute of Standards and Technology (NIST), FIPS PUB 197, U.S. Department of Commerce.

Aly, A., Ashur, T., Ben-Sasson, E., Dhooghe, S., Szepieniec, A. (2020). Design of symmetric-key primitives for advanced cryptographic protocols. *IACR Trans. Symm. Cryptol.*, 2020(3), 1–45.

Augot, D. and Finiasz, M. (2013). Exhaustive search for small dimension recursive MDS diffusion layers for block ciphers and hash functions. In *ISIT 2013*. IEEE.

Augot, D. and Finiasz, M. (2015). Direct construction of recursive MDS diffusion layers using shortened BCH codes. In *FSE 2014*, vol. 8540 of *Lecture Notes in Computer Science*, Cid, C., Rechberger, C. (eds). Springer.

Banik, S., Bogdanov, A., Isobe, T., Shibutani, K., Hiwatari, H., Akishita, T., Regazzoni, F. (2015). Midori: A block cipher for low energy. In *ASIACRYPT 2015, Part II*, vol. 9453 of *Lecture Notes in Computer Science*, Iwata, T., Cheon, J.H. (eds). Springer.

Beierle, C., Kranz, T., Leander, G. (2016). Lightweight multiplication in $GF(2^n)$ with applications to MDS matrices. In *CRYPTO 2016, Part I*, vol. 9814 of *Lecture Notes in Computer Science*, Robshaw, M., Katz, J. (eds). Springer.

Benadjila, R., Billet, O., Gilbert, H., Macario-Rat, G., Peyrin, T., Robshaw, M., Seurin, Y. (2009). Sha-3 proposal: Echo. Submission to NIST.

Borghoff, J., Canteaut, A., Güneysu, T., Kavun, E.B., Knežević, M., Knudsen, L.R., Leander, G., Nikov, V., Paar, C., Rechberger, C. et al. (2012). PRINCE – A low-latency block cipher for pervasive computing applications – Extended abstract. In *ASIACRYPT 2012*, vol. 7658 of *Lecture Notes in Computer Science*, Wang, X., Sako, K. (eds). Springer.

Boyar, J., Matthews, P., Peralta, R. (2008). On the shortest linear straight-line program for computing linear forms. In *Mathematical Foundations of Computer Science 2008*, Ochmański, E., Tyszkiewicz, J. (eds). Springer, Berlin, Heidelberg.

Boyar, J., Matthews, P., Peralta, R. (2013). Logic minimization techniques with applications to cryptology. *Journal of Cryptology*, 26(2), 280–312.

Daemen, J. and Rijmen, V. (2001). The wide trail design strategy. In *8th IMA International Conference on Cryptography and Coding*, vol. 2260 of *Lecture Notes in Computer Science*, Honary, B. (ed.). Springer.

Duval, S. and Leurent, G. (2018). MDS matrices with lightweight circuits. *IACR Trans. Symm. Cryptol.*, 2018(2), 48–78.

Guo, J., Peyrin, T., Poschmann, A. (2011). The PHOTON family of lightweight hash functions. In *CRYPTO 2011*, vol. 6841 of *Lecture Notes in Computer Science*, Rogaway, P. (ed.). Springer.

Kranz, T., Leander, G., Stoffelen, K., Wiemer, F. (2017). Shorter linear straight-line programs for MDS matrices. *IACR Trans. Symm. Cryptol.*, 2017(4), 188–211.

Kwon, D., Kim, J., Park, S., Sung, S.H., Sohn, Y., Song, J.H., Yeom, Y., Yoon, E.-J., Lee, S., Lee, J. et al. (2004). New block cipher: ARIA. In *ICISC 03*, vol. 2971 of *Lecture Notes in Computer Science*, Lim, J.I., Lee, D.H. (eds). Springer.

Li, Y. and Wang, M. (2016). On the construction of lightweight circulant involutory MDS matrices. In *FSE 2016*, vol. 9783 of *Lecture Notes in Computer Science*, Peyrin, T. (ed.). Springer.

Li, S., Sun, S., Li, C., Wei, Z., Hu, L. (2019a). Constructing low-latency involutory MDS matrices with lightweight circuits. *IACR Trans. Symm. Cryptol.*, 2019(1), 84–117.

Li, S., Sun, S., Shi, D., Li, C., Hu, L. (2019b). Lightweight iterative MDS matrices: How small can we go? *IACR Trans. Symm. Cryptol.*, 2019(4), 147–170.

MacWilliams, F.J. and Sloane, N.J.A. (1977). *The Theory of Error Correcting Codes*. North Holland.

Rijmen, V., Daemen, J., Preneel, B., Bossalaers, A., De Win, E. (1996). The cipher SHARK. In *FSE'96*, vol. 1039 of *Lecture Notes in Computer Science*, Gollmann, D. (ed.). Springer.

Satoh, A., Morioka, S., Takano, K., Munetoh, S. (2001). A compact Rijndael hardware architecture with S-box optimization. In *ASIACRYPT 2001*, vol. 2248 of *Lecture Notes in Computer Science*, Boyd, C. (ed.). Springer.

Sim, S.M., Khoo, K., Oggier, F.E., Peyrin, T. (2015). Lightweight MDS involution matrices. In *FSE 2015*, vol. 9054 of *Lecture Notes in Computer Science*, Leander, G. (ed.). Springer.

Vaudenay, S. (1995). On the need for multipermutations: Cryptanalysis of MD4 and SAFER. In *FSE'94*, vol. 1008 of *Lecture Notes in Computer Science*, Preneel, B. (ed.). Springer.

Xiang, Z., Zeng, X., Lin, D., Bao, Z., Zhang, S. (2020). Optimizing implementations of linear layers. *IACR Trans. Symm. Cryptol.*, 2020(2), 120–145.

8

S-boxes

Christina Boura

University of Paris-Saclay, UVSQ, CNRS, Versailles, France

Nonlinearity is essential for achieving security, and the design of a nonlinear function having good cryptographic properties is a crucial problem. However, applying a single large nonlinear function to the whole state is very expensive both in terms of time and memory. For this reason, it is common to divide the internal state into small words (typically 3–8 bits) and apply a small nonlinear function, called substitution box, or simply *S-box* to each word independently. Mathematically, an S-box can be seen as a vectorial Boolean function $S : \mathbb{F}_2^n \to \mathbb{F}_2^m$ and can be described by its m coordinates $s_0, s_1, \ldots, s_{m-1}$, where each coordinate is a Boolean function of n variables:

$$S(x) = (s_0(x), s_1(x), \ldots, s_{m-1}(x)), \quad x \in \mathbb{F}_2^n.$$

EXAMPLE 8.1.– The following table represents a randomly generated S-box $S : \mathbb{F}_2^3 \to \mathbb{F}_2^3$.

x	0	1	2	3	4	5	6	7
$s_0(x)$	1	1	0	1	0	1	0	0
$s_1(x)$	1	0	1	1	0	0	1	0
$s_2(x)$	0	0	1	1	0	1	0	1
$S(x)$	3	1	6	7	0	5	2	4

The last row of the above table is what is typically called the *look-up table* representation of an S-box and it is the most common representation, especially when

n is small and when the S-box does not have some simple algebraic description that can be used instead. While theoretically the values of n and m can be different, for the vast majority of S-boxes that can be found in the literature, $n = m$ and the S-box is a permutation. This is a convenient choice for SPN constructions, where all components should be invertible and is a good choice in general as bijectivity helps avoid trivial biases. Some notable exceptions to the above rule are the S-boxes of DES and PICARO (Piret et al. 2012). From now on, we will focus on the case $n = m$, but all properties that will be defined in the following can be naturally extended to the case $n \neq m$. The most popular values for n are 4 and 8, followed by S-boxes of size 3 and 5. Some S-boxes of size $6, 7$ and 9 can also be met.

For analyzing the mathematical properties of a given S-box, the look-up table representation is not convenient as it does not provide any information on the algebraic structure of the function. For this reason, it is sometimes more suitable to represent an S-box by the *algebraic normal form* (ANF) of its coordinate functions.

DEFINITION 8.1.– Let f be a Boolean function of n variables. The ANF of f is the multivariate polynomial

$$f(x) = \bigoplus_{u \in \mathbb{F}_2^n} c_f(u)x^u,$$

where $x^u = x_0^{u_0} x_1^{u_1} \cdots x_{n-1}^{u_{n-1}}$ and $c_f(u)$ can be computed by the Möbius transform as $c_f(u) = \bigoplus_{v \in \mathbb{F}_2^n, v \prec u} f(u) \in \mathbb{F}_2$, where $v \prec u$ if and only if $(u_i = 0 \Rightarrow v_i = 0)$ for all $i = 0, \ldots, n-1$.

EXAMPLE 8.2.– *The ANF of the three coordinates s_0, s_1, s_2 of the S-box* $[3, 1, 6, 7, 0, 5, 2, 4]$. The variable x is a 3-bit vector (x_0, x_1, x_2):

$$S(x) = \begin{cases} s_0(x) &= x_0x_1 + x_0x_2 + x_1x_2 + x_1 + x_2 + 1 \\ s_1(x) &= x_0x_1 + x_0x_2 + x_0 + x_1x_2 + x_2 + 1 \\ s_2(x) &= x_0x_2 + x_1x_2 + x_1 \end{cases}$$

By fixing a basis for the vectorial space $\mathbb{F}_2^n$, we can identify an isomorphism between $\mathbb{F}_2^n$ and the finite field $\mathbb{F}_{2^n}$. In this way, a vectorial Boolean function $S : \mathbb{F}_2^n \to \mathbb{F}_2^n$ can equivalently be written as a univariate polynomial over $\mathbb{F}_{2^n}$ in a unique way:

$$S(x) = \sum_{i=0}^{2^n-1} b_i x^i, \quad b_i \in \mathbb{F}_{2^n}. \qquad [8.1]$$

This representation can easily be obtained by the discrete Fourier Transform of F (aka Mattson-Solomon transform).

EXAMPLE 8.3.– *Univariate representation of the S-box [3, 1, 6, 7, 0, 5, 2, 4]*. The univariate representation of this S-box over $\mathbb{F}_{2^3} = \mathbb{F}_2[x]/(x^3 + x + 1)$ is

$$S(x) = \alpha^6 x^6 + \alpha^5 x^5 + \alpha^2 x^4 + \alpha^6 x^3 + \alpha^4 x^2 + \alpha^5 x + \alpha^3,$$

where α is a root of $x^3 + x + 1$. In this example, $\mathbb{F}_2^3$ was identified with $\mathbb{F}_{2^3}$ by the basis $\{1, \alpha, \alpha^2\}$. The use of a different irreducible polynomial instead of $x^3 + x + 1$ would of course have led to a different univariate polynomial representation.

The univariate representation is not interesting for all kind of S-boxes. We tend mainly to represent an S-box by its univariate form if this form presents some mathematical or implementation interest. This is notably the case for the functions whose univariate representation contains, up to a change of variables, a single monomial. Those functions are called *power* functions. Some famous power functions are $x \mapsto x^{2^n - 2}$, called the *inversion* over $\mathbb{F}_{2^n}$ and the function $x \mapsto x^3$ at some smaller extent. The most famous example of the first category is without doubt the AES S-box (affine equivalent to the inversion), while the *cube* function was originally used inside the KN-cipher (Nyberg and Knudsen 1995) and is present notably in the more recent MiMC construction (Albrecht et al. 2016).

8.1. Important design criteria

A cipher should be designed to resist basic state-of-the-art attacks, notably differential, linear, algebraic, integral and other classical cryptanalysis techniques. As the S-box is typically the only nonlinear component of the cipher, the resistance of the entire construction heavily depends on the properties of the underlying S-box.

8.1.1. *Differential properties*

Differential cryptanalysis (see Chapter 1 of volume 2) exploits differentials, that is, pairs of input–output differences (a, b) that appear with high probability. For evaluating the resistance of a cipher against this type of attacks, it is therefore relevant to evaluate the maximum probability that a given input difference yields a given output difference through the S-box. This property can be summarized in the so-called *difference distribution table* (DDT).

DEFINITION 8.2 (DDT and differential uniformity).– Let S be an S-box from $\mathbb{F}_2^n$ into $\mathbb{F}_2^n$. The DDT of S is the two-dimensional table defined by $\delta_S(a, b) = \#\{x \in \mathbb{F}_2^n : S(x) \oplus S(x \oplus a) = b\}$, for all $a, b \in \mathbb{F}_2^n$. An important characteristic of the DDT introduced in Nyberg (1993) is the differential uniformity of S, denoted by δ_S and defined as the highest non-trivial value in the DDT, that is,

$$\delta_S = \max_{a, b \in \mathbb{F}_2^n, a \neq 0} \delta_S(a, b).$$

One can easily see that all values inside DDT are even. Indeed, if x is a solution of the equation $S(x) \oplus S(x \oplus a) = b$, then $x \oplus a$ is a solution too. The lower the differential uniformity is, the better an S-box resists differential cryptanalysis. Indeed, the highest probability for a differential pattern to go through this S-box successfully is equal to $\delta_S/2^n$, which is lower when δ_S is small. The wide trail argument (Daemen and Rijmen 2001) relies on this bound on the differential probability at the S-box level. The optimal value for δ_S is 2, and functions reaching this minimal value are called *almost perfect nonlinear* (APN). APN permutations are quite complex mathematical objects for which very little is known and this despite more than 30 years of research. However, in the case of characteristic two finite fields of odd extension degree, some infinite families of APN permutations are known. For example, the cube function $x \mapsto x^3$ and the inverse function $x \mapsto x^{2^n-2}$ are known to be APN for any odd n. However, on characteristic two finite fields of even extension degree, which are significantly more important in the context of symmetric-key cryptography, the mere existence of APN permutations is an open problem. It was proved that APN permutations do not exist for $n = 4$, and for $n = 6$ a single permutation (up to CCZ-equivalence) was presented by Browning et al. (2010). On the one hand, it is an open problem whether there are other APN permutations for $n = 6$ and, on the other hand, the existence of an APN permutation for $n \geq 8$, n even, remains an open problem as well, known as the *big APN problem*.

The DDT of the S-box $S = [3,1,6,7,0,5,2,4]$ can be visualized on the left of Figure 8.1. The rows correspond to the input difference a and the columns to the output difference b. For better readability, all 0s were replaced by ".". We see from this table that the differential uniformity of this S-box is 4. The lower the differential uniformity, the better the resistance against differential cryptanalysis.

a/b	0	1	2	3	4	5	6	7
0	8	.	.	.	.	.	.	.
1	.	2	2	.	.	2	2	.
2	.	2	2	.	.	2	2	.
3	.	.	.	.	4	.	.	4
4	.	.	.	4	4	.	.	.
5	.	2	2	.	.	2	2	.
6	.	2	2	.	.	2	2	.
7	.	.	.	4	.	.	.	4

a/b	0	1	2	3	4	5	6	7
0	4	.	.	.	.	.	.	.
1	.	2	-2	.	2	.	.	2
2	.	-2	2	.	2	.	.	2
3	.	.	.	4	.	.	.	.
4	.	-2	-2	.	.	-2	2	.
5	.	.	.	.	-2	-2	-2	2
6	.	.	.	.	2	-2	-2	-2
7	.	-2	-2	.	.	2	-2	.

Figure 8.1. *The DDT (on the left) and the LAT (on the right) of the S-box $S = [3,1,6,7,0,5,2,4]$*

S-boxes sharing the same DDT. An interesting remark is that different S-boxes can share the same DDT. It is for example easy to see that given an S-box $S_1 : \mathbb{F}_2^n \to \mathbb{F}_2^n$, all S-boxes S_2 such that $S_2(x) = S_1(x \oplus c) \oplus d$, for all $x \in \mathbb{F}_2^n$ have the same DDT as S_1 for any value of $c, d \in \mathbb{F}_2^n$. However, it is a highly non-trivial question to decide whether given an S-box S there are more S-boxes, other than these trivial ones, to share the same DDT as S. In 2019, two different algorithms for reconstructing all functions from a given DDT were provided (Boura et al. 2019; Dunkelman and Huang 2019).

8.1.2. *Linear properties*

Linear attacks (see Chapter 2 of volume 2) exploit *biased* linear Boolean relations between the input, output and the key bits of the cipher (typically a reduced version of it). Exactly as in the case of differential cryptanalysis, the resistance of an S-box to linear cryptanalysis can be summarized in a table called the *linear approximation table* (LAT).

DEFINITION 8.3 (Linear Approximation Table).– Let S be an S-box from $\mathbb{F}_2^n$ into $\mathbb{F}_2^n$. The linear approximation table of S is the two-dimensional table defined by:

$$\mathcal{L}_S(a,b) = \frac{1}{2} \sum_{x \in \mathbb{F}_2^n} (-1)^{a \cdot x \oplus b \cdot S(x)},$$

where $a \cdot b$ denotes the classical scalar product of two vectors $a, b \in \mathbb{F}_2^n$, for all $a, b \in \mathbb{F}_2^n$. The vectors a and b are called the input and output masks, respectively, and the quantity $\sum_{x \in \mathbb{F}_2^n} (-1)^{a \cdot x \oplus b \cdot S(x)}$ is known as the *Walsh coefficient* of the component function $b \cdot S$, at point a.

A good indicator of the success of a linear attack is the highest magnitude of the non-trivial elements of the LAT. The higher these coefficients, the more efficient the attack. Thus, the main design criterion for an S-box in terms of linearity is that the absolute value of the highest coefficient in the LAT is as low as possible. This is measured using the notion of *linearity* $\mathcal{L}_S$:

$$\mathcal{L}_S = 2 \max_{a,b \in \mathbb{F}_2^n, b \neq 0} |\mathcal{L}_S(a,b)|.$$

REMARK 8.1.– In some surveys and articles, the coefficient $\mathcal{L}(a,b)$ of the LAT is defined as $\sum_{x \in \mathbb{F}_2^n} (-1)^{a \cdot x \oplus b \cdot S(x)}$. In these cases, the linearity is defined as $\mathcal{L}_S = \max_{a,b \in \mathbb{F}_2^n, b \neq 0} |\mathcal{L}_S(a,b)|$. Therefore, no matter the definition used for the coefficients of the LAT, the linearity of the S-box remains the same.

The LAT of the S-box $S = [3,1,6,7,0,5,2,4]$ is depicted on the right part of Figure 8.1. As seen from this table, the linearity of this S-box is 8.

PROPOSITION 8.1 (Chabaud and Vaudenay 1994; Carlet et al. 1998).– Let S be an S-box from $\mathbb{F}_2^n$ into $\mathbb{F}_2^n$. Then, $\mathcal{L}_S \geq 2^{\frac{n+1}{2}}$.

S-boxes for which this inequality is an equality are called *almost bent* (AB) functions. AB functions exist only for odd dimensions n. For even n, this bound is not reached (as linearity must be an integer) and the lowest possible value for the linearity is not known. For an n-bit S-box, the best known value for the linearity when n is even is $2^{\frac{n}{2}+1}$ and this value is reached for very few families of S-boxes, for example, S-boxes based on the inversion over the finite field $\mathbb{F}_{2^n}$, as the S-box of AES.

PROPOSITION 8.2 (Chabaud and Vaudenay 1994; Carlet et al. 1998).– If an S-box is AB, then it is also APN.

The inverse of the above proposition does not hold in general. However, it was proved in Carlet et al. (1998) that the two notions coincide for quadratic functions in odd dimension.

8.1.3. *Algebraic properties*

An important notion for an S-box is its algebraic degree. This quantity plays a role in the success of attacks such as algebraic, higher order differential, or division property-based attacks (see Chapter 10 of volume 2). The (multivariate) algebraic degree of a Boolean function is defined as the maximum number of variables in a term of its ANF. We define the algebraic degree of an S-box in function of the algebraic degree of its coordinates.

DEFINITION 8.4.– The *(multivariate) algebraic degree*, $\deg(S)$, of an S-box S is defined as the maximum of the algebraic degrees of its coordinates.

As previously seen, the algebraic degree of all three coordinates s_0, s_1 and s_2 of $S = [3,1,6,7,0,5,2,4]$ is 3. Therefore, the algebraic degree of this S-box S is 3.

An interesting remark concerns the maximum algebraic degree of a permutation S. This result is a special case of proposition 1 in Boura et al. (2011). Another remark is that the algebraic degree of S and the algebraic degree of the inverse permutation S^{-1} are strongly related. Both results are summarized in the following proposition.

PROPOSITION 8.3.– Let S be a permutation of $\mathbb{F}_2^n$. Then, $\deg(S) \leq n - 1$. Moreover, $\deg(S^{-1}) = n - 1$ if and only if $\deg(S) = n - 1$.

For a proof of the above result and for more details on how the algebraic degree of a permutation is related to the one of its inverse, see Boura and Canteaut (2013).

Ideally, an S-box S of n bits should be chosen to have maximum algebraic degree $n - 1$ and it is even better if all its components $\lambda \cdot S$, $\lambda \neq 0$ have algebraic degree $n - 1$. This is for example the case of the AES S-box, where all its 255 non-trivial components are of algebraic degree 7. However, such S-boxes need usually a high number of AND gates to be implemented and can therefore be expensive and badly adapted for some particular scenarios (e.g. ciphers to be used inside MPC, FHE, or zero-knowledge protocols, or that should be easily masked) or environments (e.g. ultra-lightweight cryptography).

Another important notion is the *univariate algebraic degree* of an S-box S, whose role is notably essential in interpolation attacks (Jakobsen and Knudsen 1997) (see Chapter 10 of volume 2).

DEFINITION 8.5.– Let $S(x) = \sum_{i=0}^{2^n-1} b_i x^i$, $b_i \in \mathbb{F}_{2^n}$, be the univariate representation of an S-box S. The *univariate algebraic degree* of S is defined as

$$\deg^U(S) = \max\{wt(i) : 0 \leq i < 2^n \text{ and } b_i \neq 0\}.$$

The higher this algebraic degree, the better it is, even if today relatively little is known on the influence of the univariate algebraic degree on the cipher's security, as well as the consequences of the use of a monomial function as an S-box. This last remark does not apply for the inverse function $x \mapsto x^{2^n-2}$ that is relatively well studied.

8.1.4. *Other properties*

Beyond the classical differential, linear or basic algebraic attacks, the development of other cryptanalysis techniques led to the development of new criteria for the design of S-boxes. To resist division property cryptanalysis, a design criterion for S-boxes was proposed in Boura and Canteaut (2016). A little bit later, Cid et al. (2018) proposed the notion of *boomerang connectivity table (BCT)* to evaluate the resistance of an S-box to boomerang cryptanalysis (see Chapter 6 of volume 2). The notion of *boomerang uniformity* (Boura and Canteaut 2018), defined as the maximal value in a BCT, provides a concrete design criterion for S-boxes in this case.

8.2. Popular S-boxes for different dimensions

As most processor registers are of size 32 or 64 bits, it is convenient for software implementations to design cryptographic primitives working on power-of-2 bit-size blocks (e.g. 64, 128, 256 bits). This is why S-boxes of 4 and 8 bits have always been extremely popular choices. However, as seen above, S-boxes defined on an odd number of variables offer in general better differential and linear properties. In this section, we will review for each one of these dimensions (4, 8 and odd) the most popular S-box choices. All S-boxes will be given upon an equivalence relation, called *affine equivalence*, that keeps invariant the most important security properties. This equivalence relation is defined as follows:

DEFINITION 8.6.– Two n-bit S-boxes S_1 and S_2 are called *affine equivalent* if there exist two affine permutations A_1, A_2 of $\mathbb{F}_2^n$ such that $S_2 = A_1 \circ S_1 \circ A_2$.

It is well known (see, for example, Carlet et al. (1998) or Nyberg (1993)) that two S-boxes in the same affine equivalence class share the same linearity $\mathcal{L}_S$ and differential uniformity δ_S. Other properties also remain unchanged, for example, the boomerang uniformity (Boura and Canteaut 2018) or the algebraic degree. This last fact is trivial, as the transformations applied are affine.

8.2.1. *S-boxes with an odd number of variables*

When n is odd, AB permutations exist. These permutations offer, as seen above, the best resistance against differential and linear attacks. Different families of AB permutations are known today. The first ones to be discovered were monomial ones, for example, of the type $x \mapsto x^t$. All known AB exponents are summarized in Table 8.1. In the same table, all known APN exponents but that are not AB are also mentioned.

Property	Name	Exponent t
AB	Gold	$2^k + 1$ with $\gcd(k, n) = 1$, $\quad 1 \leq k \leq t$
	Kasami	$2^{2k} - 2^k + 1$ with $\gcd(k, n) = 1$, $\quad 2 \leq k \leq t$
	Welch	$2^s + 3$
	Niho	$2^s + 2^{\frac{s}{2}} - 1$, if s is even
		$2^s + 2^{\frac{3s+1}{2}} - 1$, if s is odd
APN	Inverse	$2^{2s} - 1$
	Dobbertin	$2^{4k} + 2^{3k} + 2^{2k} + 2^k - 1$, if $n = 5k$

Table 8.1. *AB and APN exponents on $\mathbb{F}_{2^n}$ with $n = 2s + 1$*

8.2.2. *4-bit S-boxes*

As the dimension is small, all 4-bit S-boxes were successfully classified up to affine equivalence. As shown in Cannière (2007), there are in total 302 classes. We can see through this classification, that APN permutations do not exist in this dimension. The best that we can hope for in terms of differential uniformity and linearity is $\delta_S = 4$ and $\mathcal{L}_S = 16$ and permutations having these properties are considered as optimal. Leander and Poschmann provided 16 affine equivalent classes of optimal permutations (Leander and Poschmann 2007). All of these permutations are of algebraic degree 3 but only half of them have all of their components of this maximal degree. Choosing one of the above S-boxes is a perfect choice in terms of security. However, for some environments or applications, physical constraints may apply, and in these cases it is fundamental to have an efficient hardware and/or bit-sliced implementation for the S-box. In the case of 4-bit S-boxes, Ullrich et al. (2011) performed a search of all 4-bit S-boxes having optimal differential uniformity and linearity but also a minimal bit-slice implementation. This search led to the *Class 13* set of S-boxes, whose members have a very simple circuit implementation and have been used inside different ciphers.

8.2.3. *8-bit S-boxes*

In dimension 8, classification is no longer possible and very little is known about the design of S-boxes having good properties for this value of n. The best known differential uniformity in this dimension is $\delta_S = 4$, while the best known nonlinearity is $\mathcal{L}_S = 32$. These optimal values are reached by the inversion, $x \mapsto x^{2^n - 2}$ and in this dimension we do not know any other permutation doing so. This is why the inversion is a very popular choice for 8-bit S-boxes.

Another popular way of constructing 8-bit S-boxes is by building them using smaller components, for example, 4-bit S-boxes and a block-based structure. This approach has obvious implementation advantages, as it is much easier to implement few layers of 4-bit S-boxes than an 8-bit S-box without some particular structure. This strategy leads also to obvious circuit optimizations. Popular structures for building big S-boxes from smaller ones are the Feistel, MISTY, LAI-MASSEY or one or two layers of an SPN structure. More details on these constructions and other popular ways of building 8-bit S-boxes can be found in Perrin (2017).

8.3. Further reading

Readers interested in the mathematical properties of S-boxes can find a more detailed presentation in the *Lecture Notes* of Canteaut (2016) or can read Chapter 8 of the PhD thesis of Perrin (2017). Furthermore, different libraries exist for computing the different representations of a given S-box, its cryptographic properties or to check if two S-boxes are affine, extended-affine or CCZ-equivalent. We can cite the Sage module SBox (The Sage Development Team 2021), the Sage library S-boxU (Perrin 2021) or the platform PEIGEN (Bao et al. 2019).

8.4. References

Albrecht, M.R., Grassi, L., Rechberger, C., Roy, A., Tiessen, T. (2016). MiMC: Efficient encryption and cryptographic hashing with minimal multiplicative complexity. In *ASIACRYPT 2016, Proceedings, Part I*, vol. 10031 of *Lecture Notes in Computer Science*, Cheon, J.H., Takagi, T. (eds).

Bao, Z., Guo, J., Ling, S., Sasaki, Y. (2019). PEIGEN – A platform for evaluation, implementation, and generation of S-boxes. *IACR Trans. Symmetric Cryptol.*, 2019(1), 330–394.

Boura, C. and Canteaut, A. (2013). On the influence of the algebraic degree of f^{-1} on the algebraic degree of G ∘ F. *IEEE Trans. Inf. Theory*, 59(1), 691–702.

Boura, C. and Canteaut, A. (2016). Another view of the division property. In *CRYPTO 2016, Proceedings, Part I*, vol. 9814 of *Lecture Notes in Computer Science*, Robshaw, M., Katz, J. (eds). Springer.

Boura, C. and Canteaut, A. (2018). On the boomerang uniformity of cryptographic S-boxes. *IACR Trans. Symmetric Cryptol.*, 2018(3), 290–310.

Boura, C., Canteaut, A., Cannière, C.D. (2011). Higher-order differential properties of Keccak and *Luffa*. In *FSE 2011*, vol. 6733 of *Lecture Notes in Computer Science*. Joux, A. (ed.). Springer.

Boura, C., Canteaut, A., Jean, J., Suder, V. (2019). Two notions of differential equivalence on S-boxes. *Des. Codes Cryptogr.*, 87(2–3), 185–202.

Browning, K., Dillon, J., McQuistan, M., Wolfe, A. (2010). An APN permutation in dimension six. *Finite Fields: Theory and Applications*, 518, 33–42.

Cannière, C.D. (2007). Analysis and design of symmetric encryption algorithms. PhD Thesis, KU Leuven.

Canteaut, A. (2016). Lecture notes on cryptographic boolean functions [Online]. Available at: https://www.rocq.inria.fr/secret/Anne.Canteaut/poly.pdf.

Carlet, C., Charpin, P., Zinoviev, V.A. (1998). Codes, bent functions and permutations suitable for DES-like cryptosystems. *Des. Codes Cryptogr.*, 15(2), 125–156.

Chabaud, F. and Vaudenay, S. (1994). Links between differential and linear cryptanalysis. In *EUROCRYPT '94*, vol. 950 of *Lecture Notes in Computer Science*, Santis, A.D. (ed.). Springer.

Cid, C., Huang, T., Peyrin, T., Sasaki, Y., Song, L. (2018). Boomerang connectivity table: A new cryptanalysis tool. In *EUROCRYPT 2018, Part II*, vol. 10821 of *Lecture Notes in Computer Science*, Nielsen, J.B., Rijmen, V. (eds). Springer.

Daemen, J. and Rijmen, V. (2001). The wide trail design strategy. In *Cryptography and Coding, 8th IMA International Conference, Cirencester, UK, December 17–19, 2001, Proceedings*, vol. 2260 of *Lecture Notes in Computer Science*, Honary, B. (ed.). Springer.

Dunkelman, O. and Huang, S. (2019). Reconstructing an S-box from its difference distribution table. *IACR Trans. Symmetric Cryptol.*, 2019(2), 193–217.

Jakobsen, T. and Knudsen, L.R. (1997). The interpolation attack on block ciphers. In *FSE '97*, vol. 1267 of *Lecture Notes in Computer Science*, Biham, E. (ed.). Springer.

Leander, G. and Poschmann, A. (2007). On the classification of 4 bit S-boxes. In *WAIFI 2007*, vol. 4547 of *Lecture Notes in Computer Science*, Carlet, C., Sunar, B. (eds). Springer.

Nyberg, K. (1993). Differentially uniform mappings for cryptography. In *EUROCRYPT '93*, vol. 765 of *Lecture Notes in Computer Science*, Helleseth, T. (ed.). Springer.

Nyberg, K. and Knudsen, L.R. (1995). Provable security against a differential attack. *J. Cryptol.*, 8(1), 27–37.

Perrin, L. (2017). Cryptanalysis, reverse-engineering and design of symmetric cryptographic algorithms. Doctoral Thesis [Online]. Available at: http://hdl.handle.net/10993/31195.

Perrin, L. (2021). SboxU: S-box analysis utils [Online]. Available at: https://who.paris.inria.fr/Leo.Perrin/teaching/sboxu.html.

Piret, G., Roche, T., Carlet, C. (2012). PICARO – A block cipher allowing efficient higher-order side-channel resistance. In *ACNS 2012*, vol. 7341 of *Lecture Notes in Computer Science*, Bao, F., Samarati, P., Zhou, J. (eds). Springer.

The Sage Development Team (2021). S-boxes and their algebraic representations [Online]. Available at: https://doc.sagemath.org/html/en/reference/cryptography/sage/crypto/sbox.html.

Ullrich, M., Cannière, C.D., Indesteege, S., Küçük, Ö., Mouha, N., Preneel, B. (2011). Finding optimal bitsliced implementations of 4×4-bit S-boxes. *SKEW 2011, Symmetric Key Encryption Workshop*, Lyngby, Denmark.

9

Rationale, Backdoors and Trust

Léo PERRIN

Inria, Paris, France

What makes a primitive "trustworthy"? As these algorithms are the root of most cybersecurity, we need to be able to trust them to provide the security level we demand from them. At the same time, it is impossible to "prove" that a primitive is secure. It is sometimes possible to prove that the complexity of attacking them is the same as the complexity of solving a specific mathematical problem, as is the case for Diffie-Hellman and the DH problem (which is related to the discrete logarithm). Nevertheless, such an approach merely moves the problem instead of solving it: we still need to trust that no solution to the mathematical problem will be found in the foreseeable future. Ultimately, it is not really possible to *know* that a primitive is secure. However, it is possible to have reasonably *trustworthy* primitives.

We may then go back to the opening question: what does it mean for a primitive to be trustworthy? We do not pretend to answer this question completely. Indeed, trust is by definition a personal notion, and the weight each person gives to each possible criteria may as well be considered axiomatic. For instance, the mere fact that an algorithm has been standardized by the authorities of a specific country is sufficient for some to distrust it, regardless of the merits or the history of said primitive. And we may imagine that this standardization has the opposite effect on other people! At the same time, we can imagine simple and tangible guidelines that, if followed, will contribute to convincing experts that a primitive is trustworthy.

Symmetric Cryptography 1,
coordinated by Christina BOURA and María NAYA-PLASENCIA. © ISTE Ltd 2023.

The aim of this chapter is to discuss such guidelines and the context in which they are needed. In other words, we try to answer a narrower but better specified question:

What are the properties that will lead experts to trust a primitive?

To this end, we first give an outline of the lifecycle of a cryptographic primitive (section 9.1). It corresponds to an idealized view that, fortunately, also corresponds to some real world cases. Then, in section 9.2, we study algorithms with a very different lifecycle, and which should indeed not be trusted as a consequence. These fall into two big categories: "a priori honest blunders" where the primitive simply turned out to be flawed despite what was probably the best efforts of their designers, and primitives for which undisclosed properties were identified by third parties, including backdoors. Finally, section 9.3 builds upon these examples to discuss approaches that should increase the level of trust a primitive gathers among experts.

9.1. Lifecycle of a cryptographic primitive

Though there are important exceptions (that will be discussed later), the life time of a cryptographic primitive is divided into three main phases: the design, the public analysis and the deployment. The boundaries between these phases correspond to two discrete events: the design ends when the algorithm is published, and the deployment starts when the primitive has been approved in some way, for example, when it has been standardized. While the public analysis starts at publication, it does not stop when the algorithm is approved: it has to continue, as we will see later.

9.1.1. *Design phase*

During the design phase, the authors of the primitive first need to decide what the scope statement of the primitive is. It could be the outcome of their own research (e.g. to showcase a new design approach), or it could be guided by a specific use case: for a primitive to be submitted to the NIST lightweight cryptography standardization effort, some form of lightweightness must be a target.

In the case of symmetric cryptography, the designers first construct a round function, and then choose a number of rounds. This choice is difficult and corresponds to a tradeoff between security and efficiency: the more rounds, the more secure the primitive, but the slower it is. Thus, in order to make an informed decision, it is necessary to carefully assess this security level: how many rounds can be proven secure against differential and linear attacks? How efficient could a key-recovery algorithm be (if relevant)? What is the highest number of rounds attacked using any attack?

Interpreting these data is difficult. In particular, while the authors should have done their best to identify the strongest attacks, others are likely to improve them. Thus, a primitive is expected to have a *security margin*, that is, to have more rounds than can be argued secure at the time of design in order to account for later attack improvements.

Once this process is finished, a paper is submitted to a conference, or to a specific call for primitives (such as a NIST competition). This paper contains:

– a specification, in order to precisely describe the primitive;

– a *design rationale* describing and justifying the choices made during the design process, which should in particular justify the number of rounds chosen;

– a description of the first cryptanalysis performed by the authors.

9.1.2. *Public cryptanalysis*

This phase is the longest, and yet it is conceptually the simplest: cryptographers try to find flaws in the published algorithm. These rarely lead to practical cryptanalysis at first: if the primitive has been designed using a rigorous application of state-of-the-art techniques, then it is unlikely that it falls to a practical attack right away. Instead, the focus of the academic community is in finding attacks that target a *round-reduced* version of the primitive, that is, a weakened instance. The corresponding attacks are a priori of little practical interest since such instances do not conform to the specification. Yet, such attacks can have two consequences. First, if they can only successfully target substantially weaker instances, then the trust in the primitive is increased; the conclusion in this case being that, despite their best efforts, a team of cryptographers could not find any flaw of great importance. After all, a negative result is still a result. On the other hand, in the second case, the attack might work against more rounds than foreseen by the designers, or suggest an attack direction that they did not investigate. Even if the attack found does not threaten the full round primitive, it may still invite caution about this specific primitive.

9.1.3. *Deployment?*

If a worrying flaw is found during the public analysis phase, then the primitive is essentially discarded. For example, during a multi-round NIST competition, the algorithm would simply not make it to the next round. On the other hand, once it has gathered the trust of the community, this algorithm might eventually get deployed by the industry in actual products, for example, within TLS or in some physical devices like smartcards. This endorsement often takes the form of a standardization or normalization. Indeed, since the algorithm has to be used by multiple devices or applications from multiple institutions, a common reference for their description is needed.

However, even though many primitives are considered secure, only a small fraction of them makes it to this phase. For most of them, while public analysis remains an open problem, deployment will in practice never happen. They will advance our knowledge of cryptography, and provide new research directions, but they are unlikely to be given attention outside academia; not because there is something inherently wrong with them, but rather because there are many primitives of each type.

OBSERVATION.– Most of algorithms from the literature are *never* used in practice.

This observation has a crucial corollary that must be kept in mind when discussing the use of a specific primitive. Suppose that a decision must be taken about whether to use a specific algorithm or not. The question is not "is there a reason to refuse to use it?" but rather "is there a reason to prefer it over all the others?" As a result, we can afford a great deal of caution when choosing which primitive will make it to the deployment phase since there is a plethora to choose from.

9.1.4. *The limits of this process*

Usually, the design is made by teams consisting of between 1 and 15 well-identified cryptographers. The analysis is performed by the whole cryptographic community, and the deployment is of course handled by developers, be they working for the industry, open-source projects, etc. The story of the AES (2001) block cipher corresponds exactly to this idealized process, but there are of course exceptions: some proprietary ciphers were neither published nor publicly analyzed before their deployment (see section 9.2.1), and the identity of their designers remains a mystery. The situation is similar for some national standards such as the Russian hash function STREEBOG (Federal Agency on Technical Regulation and Metrology 2012).

9.2. When a selection process fails

The algorithms whose development failed to adhere to this process can be sorted into two categories. The first contains proprietary ciphers designed and deployed in industrial products without any input from the cryptography community. The second contains backdoored primitives, that is, algorithms that were intended to have a hidden flaw, the secrecy surrounding their design then being intended to preserve it.

Regardless of the specifics of the flawed reasoning behind the design of these algorithms, their mere presence is a problem. This might seem counterintuitive: after all, if a primitive is not trustworthy, then we could simply refuse to use it. However, the physical devices running them might not allow updates of their cryptography stack, or the support of legacy encryption might be necessary to preserve backward compatibility. As a result, the RC2 block cipher, which uses a 40-bit key, was explicitly mentioned in the standard of the (now deprecated) TLS 1.1 published in 2006. More generally, once a cipher has been "approved" for a certain use, it takes a lot of effort to walk back this approval. This situation is akin to environmental pollution: it is much more difficult to undo damage than it is to make it.

9.2.1. *Under-engineered algorithms*

9.2.1.1. *Proprietary/legacy algorithms*

The first group of algorithms in this category contains proprietary primitives that were designed behind closed doors and whose specification was usually intended to remain secret. A list of these algorithms is provided in Biryukov and Perrin (2017, Table 3), which is reproduced below (Table 9.1) with the addition of GEA-1/2 (Beierle et al. 2021). Many share a similar story: first they were deployed, then they were reverse-engineered from the products using them, and finally flaws were identified.

Intended platform	Name	Key	IS	IV	Attack time
Cell phones	A5/1	64	64	22	2^{24}
	A5/2	64	81	22	2^{16}
	CMEA†	64	16–48	–	2^{32}
	ORYX	96	96	–	2^{16}
	GEA-1	64	96	33	2^{40}
	GEA-2	64	97	33	$2^{45.1}$
Satellite phones	A5-GMR-1	64	82	19	$2^{38.1}$
	A5-GMR-2	64	68	22	2^{28}
Cordless phones	DSC	64	80	35	2^{34}
Atmel chips	SECUREMEM.	64	109	128	$2^{29.8}$
	CRYPTOMEM.	64	117	128	2^{50}
Car key/ immobilizer	HITAG2	48	48	64	2^{35}
	MEGAMOS	96	57	56	2^{48}
	KEELOQ†	64	32	–	$2^{44.5}$
	DST40†	40	40	–	2^{40}
Smart cards	ICLASS	64	40	–	2^{40}
	CRYPTO-1	48	48	96	2^{32}
DVD players	CSS	40	42	–	2^{40}
	CRYPTOMERIA†	56	64	–	2^{48}
Digital televisions	CSA-BC†	64	64	–	2^{64}
	CSA-SC	64	103	64	$2^{45.7}$
Amazon Kindle	PC-1	128	152	–	2^{31}
Secure token	SECURID‡	64	64	–	2^{44}
Bluetooth devices	E0	128	128	–	2^{27}

Table 9.1. *(Biryukov and Perrin 2017) Proprietary/legacy primitives. Block ciphers are marked with "†", MACs with "‡" and unmarked primitives are stream ciphers*

Many of these algorithms were essentially broken by design because of their very small key size. While performance optimization probably played a role, we can surmise that export control laws played a significant role in the decision to use such short keys (see section 9.2.1.2). The obscurity surrounding their design process makes it difficult to accurately estimate the date of their design; but we can still expect their old age to play a role as well. Indeed, it is impossible for algorithm designers to implement counter-measures against cryptanalysis techniques that are not known yet.

9.2.1.2. *Legal requirements*

Programs implementing cryptographic primitives used to be considered like ammunition in the United States, and as such their export was restricted unless the key size was limited (similar limitations were enforced in other countries as well). Most prominently, the NSA was involved in the design of the DES (1977). Some contradictory statements have been made about this involvement, as listed in Schneier (1996): while it seems like the agency modified the S-boxes to improve the resilience of the cipher against differential attack, a technique that was unknown in academia at the time, it is on the other hand quite clear that it is responsible for a decrease in the key size. Thus, while the spying agency may have improved the resistance of the DES against some attacks, its contribution to the security of the cipher remains substantially negative overall as a consequence of this shortening.

9.2.2. *Primitives with hidden properties*

The whole purpose of cryptographic algorithms is to provide security guarantees. However, for a surprisingly high number of primitives, this security was purposefully crippled: their aim was to provide *some* security, *but not too much*. There is always a trade-off between security and performance,[1] but that is not the security reduction discussed in this section. The aim pursued here is not to obtain a given property at the expense of security (i.e. decrease the number of rounds to improve throughput); instead, it is to reduce security for the sake of reducing the security. In other words, we are discussing the case where the algorithm is *backdoored*, that is, where a security flaw was purposefully introduced. In general, the design of backdoored primitives corresponds to *kleptography*, as introduced in Young and Yung (1997). In the case of symmetric cryptographic primitives, the techniques for inserting a backdoor have been an active research area. First, S-box based methods were investigated in Paterson (1999). These were refined much more recently in Bannier et al. (2016). Another direction was explored that relies on inserting secret

---

1 The identity cipher, that is, the operation mapping each plaintext to each-self, will always be the fastest encryption algorithm. Thus, using any non-trivial encryption or authentication means that it is acceptable to lose performance in the name of security.

vulnerability against linear attacks (Rijmen and Preneel 1997), but it proved less promising (Wu et al. 1998). However, this idea is getting renewed attention (Posteuca and Ashur 2021) and seems applicable even in the absence of S-boxes.

Weakening the security provided by a component would be unacceptable in other contexts. Who would suggest weakening seatbelts in cars? Yet, the security provided by cryptography in general is regularly the target of various politicians who wish law enforcement were capable of bypassing encryption in some cases (pedopornography, terrorism, etc.). This problem is sometimes magnified by the fact that the institutions supposed to secure communications are the same law enforcement agencies that would use such backdoors. Nevertheless, in practice, it seems impossible to introduce a flaw[2] with the following properties:

– usability: the flaw is significant enough that its intended users are capable of using it to break the security properties;

– stealth: the flaw cannot be spotted after an analysis of the specification.

To support the claim that stealth cannot be achieved, we will consider three examples. The first (DUAL_EC) will show that backdoors can be easy to spot. The second (STREEBOG and KUZNYECHIK) will provide evidence that very subtle structures can still be detected, thus showing that hiding a backdoor in plain sight would be extremely hard in practice. As a result, it seems necessary for a backdoor to exist that the specification of the algorithm be kept secret. While it is a hindrance, the last example (GPRS encryption) will show that it is not sufficient.

9.2.2.1. *DUAL_EC*

The most prominent one has to be DUAL_EC (Bernstein et al. 2015). This algorithm is a pseudo-random number generator (PRNG), meaning that it takes as input a seed of a given length and outputs an arbitrarily long bit string. Once seeded, the output of such an algorithm is typically used to generate both cryptographic keys (that are supposed to be secret) and nonces (that are supposed to be public). In such a context, a deeply flawed PRNG could allow an attacker to deduce a cryptographic key from the nonce, and in fact there are reasons to believe that DUAL_EC was intended to allow such a recovery. Indeed, the knowledge of the private key used by its inner public key cryptosystem allows an attacker to perform the type of cryptanalysis described above. This fact was quickly identified (Shumow and Ferguson 2007), but the algorithm ended up in some products from the RSA company anyway (Bernstein et al. 2015). This use is rather puzzling: independently

---

2 Other techniques based on key-escrow have been considered to solve the same problem without weakening encryption. The *Clipper Chip* is a high-profile example of this approach. It does not imply any weakening of the primitives themselves, and is therefore not within the scope of this chapter. Nevertheless, as shown by the example of the Clipper Chip, this method has its own problems, and fails in practice.

from the backdoor, the performances of this PRNG were poor (both in terms of speed and in terms of security).

9.2.2.2. STREEBOG *and* KUZNYECHIK

The second example is not an evidence of backdoor per se. Rather, it highlights the difficulty of hiding information in plain sight: in practice, a stealthy backdoor could not be hidden in an algorithm with a public specification. STREEBOG and KUZNYECHIK are the standard hash function and block cipher in the Russian federation at the time of writing. These symmetric primitives both rely on the same 8-bit S-box, denoted π' in the original specifications, and usually nicknamed π. This S-box was only specified via its lookup table. While it is indeed all that is needed in a *specification*, it does not provide cryptanalysts with the information they need in order to perform a proper security analysis. Worse, the authors of these algorithms repeatedly claimed that this component had been generated using a pseudo-random process,[3] as summarized by Bonnetain et al. (2019). In that paper, the authors built upon the main result of Perrin (2019) to conclusively prove that the randomness claimed by its authors is incoherent with the properties of π. Indeed, π has a so-called "TKlog" structure, a style of construction with very strong algebraic properties. More precisely, it is defined over the finite field $\mathbb{F}_{2^8}$ and is such that $\pi(a \times \mathbb{F}_{2^4}^*) = L(a) + \mathbb{F}_{2^4}^*$: it maps multiplicative cosets of the subfield to additive subsets of the subfield. Moreover, the restriction of π to each multiplicative coset is always essentially the same function. It is also remarkable that additive cosets (but not multiplicative cosets) were proved to be a promising direction to insert backdoors in block ciphers in Bannier et al. (2016).

While the purpose of the TKlog (Perrin 2019) remains unclear[4], these results show that it would be in practice extremely difficult (if not impossible) to have a stealthy backdoor: the technique for its exploitation might remain hidden, but the potential presence of a backdoor will be identified provided that cryptographers can analyze the algorithm.

9.2.2.3. *GPRS encryption*

The latest example is from Beierle et al. (2021). In this paper, the authors identify a backdoor in one of the standard algorithms used to encrypt some cell phone communications. The backdoor relies on sophisticated properties of the key-schedule to allow efficient divide-and-conquer attacks. It took many years to spot this flaw, the main reason being the fact that this encryption algorithm was a trade secret. As a result, cryptanalysts could not simply investigate the properties of the cipher. Instead,

---

3 More specifically, they specifically told yours truly during a conversation taking place during an ISO meeting that a Fisher-Yates shuffle was used.

4 There is to the best of our knowledge no published cryptanalysis that leverages it.

it was first necessary for a third party to reverse-engineer the specification of the algorithm in order then to allow researchers to recover the backdoor. Still, as we can see, this task was eventually successful. Thus, hiding the specification of an algorithm is not sufficient to ensure the stealth of a backdoor, even if it can protect it for some time.

9.3. Can we trust modern algorithms?

9.3.1. *Standardization and normalization*

Standards and *norms* are related but different concepts.

Informally, the use of a standard is advised, while norms are binding (their use is mandatory). In cryptography, the most relevant standardizing bodies are probably the IETF (which is in charge of RFCs, the de facto web standards) and the American NIST (an agency of the United States Department of Commerce). The importance of the web does not need explaining; as for NIST, its standards have been very widely adopted (including by the IETF). For instance, its *advanced encryption standard* (AES) is arguably the most successful block cipher. Other notable standardizing bodies include the international ISO/IEC and various regional bodies such as the Russian "Technical Committee 26" (issuing *GOST* standards) or the Chinese State "Cryptography Administration".

While a standard is merely a specification, it also emphasizes that the use of this algorithm is encouraged by the standardizing body.[5] This explains why SHA-1 has been *deprecated* (see Chapter 15 of volume 2): it is not sufficient that the algorithm is known to be insecure, standardizing bodies have to explicitly mark it as such. The case of SHA-1 also highlights another property of standards and norms: there is a great asymmetry between the difficulty of preventing a standardization, and the one of deprecating a standard. Indeed, given the vast array of primitives of all types that are available, deciding not to standardize a specific primitive is not that heavy a decision. On the other hand, *after* a primitive is standardized, it is extremely difficult to deprecate it.

The difficulty of removing already standardized algorithms compounds with the conflictive incentives of some spying agencies: the latter have successfully pushed

---

5 The situation for the IETF is more complicated. Its standards are *Request For Comments (RFC)*, such as RFC8446 which specifies TLS 1.3. However, these RFC can have different origins which are specified by the "Category" keyword at the top of each of them. In the case of RFC8446, we can see that it is in the "Standards Track", that is, that it is a "real" standard. On the other hand, the RFC specifying the hash function Streebog (RFC6986) is in the category "Informational", meaning that it is *not* an IETF standard.

for the standardization of purposefully under-engineered algorithms (e.g. the DES), and then those remain standards for much longer than is desirable. In Dunkelman and Perrin (2019), a technique is suggested to secure standardization processes against under-engineered ciphers. It relies on assessing the design process rather than the primitive itself, and achieves this by forcing designers to provide a clear specification of this process that is then evaluated in a multi-stage mechanism.

9.3.2. *Some rules of thumb*

As we have seen, unfortunately, an algorithm being standardized does not mean that it is secure. Below, we provide some simple rules of thumb, which are of course imperfect, but should help the reader to make a more informed choice about which standardized primitive to use in their program.

Rule 1

Have the designers (honestly) explained their design process?

If a design process such as the one from Dunkelman and Perrin (2019) was used, then this property is ensured. However, even if it is not the case, it is still possible to verify if the designers have provided convincing arguments for their design choices. In light of section 9.2.2, we also have to specify that the explanations must be truthful.

Rule 2

What is the reasoning behind the computation of the number of rounds?

The aim of this rule is to verify two points. First, the authors of the primitive have provided a clear description of their best attacks as it is an important step when choosing a number of rounds. Second, it implies checking the security margin, and seeing whether it is aligned with what is comfortable for the application considered.

Rule 3

What is the state of the public analysis of the algorithm?

The aim of this rule is straightforward: it is to assess whether the algorithm has withstood the test of time. For example, it is fair to assume that a primitive about which many papers have been published has received substantial attention, as is the case, for instance, for the AES. However, the converse is wrong, and counting the papers published at academic conferences that present attacks against an algorithm is an imperfect metric. Indeed, the fact that unsuccessful attacks do not get published means that an algorithm for which the designers published a thorough analysis might perform poorly for that metric without it being an indication of a low security. The following aspects should then be taken into account as well.

– Is it designed to ease third party analysis? If it is not the case, then a lack of publication could mean that cryptographers simply focused their attention on better designed algorithms. In this case, a lack of published cryptanalysis could mean that little analysis was performed, and not that attack attempts were unsuccessful.

– Is it a high profile target? If an algorithm is the finalist of a NIST competition, or if it is an important standard, then we can assume that cryptographers try to attack it. In this case, lack of published analysis could be an indication of security. Still, "high profile" can be hard to define: implementers and cryptanalysts may use different criteria to decide which algorithm is the most interesting to look at.

9.4. References

AES (2001). Advanced encryption standard (AES). National Institute of Standards and Technology (NIST), FIPS PUB 197, U.S. Department of Commerce.

Bannier, A., Bodin, N., Filiol, E. (2016). Partition-based trapdoor ciphers. Cryptology ePrint Archive, Report 2016/493 [Online]. Available at: https://eprint.iacr.org/2016/493.

Beierle, C., Derbez, P., Leander, G., Leurent, G., Raddum, H., Rotella, Y., Rupprecht, D., Stennes, L. (2021). Cryptanalysis of the GPRS encryption algorithms GEA-1 and GEA-2. In *EUROCRYPT 2021, Part II*, vol. 12697 of *Lecture Notes in Computer Science*, Canteaut, A., Standaert, F. (eds). Springer.

Bernstein, D.J., Lange, T., Niederhagen, R. (2015). Dual EC: A standardized back door. Cryptology ePrint Archive, Report 2015/767 [Online]. Available at: https://eprint.iacr.org/2015/767.

Biryukov, A. and Perrin, L. (2017). State of the art in lightweight symmetric cryptography. Cryptology ePrint Archive, Report 2017/511 [Online]. Available at: https://eprint.iacr.org/2017/511.

Bonnetain, X., Perrin, L., Tian, S. (2019). Anomalies and vector space search: Tools for S-Box analysis. In *ASIACRYPT 2019, Part I*, vol. 11921 of *Lecture Notes in Computer Science*, Galbraith, S.D., Moriai, S. (eds). Springer.

DES (1977). Data encryption standard. National Bureau of Standards, NBS FIPS PUB 46, U.S. Department of Commerce.

Dunkelman, O. and Perrin, L. (2019). Adapting rigidity to symmetric cryptography: Towards "unswerving" designs. In *ACM Workshop on Security Standardisation Research Workshop, SSR'19*. Association for Computing Machinery.

Federal Agency on Technical Regulation and Metrology (2012). Information technology – Data security: Hash function [Online]. Available at http://wwwold.tc26.ru/en/standard/gost/GOSTR3411-2012eng.pdf.

Paterson, K.G. (1999). Imprimitive permutation groups and trapdoors in iterated block ciphers. In *FSE '99*, vol. 1636 of *Lecture Notes in Computer Science*, Knudsen, L.R. (ed.). Springer.

Perrin, L. (2019). Partitions in the S-box of Streebog and Kuznyechik. *IACR Trans. Symmetric Cryptol.*, 2019(1), 302–329.

Posteuca, R. and Ashur, T. (2021). How to backdoor a cipher. Cryptology ePrint Archive, Report 2021/442 [Online]. Available at: https://eprint.iacr.org/2021/442.

Rijmen, V. and Preneel, B. (1997). A family of trapdoor ciphers. In *FSE '97*, vol. 1267 of *Lecture Notes in Computer Science*, Biham, E. (ed.). Springer.

Schneier, B. (1996). *Applied Cryptography*, 2nd edition, John Wiley & Sons, Inc.

Shumow, D. and Ferguson, N. (2007). On the possibility of a back door in the NIST SP800-90 Dual EC PRNG. CRYPTO 2007 Rump Session [Online]. Available at: http://rump2007.cr.yp.to/15-shumow.pdf.

Wu, H., Bao, F., Deng, R.H., Ye, Q. (1998). Cryptanalysis of Rijmen-Preneel trapdoor ciphers. In *ASIACRYPT '98*, vol. 1514 of *Lecture Notes in Computer Science*, Ohta, K., Pei, D. (eds). Springer.

Young, A.L. and Yung, M. (1997). Kleptography: Using cryptography against cryptography. In *EUROCRYPT '97*, vol. 1233 of *Lecture Notes in Computer Science*, Fumy, W. (ed.). Springer.

PART 2

Security Proofs for
Symmetric-key Algorithms

10

Modeling Security

Bart MENNINK

Radboud University, Nijmegen, The Netherlands

This chapter will be concerned with how to formalize security of cryptographic primitives. We will take stream ciphers as a running example through sections 10.1–10.5, and extend our formalization to block ciphers in section 10.6.

10.1. Different types of adversary models

Consider a modern stream cipher of the form $SC : \{0,1\}^k \times \{0,1\}^d \to \{0,1\}^*$ that takes as input a key K, a diversifier D and that outputs an arbitrarily large keystream. When we fix the key, the stream cipher becomes a function mapping a diversifier D to a keystream s. We denote this function as $SC_K : \{0,1\}^d \to \{0,1\}^*$.

There are different types of adversaries one might consider. Differences are in the amount of information that it obtains. For example, if SC_K is used to encrypt a message m, an adversary may know a small portion of the message m. For example, m is an official letter with some standard heading. In this case, we speak of a *known plaintext adversary*. The adversarial knowledge about the message may be more subtle. For example, it may only know that it is ASCII encoded English text, or just know it is the letter *when it sees it*. Here, one typically speaks of a *ciphertext-only* adversary. In these cases, finding the key K by exhaustive key search is still possible if the message is long enough, but it may be trickier to implement.

The adversarial knowledge about the message may likewise be much more. For example, the adversary may be able to choose the message itself and receive the corresponding ciphertext. Clearly, this will give the adversary knowledge of a keystream s corresponding to one diversifier, but one would like that it reveals nothing about keystreams from different diversifiers.

In general, when evaluating a cipher, one assumes the most powerful adversary model. If it is secure in that model, it is also secure in many weaker models.

10.2. When is an attack considered successful?

Clearly, if the adversary manages to recover the key K, it can compute the keystream s for any value of the diversifier D by means of running SC_K. However, this is not the only way for the adversary to break it.

Suppose it can *predict* part of a new keystream: after having learned many (D, s) tuples for different diversifiers, it happens to know that for a specific new diversifier $D^\star$, with high probability the keystream is equal to $s^\star$. If one would use $D^\star$, then it can use this information to recover the plaintext from a ciphertext where $SC_K(D^\star)$ was used as keystream. Clearly, this should also be considered as an attack.

As said, key recovery allows the adversary to predict a keystream but the converse is not true. If the adversary can predict part of a new keystream, it might not be able to recover the key. This means that a key recovery attack is (strictly) stronger than a keystream prediction attack.

We can weaken the attack even further. Suppose that the adversary can spot certain *regularities* in a keystream. For example, after having learned many (D, s) tuples, it can do basic statistical analysis and observe that the number of ones in all keystream sequences s is much more than 50%. Should this be considered as a valid attack, even though it does not lead to the adversary recovering the key or to recover plaintext from particular ciphertexts?

In general, we want SC_K to "look like" a function that responds randomly for each input. We will consider a theoretical function that behaves ideally in this respect: the *random oracle*.

10.3. Random oracle

A random oracle is an ideal cryptographic primitive that generates a random response to each query (and the same response for queries with the same argument). It is not a practical function, but it can be described by an algorithm that clarifies the properties of its outputs. It accepts inputs of arbitrary size and generates infinite streams, and it is denoted "$\mathcal{RO}$". The idea of a random oracle was first formalized in a seminal work of Bellare and Rogaway (1993). It has found myriad use cases in cryptography.

We first give the algorithm for a random oracle that returns strings s of fixed length and will deal with the infinite length in a later stage. $\mathcal{RO}$ maintains an archive $\mathcal{L}$ that contains tuples (m, s). We call an algorithm that keeps a state between queries *stateful*. We abuse notation somewhat by saying that $m \in \mathcal{L}$ if there is a tuple (m, s) in $\mathcal{L}$ with first member m. For $m \in \mathcal{L}$, we denote by s_m the second member of the tuple (m, s)

Initially, the archive $\mathcal{L}$ is empty. If $\mathcal{RO}$ is queried with an input m, it integrates the query in the archive $\mathcal{L}$:

– If $m \notin \mathcal{L}$, $\mathcal{RO}$ generates a uniformly random string s, and stores (m, s) in $\mathcal{L}$.

Then it returns s_m to the query.

We wish our $\mathcal{RO}$ oracle to be usable as a stream cipher, and that implies that it must be able to return an output s of arbitrary length. Concretely, we adapt the query interface to $\mathcal{RO}$ by also including the desired length of s, denoted by ℓ. The algorithm now becomes the following. If $\mathcal{RO}$ is queried with (m, ℓ), it integrates the query in the archive $\mathcal{L}$:

– if $m \in \mathcal{L}$ and s_m is shorter than ℓ bits, $\mathcal{RO}$ updates (m, s) in the archive by appending enough uniform random bits to s so that its length becomes ℓ;

– if $m \notin \mathcal{L}$, $\mathcal{RO}$ generates a uniformly random string s and stores (m, s) in $\mathcal{L}$.

Then it returns the first ℓ bits of s_m to the query.

10.4. Distinguishing advantage

We consider an adversary to be successful if it finds an attack that has a success probability that is higher than the one in the security claim that comes with the cryptographic primitive. This section is about how we can express such a claim. In a claim, one takes the strongest possible attacker model and if a cryptographic primitive is secure in that model, it is also secure in all weaker attacker models.

Behind the back of the adversary, we secretly select either SC_K or $\mathcal{RO}$. Either function is chosen with probability 0.5: we generate a random bit $b \xleftarrow{\$} \{0, 1\}$, and select SC_K if $b = 1$ and $\mathcal{RO}$ if $b = 0$. We do not reveal our choice to the adversary. However, the adversary would like to know this.

To measure the success probability that the adversary has in guessing b, we consider the experiment shown in Figure 10.1. In this figure, the adversary is in either of two worlds: the "real world" where it speaks with SC_K and the "ideal world" where it speaks with $\mathcal{RO}$. As the adversary does not know whether it is in the real or ideal world, we call the entity that is either SC_K or $\mathcal{RO}$ the "oracle". It can "query" its oracle. In a query it gives as input a diversifier D and requested stream length ℓ and its oracle responds with a keystream s of ℓ bits. In the real world, this keystream satisfies $s = SC_K(D, \ell)$ and in the ideal world it satisfies $s = \mathcal{RO}(D, \ell)$.

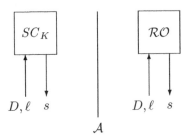

Figure 10.1. *Distinguishing experiment for stream ciphers*

The adversary can send a number of queries to its oracle, and eventually, it must guess whether it is in the real or in the ideal world. It does so by returning a bit $b' \in \{0, 1\}$: $b' = 1$ if it thinks it is in the real world and $b' = 0$ if it thinks it is in the ideal world.

The adversary succeeds if $b' = b$, and we denote this by the event success. Clearly, a naive adversary has a success probability of $1/2$: it may simply make no queries and toss a coin to determine b'. Therefore, its goal would be to succeed in guessing b with probability significantly larger than $1/2$. In other words, any adversary that succeeds with probability *significantly more than* $1/2$ can distinguish. When considering such an adversary in a formal way, it is simply an algorithm. We denote such an adversary by $\mathcal{A}$. We now define the (probability) *distance* between the real world and the ideal world with respect to an adversary $\mathcal{A}$:

$$\Delta_{\mathcal{A}}(SC_K; \mathcal{RO}) = \mathbf{Pr}\left(\mathcal{A}^{SC_K} = 1\right) - \mathbf{Pr}\left(\mathcal{A}^{\mathcal{RO}} = 1\right). \qquad [10.1]$$

In other words, this distance is the difference between the probability that the adversary $\mathcal{A}$ returns $b' = 1$ in the real world minus the probability that it returns $b' = 1$ in the ideal world.

This distance is equal to two times the success probability of the adversary $\mathcal{A}$ minus 1:

$$\Delta_{\mathcal{A}}(SC_K; \mathcal{RO}) = 2\mathbf{Pr}\left(\text{success}\right) - 1.$$

This can be seen by basic probability theory:

$$
\begin{aligned}
\Delta_{\mathcal{A}}(SC_K; \mathcal{RO}) &= \mathbf{Pr}\left(\mathcal{A}^{SC_K} = 1\right) - \mathbf{Pr}\left(\mathcal{A}^{\mathcal{RO}} = 1\right) \\
&= \mathbf{Pr}\left(b' = 1 \mid b = 1\right) - \mathbf{Pr}\left(b' = 1 \mid b = 0\right) \\
&= \mathbf{Pr}\left(b' = 1 \mid b = 1\right) - \left(1 - \mathbf{Pr}\left(b' = 0 \mid b = 0\right)\right) \\
&= \mathbf{Pr}\left(b' = 1 \mid b = 1\right) + \mathbf{Pr}\left(b' = 0 \mid b = 0\right) - 1 \\
&= \frac{\mathbf{Pr}\left(b' = 1 \wedge b = 1\right)}{\mathbf{Pr}\left(b = 1\right)} + \frac{\mathbf{Pr}\left(b' = 0 \wedge b = 0\right)}{\mathbf{Pr}\left(b = 0\right)} - 1 \\
&= 2\left(\mathbf{Pr}\left(b' = 1 \wedge b = 1\right) + \mathbf{Pr}\left(b' = 0 \wedge b = 0\right)\right) - 1 \\
&= 2\mathbf{Pr}\left(b' = b\right) - 1 \\
&= 2\mathbf{Pr}\left(\mathsf{success}\right) - 1.
\end{aligned}
$$

We call $\Delta_{\mathcal{A}}(SC_K; \mathcal{RO})$ *the advantage of $\mathcal{A}$ in distinguishing SC_K from $\mathcal{RO}$.* In literature, it is also known as the advantage of $\mathcal{A}$ in breaking the pseudorandom function (PRF) security of SC_K, and it is denoted as $\mathrm{Adv}^{\mathrm{prf}}_{SC}(\mathcal{A})$.

DEFINITION 10.1 (Pseudorandom Function Security).– Let SC be a stream cipher with key size k. Let K be randomly drawn from the set of all keys. The advantage of an adversary $\mathcal{A}$ in distinguishing SC_K from a random oracle $\mathcal{RO}$ is defined as

$$
\mathrm{Adv}^{\mathrm{prf}}_{SC}(\mathcal{A}) = \Delta_{\mathcal{A}}(SC_K; \mathcal{RO}). \tag{10.2}
$$

10.5. Understanding the distinguishing advantage

There is no way to prove an upper bound for $\mathrm{Adv}^{\mathrm{prf}}_{SC}(\mathcal{A})$ for any concrete stream cipher, but it makes sense to claim such a bound. Breaking the cipher then simply corresponds with coming up with an algorithm $\mathcal{A}'$ with $\mathrm{Adv}^{\mathrm{prf}}_{SC}(\mathcal{A}')$ higher than the one claimed. To understand what kind of claims we can make for a stream cipher SC, we first have to quantify the complexity of an adversary.

10.5.1. *Adversarial complexity*

There are two types of information that $\mathcal{A}$ might learn about its oracle.

First off, $\mathcal{A}$ can query its oracle, SC_K or $\mathcal{RO}$. These queries are called *online queries* (as in the real world these queries correspond to conversations with the keyed instance of SC_K), and they are stored in a query history Q_d. Clearly, the advantage of $\mathcal{A}$ in distinguishing SC_K from $\mathcal{RO}$ increases with the number of queries that $\mathcal{A}$

makes. We could try to express the claimed advantage as a function of the number of queries. However, in many cases this is not a representative metric for the attack complexity. What is much more representative is the total number of bits sent to and received from the oracle. In this case, it is the number of diversifier bits sent and keystream bits received in all queries. We define by $|Q_d|$ the number of diversifier and keystream bits in Q_d. It is called the *online* or *data* complexity.

The second source of information of $\mathcal{A}$ comes from evaluations of SC for arbitrarily chosen keys. For this, $\mathcal{A}$ need not be connected with its oracle: as the specification of SC is known, $\mathcal{A}$ can implement it and run it offline. For this reason, these evaluations are called *offline evaluations*. They are stored in a query history Q_c. As mentioned above, what matters for Q_c is the number of keystream bits, and we define by $|Q_c|$ the number of keystream bits in Q_c. It is called the *offline* or *computational* complexity.

In practice, measuring $|Q_c|$ is subtle. The reason for this is that it, intuitively, measures the maximum number of evaluations of SC that adversary $\mathcal{A}$ can compute offline in a certain amount of time. A typical normalization that is often considered is that generating one keystream bit takes one unit of time, but it may be that the adversary can use its time more efficiently so as to compute more than $|Q_c|$ keystream bits in time $|Q_c|$.

On the other side, $|Q_c|$ not only covers function evaluations but also other computations that are relevant to the scheme but cannot be expressed as a function of the number of evaluations of SC. For example, if the distinguisher has gathered a certain set of oracle-responses and a certain set of offline primitive evaluations, it may have to do linear algebra computations to make up its decision based on the gathered data.

These two inaccuracies in the time parameter are generally neglected. One typically assumes that time is scaled and normalized and that $|Q_c|$ time allows for the generation of $|Q_c|$ keystream bits of SC.

10.5.2. *Claiming security*

Having discussed adversarial complexities, we can now discuss what claims one may make for stream ciphers. Consider a given stream cipher SC with k-bit key. A typical claim that the designers may have posed for this stream cipher is the following:

CLAIM 10.1.– Let SC be a stream cipher with key size k. There exists no adversary $\mathcal{A}$ with computational complexity $|Q_c|$ less than 2^{k-1} that succeeds in distinguishing SC_K from a random oracle with advantage more than $1/2$.

This claim captures the idea that there should be no attacks more efficient than exhaustive key search. However, it is rather vague about the advantage of adversaries with limited resources. The following claim is much more clear:

CLAIM 10.2.– Let SC be a stream cipher with key size k. For any adversary $\mathcal{A}$ with computational complexity $|Q_c|$,

$$\text{Adv}_{SC}^{\text{prf}}(\mathcal{A}) \leq \frac{|Q_c|}{2^k}.$$

10.5.3. *Breaking claims*

The above-mentioned claims cannot be proven. However, it is possible to disprove them. This happens by means of attacks.

Again, consider the stream cipher SC with k-bit key that serves as running example, and assume that the designers posed claim 10.2. Suppose a team of researchers finds an attack on SC: they show that SC_K can be distinguished from a random oracle $\mathcal{RO}$ with probability 1 using computational complexity $2^{k/2}$. Formally, this means that this team of researchers has described an adversary $\mathcal{A}'$ with computational complexity $|Q_c| = 2^{k/2}$ such that

$$\text{Adv}_{SC}^{\text{prf}}(\mathcal{A}') = 1.$$

This is better than the claimed bound of claim 10.1, and the adversary is thus considered to be a valid attack on the scheme.

10.6. Adaptation to block ciphers

The above description of distinguishing advantages is for functions that should behave like a random oracle. The situation for a block cipher is different. A block cipher takes as input a k-bit key K and a n-bit plaintext m and *bijectively* transforms it to a n-bit ciphertext c. For a fixed key, it is a permutation on n-bit strings. This makes the situation different from before, where the function was compared with a random oracle that has collisions and variable-length outputs.

We will use an adaptation of the pseudorandom function security of definition 10.1 to block ciphers. In the new thought experiment, we compare a block cipher E_K with a random permutation $\mathcal{P}$. This function $\mathcal{P}$ is defined similarly as a random oracle, with the difference that it is for n-bit length inputs and outputs only, and that it never responds with the same value to two different values. Alternatively, one may consider $\mathcal{P}$ to be uniformly randomly drawn from the set of all n-bit permutations.

10.6.1. *Distinguishing advantage*

The distinguishing advantage remains mainly unchanged: adversary $\mathcal{A}$ is either in the "real world", talking to E_K, or in the "ideal world", talking to $\mathcal{P}$. It can make queries to its oracle, and in the end, it has to guess whether it is in the real world or the ideal world. The *distance* between the real world and the ideal world with respect to adversary $\mathcal{A}$ is now defined as

$$\Delta_{\mathcal{A}}(E_K; \mathcal{P}) = \mathbf{Pr}\left(\mathcal{A}^{E_K} = 1\right) - \mathbf{Pr}\left(\mathcal{A}^{\mathcal{P}} = 1\right). \qquad [10.3]$$

We call $\Delta_{\mathcal{A}}(E_K; \mathcal{P})$ *the advantage of $\mathcal{A}$ in distinguishing E_K from $\mathcal{P}$*. In literature, it is also known as the advantage of $\mathcal{A}$ in breaking the pseudorandom permutation (PRP) security of E_K, and it is denoted $\mathrm{Adv}_E^{\mathrm{prp}}(\mathcal{A})$.

DEFINITION 10.2 (Pseudorandom Permutation Security).– Let E be a block cipher with key size k. Let K be randomly drawn from the set of all keys. The advantage of an adversary $\mathcal{A}$ in distinguishing E_K from a random permutation $\mathcal{P}$ is defined as

$$\mathrm{Adv}_E^{\mathrm{prp}}(\mathcal{A}) = \Delta_{\mathcal{A}}(E_K; \mathcal{P}). \qquad [10.4]$$

For block ciphers, one often measures the complexity of an adversary in the number of input blocks to the oracle, rather than in the number of bits. As E_K and $\mathcal{P}$ are of fixed length n bits only, this is just a convention: there is a one-to-one correspondence.

Sometimes, a block cipher E_K is used in such a way that the adversary learns evaluations of the form $c = E_K(m)$ as well as evaluations of the form $m = E_K^{-1}(c)$. In this case, we must *expand* our real world and our ideal world to also include the inverses E_K^{-1} and $\mathcal{P}^{-1}$. The *distance* between the real world and the ideal world with respect to adversary $\mathcal{A}$ is now defined as

$$\Delta_{\mathcal{A}}(E_K, E_K^{-1}; \mathcal{P}, \mathcal{P}^{-1}) = \mathbf{Pr}\left(\mathcal{A}^{E_K, E_K^{-1}} = 1\right) - \mathbf{Pr}\left(\mathcal{A}^{\mathcal{P}, \mathcal{P}^{-1}} = 1\right).$$
$$[10.5]$$

We call $\Delta_{\mathcal{A}}(E_K, E_K^{-1}; \mathcal{P}, \mathcal{P}^{-1})$ *the advantage of $\mathcal{A}$ in distinguishing (E_K, E_K^{-1}) from $(\mathcal{P}, \mathcal{P}^{-1})$*. In literature, it is also known as the advantage of $\mathcal{A}$ in breaking the strong pseudorandom permutation (SPRP) security of E_K, and it is denoted $\mathrm{Adv}_E^{\mathrm{sprp}}(\mathcal{A})$.

DEFINITION 10.3 (Strong Pseudorandom Permutation Security).– Let E be a block cipher with key size k. Let K be randomly drawn from the set of all keys. The advantage of an adversary $\mathcal{A}$ in distinguishing (E_K, E_K^{-1}) from a random permutation $(\mathcal{P}, \mathcal{P}^{-1})$ is defined as

$$\mathrm{Adv}_E^{\mathrm{sprp}}(\mathcal{A}) = \Delta_{\mathcal{A}}(E_K, E_K^{-1}; \mathcal{P}, \mathcal{P}^{-1}). \qquad [10.6]$$

As mentioned before, one often measures the complexity of an adversary in the number of input blocks to the oracle, rather than in the number of bits.

10.6.2. *Security of AES*

In 1998, NIST launched the advanced encryption standard (AES) contest to find a successor/replacement for DES. The contest ended on October 2, 2000, when NIST officially announced that RIJNDAEL, of (Daemen and Rijmen 2002), was selected as AES. RIJNDAEL is a family of 25 block ciphers that supports all combinations of block lengths and key lengths that are a multiple of 32 bits with a minimum of 128 bits and a maximum of 256 bits. AES is a subset of three block ciphers: AES-128, AES-192 and AES-256. All three have a block length of 128 bits and they have cipher keys of 128, 192 and 256 bits, respectively.

Given the relevance of AES, it is used millions of times per day, worldwide, one might hope for a nice upper bound on

$$\mathrm{Adv}^{\mathrm{prp}}_{\mathrm{AES}}(\mathcal{A})$$

that holds for any possible adversary $\mathcal{A}$. Unfortunately, for block ciphers the situation is not much different than for stream ciphers. We cannot prove an upper bound on $\mathrm{Adv}^{\mathrm{prp}}_{\mathrm{AES}}(\mathcal{A})$. As discussed in section 10.5, the best we can do, is to just claim an upper bound on this quantity.

For RIJNDAEL (AES), a claim was made that corresponds to the following:

CLAIM 10.3.– Consider AES with key size k. For any adversary $\mathcal{A}$ with computational complexity $|Q_c|$,

$$\mathrm{Adv}^{\mathrm{prp}}_{\mathrm{AES}}(\mathcal{A}) \leq \frac{|Q_c|}{2^k}.$$

Note that there exists an adversary whose advantage matches this bound, namely one that performs an exhaustive key search with $|Q_c|$ attempts.

The claim on AES turns out to be very useful for claiming security of cryptographic schemes that are built on top of AES. Many cryptographic encryption and authentication schemes used in practice can be considered to be built as modes of use *on top of* AES. Under the assumption that AES is secure (claim 10.3), one can abstract this cryptographic primitive and focus on the mode of use itself. This mode of use can then be formally proven secure using (mostly) probability theory and combinatorics. This approach will be demonstrated in the following chapters.

10.7. Acknowledgments

This chapter is largely inspired by the lecture notes of the course "Introduction to Cryptography" taught at Radboud University. These lecture notes are written by Daemen et al. (2020).

10.8. References

Bellare, M. and Rogaway, P. (1993). Random oracles are practical: A paradigm for designing efficient protocols. In *CCS '93*, Denning, D.E., Pyle, R., Ganesan, R., Sandhu, R.S., Ashby, V. (eds). ACM.

Daemen, J. and Rijmen, V. (2002). *The Design of* RIJNDAEL*: AES – The Advanced Encryption Standard*. Information Security and Cryptography. Springer.

Daemen, J., Mennink, B., Schoone, J. (2020). Introduction to cryptography – Lecture notes 2020.

11

Encryption and Security of Counter Mode

Bart MENNINK

Radboud University, Nijmegen, The Netherlands

In this chapter, we consider ways to encipher messages of arbitrary length using a block cipher. These ways are called *modes of use*, *modes of operation* or *modes* in short. We subdivide these modes into two types depending on how the plaintext is processed. We treat the first type, called *block encryption*, in section 11.1, and the second type, called *stream encryption*, in section 11.2. In section 11.3, we argue about security of modes.

11.1. Block encryption

We speak of *block encryption* if the ciphertext is the result of applying a block cipher to the plaintext. The simplest block encryption mode is Electronic Codebook (ECB) mode (Dworkin 2001). We first explain a degenerated version of ECB that can only encrypt messages m that have as length a multiple of the block length n. This degenerated version already reveals the most important advantages and limitations of ECB.

Suppose the length of m is $\ell \cdot n$ bits. The first step is to split the plaintext m into ℓ blocks of n bits. We let $m_1, m_2, m_3, \ldots, m_\ell$ denote these blocks. ECB encryption just consists of applying the block cipher to these blocks separately, leading to a sequence of ciphertext blocks $c_i = E_K(m_i)$. The ciphertext c is simply the concatenation of the ciphertext blocks: $c = c_1 \| c_2 \| \cdots \| c_\ell$. ECB decryption is the inverse operation:

Symmetric Cryptography 1,
coordinated by Christina BOURA and María NAYA-PLASENCIA. © ISTE Ltd 2023.

split c into blocks c_i, apply the inverse block cipher to obtain the plaintext blocks $m_i = E_K^{-1}(c_i)$ and concatenate the plaintext blocks to obtain $m = m_1 \| m_2 \| \cdots \| m_\ell$.

ECB has the advantage that both encryption and decryption of the blocks are parallelizable as they are encrypted and decrypted separately and independently of their position in the plaintext or ciphertext, respectively. The consequence of this independence is that equal blocks $m_i = m_j$ in the plaintext will give rise to equal blocks $c_i = c_j$ in the ciphertext. This implies that the security offered by ECB is quite limited.

11.1.1. *Padding*

As mentioned above, we expect encryption modes to support arbitrary-length plaintexts, that is, with length that is not necessarily a multiple of n. We can resolve this using *padding*: appending bits to the plaintext so that the result can be split into n-bit blocks.

A padding rule pad_n takes an arbitrary-length message and turns it into a string with length that is a multiple of n. ECB can now be extended to support arbitrary-length plaintexts m by including a padding step $m_1 \| \dots \| m_\ell \leftarrow \mathrm{pad}_n(m)$ prior to encryption. Decryption of c gives the padded message $m_1 \| \dots \| m_\ell$. For obtaining m, it is necessary to "undo" the padding.

A simple *injective* padding is one that adds a single one and then the minimum number of zeros:

$$\mathrm{pad}_n : m \mapsto m \| 1 \| 0^{n - |m| - 1 \bmod n}.$$

It is easy to verify that this padding operation is injective. The consequence is that the plaintext can be recovered unambiguously from an ECB-deciphered ciphertext. Namely, it suffices to remove all trailing zeros and a single 1. The resulting scheme is given in Figure 11.1.

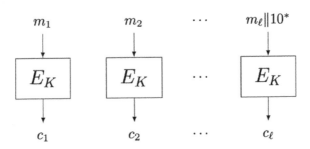

Figure 11.1. *Electronic Codebook mode*

11.1.2. *Cipher block chaining*

As mentioned previously, in ECB equal plaintext blocks result in equal ciphertext blocks: if $m_1 = m_2$ in Figure 11.1, then also $c_1 = c_2$.

One can salvage this issue by randomizing the input blocks to E_K in some way. A well-established mode that does this is cipher block chaining (CBC) (Dworkin 2001). As in ECB, the plaintext m is injectively padded to a string with length a multiple of n bits and then split into ℓ blocks $m_1, m_2, \ldots, m_\ell$. Prior to encryption with E_K, each block m_i is *randomized* by bitwise adding to it the previous block of the ciphertext c_{i-1}. In other words, we have for all $i > 1$: $c_i = E_K(m_i \oplus c_{i-1})$. For encrypting m_1, there is no *previous block of ciphertext* and there the CBC mode specifications prescribe to use a (random) initial value IV: so $c_1 = E_K(m_1 \oplus IV)$. Encryption is depicted in Figure 11.2.

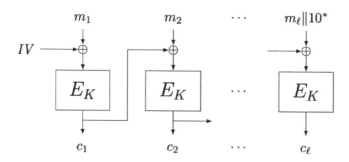

Figure 11.2. *Cipher block chaining mode encryption with random IV*

Upon decryption, m_i is obtained by applying the inverse block cipher to c_i and then *subtracting* c_{i-1}: $m_i = E_K^{-1}(c_i) \oplus c_{i-1}$. For decrypting the first block, we obviously have $m_1 = E_K^{-1}(c_1) \oplus IV$.

For a secure block cipher, ciphertext blocks c_i corresponding to different inputs will appear fully random, and hence so will the inputs to E_K and subsequently the outputs. For the input to the first application of E_K, namely $m_1 \oplus IV$ to be random, it is hence necessary for IV to be random.

Even when using a secure block cipher and random IVs, bad things can still happen. Namely, colliding inputs to E_K will still lead to equal ciphertext blocks. Such a collision leaks information about the difference between plaintext blocks: for example, $c_i = c_j$ implies $m_i \oplus c_{i-1} = m_j \oplus c_{j-1}$ and hence $m_i \oplus m_j = c_{i-1} \oplus c_{j-1}$. As c_{i-1} and c_{j-1} are known to the adversary, it learns the value of $m_i \oplus m_j$, similar to the case of re-use of a one-time pad. The collision probability depends on the total number of blocks encrypted and the block length n

and follows the birthday bound $\Pr(\text{collision}) \approx N^2 2^{-(n+1)}$ with N the total number of blocks encrypted.

Generating IV randomly is a burden as it requires the presence of a decent random generator. Moreover, Alice must send the IV along with the cryptogram c to Bob as he needs it to do the decryption. It is possible to turn the requirement of IV randomness into the requirement of a unique diversifier D by computing IV as $IV = E_K(D)$. The scheme is depicted in Figure 11.3.

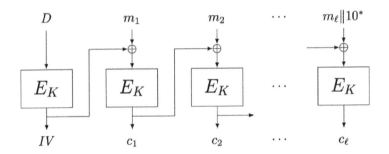

Figure 11.3. *Cipher block chaining mode with diversifier D*

CBC encryption has the disadvantage that it is inherently sequential: the encryption of plaintext block m_i cannot be started before c_{i-1} is available. This can be applied recursively and hence imposes that encryption of blocks is done serially starting with m_1 and ending with m_ℓ. Remarkably, decryption can be done in parallel as a plaintext block m_i only depends on ciphertext blocks c_{i-1} and c_i. As ECB, CBC suffers from message expansion: due to padding, the ciphertext is longer than the plaintext.

11.2. Stream encryption

As we saw in the previous section, block encryption modes have failed to deliver on their promise. Still, we are stuck with a lot of block cipher implementations, especially AES, and we may make the best of it.

For encryption, we can use block ciphers to build secure stream ciphers. These are *stream cipher modes of use* and in this chapter we will discuss two of them. The first is the output feedback (OFB) mode that is mostly of historical importance and we can use it to show what not to do. The second is counter (CTR) mode and is the only decent block cipher mode of encryption left.

Stream encryption has a number of advantages over block encryption and this immediately follows from their architecture. Recall that a stream cipher takes a diversifier D and generates a keystream s. This keystream s can then be used for encryption of a plaintext m to a ciphertext by adding the keystream: $c = p \oplus s$. Decryption consists of subtracting the keystream: $m = c \oplus s$. Sender and receiver generate the keystream s in the same way and so no *inverse function* is needed for decryption as is the case for block ciphers. Moreover, because of the fact that encryption is done by adding a keystream, there is no need for plaintext padding and hence there is no message expansion (depending on whether D/IV must be transmitted).

11.2.1. *Output feedback mode*

OFB mode (Dworkin 2001) builds a stream cipher that has updating function E_K, where each block of keystream is used to vary the next call. Its state consists of two parts: the block cipher key K that is fixed and the updating state that has length the block length n of the block cipher E. It generates n-bit keystream blocks as

$$s_i = E_K(s_{i-1}), \quad i \geq 1,$$

where $s_0 = IV$ is an initialization vector. The function is depicted in Figure 11.4.

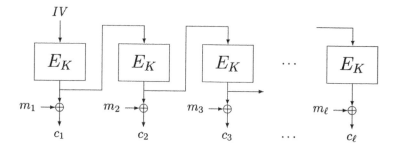

Figure 11.4. *Output feedback mode*

As we saw, a stream cipher takes as input a diversifier D and the OFB mode takes an IV. At first sight, it seems logical to take $IV = D$. However, this gives a stream cipher that can be distinguished in two queries from a random oracle:

– first query $SC_K(D, \ell = 2n)$ resulting in $s = s_1 s_2$;
– then query $SC_K(s_1, \ell = n)$.

For the OFB mode, the second query will output s_2, while for a random oracle this is very unlikely.

A solution to this is to restrict the range of diversifiers to a subset of the space of IV values. For example, one can restrict diversifiers to $r < n$ bits and build the initial value as $IV = D\|0^{n-r}$. If $n - r$ is sufficiently large, this prevents the problem discussed above as it is unlikely that s_1 will have its last $n - r$ bits equal to zero. Clearly, increasing r decreases the level of security that can be achieved.

Note that OFB is inherently serial, both for encryption and decryptiond.

11.2.2. *Counter mode*

In CTR mode (Dworkin 2001), the block cipher takes the place of the output function and the state-updating function is a simple counter. The state consists of two parts: the block cipher key K that is fixed, a counter $i \in \{0, \ldots, 2^r - 1\}$ for some $r < n$, where n is the block length of the block cipher E, and a diversifier D of length $n - r$. It generates n-bit keystream blocks as

$$s_i = E_K(D \| \text{conv}_r(i)), \quad i \geq 1,$$

where conv_r is a function that converts integers to r-bit strings. The function is depicted in Figure 11.5.

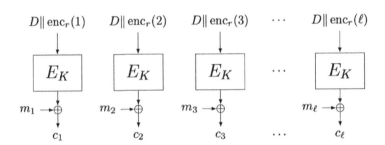

Figure 11.5. *Counter mode*

Note that the keystream length of the mode is restricted to at most 2^{n-r} blocks. It is possible to change the mode so as to allow for larger keystreams. This can be done by considering an *additive* version of CTK mode, where the counter is added to the diversifier D. After the generation of a keystream, it must be ensured that the next diversifier is set to at least the last updated block cipher input.

Unlike OFB mode, CTK mode has a very predictable cycle structure: all states are in a single cycle of length 2^n. If the described scheme for IV computation and maximum length of keystream is respected, cycles simply pose no problem.

The security of CTK mode is limited by a similar effect than OFB mode. When generating a keystream, all state values are different, implying that all keystream blocks s_t are different. This is not necessarily the case for a random oracle that will exhibit collisions between n-bit blocks in its output stream. This limits the maximum security strength of CTR mode to $n/2$ (birthday bound, see later).

Note that CTK mode is fully parallel, both for encryption and decryption.

11.3. Provable security of modes: the case of counter mode

We will demonstrate how one can formally argue that CTK mode based on AES, called CTR[AES], is a secure stream cipher. Stated differently, we will derive an expression for an upper bound on the distinguishing advantage $\text{Adv}^{\text{prf}}_{\text{CTR[AES]}}(\mathcal{A})$ of definition 10.1.

As explained in Chapter 10, we cannot prove security of any concrete encryption scheme such as CTR[AES]. Instead, we can express an upper bound on the distinguishing advantage of CTR[AES] by a sum of two terms:

– the first term that bounds the PRP security of AES. This term cannot be proven but can be given in a claim, in this case in claim 10.3;

– the second term that bounds the security of CTK mode where AES with a secret key is replaced by a random 128-bit permutation. This term can be proven (Bellare et al. 1997).

For someone who believes that claim 10.3 is valid, this reasoning provides a lower bound for the security of CTR[AES].

THEOREM 11.1 (Security of AES in counter mode).– Consider CTR mode with AES with key size k. For any adversary $\mathcal{A}$ with data complexity $|Q_d|$ blocks and computational complexity $|Q_c|$,

$$\text{Adv}^{\text{prf}}_{\text{CTR[AES]}}(\mathcal{A}) \leq \frac{\binom{|Q_d|}{2}}{2^{128}} + \text{Adv}^{\text{prp}}_{\text{AES}}(\mathcal{A}'),$$

where $\mathcal{A}'$ is an adversary with the same data complexity and almost the same computational complexity as $\mathcal{A}$. Claim 10.3 states that $\text{Adv}^{\text{prp}}_{\text{AES}}(\mathcal{A}') \leq \frac{|Q_c|}{2^k}$. For someone believing claim 10.3, theorem 11.1 implies CTR[AES] is a secure stream cipher as long as:

– the data complexity of $\mathcal{A}$ satisfies $|Q_d| \ll 2^{64}$ blocks;

– the computational complexity of $\mathcal{A}$ satisfies $|Q_c| \ll 2^k$.

The limitation in data complexity is a manifestation of the *birthday paradox*. The proof is given at very high detail in the remainder of this section.

Proof (of theorem 11.1). Consider any adversary $\mathcal{A}$ with data complexity $|Q_d|$ blocks and computational complexity $|Q_c|$. Let K be randomly drawn from the set of all keys, and let $\mathcal{RO}$ be a random oracle. From definition 10.1, we can observe that we have to bound

$$\mathrm{Adv}^{\mathrm{prf}}_{\mathrm{CTR[AES]}}(\mathcal{A}) = \Delta_{\mathcal{A}}(\mathrm{CTR[AES]}_K;\ \mathcal{RO}). \qquad [11.1]$$

Step 1: Isolating AES$_K$

Note that $\mathcal{A}$ has *indirect* access to AES_K: upon querying $\mathrm{CTR[AES]}_K$ with D it gets a sequence of values

$$\mathrm{AES}_K(D \parallel \mathrm{conv}_r(1)),\ \mathrm{AES}_K(D \parallel \mathrm{conv}_r(2)),\ \ldots.$$

As a first step, we will move to an adversary $\mathcal{A}'$ that has more power: one that can fully choose the input to AES_K. More detailed, $\mathcal{A}'$ is an adversary that has access to either AES_K or $\mathcal{RO}$ and tries to distinguish between them:

$$\Delta_{\mathcal{A}'}(\mathrm{AES}_K;\ \mathcal{RO}). \qquad [11.2]$$

The adversary $\mathcal{A}'$ will use its own oracle to *simulate* the oracle of $\mathcal{A}$ as follows. If $\mathcal{A}$ makes a query for input D and requested length ℓ bits, $\mathcal{A}'$ queries its own oracle for ℓ' blocks with ℓ' the smallest value that satisfies $\ell' \cdot n \geq \ell$:

$$D \parallel \mathrm{conv}_r(1),\ D \parallel \mathrm{conv}_r(2),\ \ldots,\ D \parallel \mathrm{conv}_r(\ell').$$

It concatenates the outputs to s and returns the first ℓ bits. In the end, $\mathcal{A}$ outputs a bit expressing its decision (see section 10.4). Adversary $\mathcal{A}'$ outputs the same decision bit. The simulation is depicted in Figure 11.6.

The step from $\mathcal{A}$ to $\mathcal{A}'$ is called a *reduction*. As $\mathcal{A}'$ uses its own oracle (namely AES_K or $\mathcal{RO}$) to simulate the oracle of $\mathcal{A}$ (namely $\mathrm{CTR[AES]}_K$ or $\mathcal{RO}$), we can conclude that $\mathcal{A}'$ correctly distinguishes its oracles if $\mathcal{A}$ manages to do so. Stated differently, the distinguishing advantage of $\mathcal{A}'$ cannot be smaller than the distinguishing advantage of $\mathcal{A}$, and the quantities of [11.1] and [11.2] satisfy

$$\mathrm{Adv}^{\mathrm{prf}}_{\mathrm{CTR[AES]}}(\mathcal{A}) = \Delta_{\mathcal{A}}(\mathrm{CTR[AES]}_K;\ \mathcal{RO}) \leq \Delta_{\mathcal{A}'}(\mathrm{AES}_K;\ \mathcal{RO}). \quad [11.3]$$

Note that $\mathcal{A}'$ has the same data complexity as $\mathcal{A}$ and a slightly larger computational complexity (because it needs to put some negligible effort in performing the simulation). However, this change in the computational complexity is negligible and typically ignored (see also the discussion of adversarial complexities in section 10.5.1).

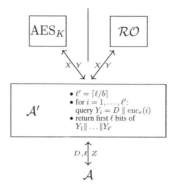

Figure 11.6. *The simulation step in the proof of theorem 11.1*

Step 2: A hybrid argument

Our goal is now to upper bound the advantage of $\mathcal{A}'$ in distinguishing AES_K from $\mathcal{RO}$ (of [11.2]), where $\mathcal{A}'$ has data complexity $|Q_d|$ blocks and computational complexity $|Q_c|$. Unfortunately, [11.2] is not quite the same as the pseudorandom permutation security of AES of definition 10.2, and we cannot readily apply claim 10.3.

Let $\mathcal{P}$ be a random permutation of the set of 128-bit strings. We have

$$\Delta_{\mathcal{A}'}(\mathrm{AES}_K;\ \mathcal{RO}) = \mathbf{Pr}\left(\mathcal{A}'^{\mathrm{AES}_K} = 1\right) - \mathbf{Pr}\left(\mathcal{A}'^{\mathcal{RO}} = 1\right)$$

$$= \left(\mathbf{Pr}\left(\mathcal{A}'^{\mathrm{AES}_K} = 1\right) - \mathbf{Pr}\left(\mathcal{A}'^{\mathcal{P}} = 1\right)\right)$$

$$+ \left(\mathbf{Pr}\left(\mathcal{A}'^{\mathcal{P}} = 1\right) - \mathbf{Pr}\left(\mathcal{A}'^{\mathcal{RO}} = 1\right)\right)$$

$$= \Delta_{\mathcal{A}'}(\mathrm{AES}_K;\ \mathcal{P}) + \Delta_{\mathcal{A}'}(\mathcal{P};\ \mathcal{RO}). \qquad [11.4]$$

Step 3: permutation-to-function switch

We now have to upper bound the remaining terms in [11.4]. The first term is exactly $\mathrm{Adv}_{\mathrm{AES}}^{\mathrm{prp}}(\mathcal{A}')$ and the subject of claim 10.3. For the second term, note that $\mathcal{A}'$ has only access to either random permutation $\mathcal{P}$ or random oracle $\mathcal{RO}$. It does not have access to any concrete keyed primitive like AES_K. The only way $\mathcal{A}'$ can learn about $\mathcal{P}$ or $\mathcal{RO}$ is by querying them. They have no algorithmic descriptions, so the adversary cannot do computations as it can do, for example, for AES. So even though $\mathcal{A}'$ has a certain computational complexity around $|Q_c|$, it cannot use this to increase its chances in distinguishing $\mathcal{P}$ from $\mathcal{RO}$. We can therefore ignore the computational complexity. For ease, we therefore move to an adversary $\mathcal{A}''$ that has data complexity $|Q_d|$ as before, but that has unbounded computational complexity. Clearly, the distinguishing advantage of $\mathcal{A}''$ cannot be smaller than the distinguishing advantage of $\mathcal{A}'$, and we have

$$\Delta_{\mathcal{A}'}(\mathcal{P}; \mathcal{RO}) \leq \Delta_{\mathcal{A}''}(\mathcal{P}; \mathcal{RO}). \tag{11.5}$$

The distance can now be measured by simple probability theory. Both $\mathcal{P}$ and $\mathcal{RO}$ return uniformly random 128-bit responses for each query, but those of $\mathcal{P}$ never collide, whereas those of $\mathcal{RO}$ may do. Adversary $\mathcal{A}''$ can thus only distinguish the two oracles if there are colliding outputs from $\mathcal{RO}$. As the data complexity of $\mathcal{A}''$ is $|Q_d|$ blocks, the probability that two of the $|Q_d|$ blocks from $\mathcal{RO}$ collide is at most $\frac{\binom{|Q_d|}{2}}{2^{128}}$. We therefore obtain

$$\Delta_{\mathcal{A}''}(\mathcal{P}; \mathcal{RO}) \leq \frac{\binom{|Q_d|}{2}}{2^{128}}. \tag{11.6}$$

Step 4

We conclude by combining the individual steps. From [11.3]–[11.6], we obtain

$$\mathrm{Adv}^{\mathrm{prf}}_{\mathrm{CTR[AES]}}(\mathcal{A}) \overset{(11.3)}{\leq} \Delta_{\mathcal{A}'}(\mathrm{AES}_K; \mathcal{RO})$$

$$\overset{(11.4)}{=} \Delta_{\mathcal{A}'}(\mathrm{AES}_K; \mathcal{P}) + \Delta_{\mathcal{A}'}(\mathcal{P}; \mathcal{RO})$$

$$\overset{(11.5)}{\leq} \Delta_{\mathcal{A}'}(\mathrm{AES}_K; \mathcal{P}) + \Delta_{\mathcal{A}''}(\mathcal{P}; \mathcal{RO})$$

$$\overset{(11.6)}{\leq} \mathrm{Adv}^{\mathrm{prp}}_{\mathrm{AES}}(\mathcal{A}') + \frac{\binom{|Q_d|}{2}}{2^n}.$$

This completes the proof.   □

11.4. Acknowledgments

This chapter is largely inspired by the lecture notes of the course "Introduction to Cryptography" taught at Radboud University. These lecture notes are written by Daemen et al. (2020).

11.5. References

Bellare, M., Desai, A., Jokipii, E., Rogaway, P. (1997). A concrete security treatment of symmetric encryption. In *FOCS '97, IEEE Computer Society*, 394–403.

Daemen, J., Mennink, B., Schoone, J. (2020). Introduction to cryptography – Lecture notes 2020.

Dworkin, M. (2001). NIST SP 800-38A: Recommendation for block cipher modes of operation: Methods and techniques.

12

Message Authentication and Authenticated Encryption

Tetsu IWATA

Nagoya University, Japan

In this chapter, we consider the provable security of message authentication and authenticated encryption. In section 12.1, we formalize a message authentication code and discuss the security definition. We introduce a universal hash function and show an example of the provable security result of Wegman-Carter-Shoup authenticator. In section 12.2, we consider authenticated encryption and show an example of the provable security result of Galois/counter mode.

12.1. Message authentication

A message authentication code (MAC) is used to ensure data integrity, that is, it is used to detect possibly malicious manipulation of messages during their transmission. A MAC scheme consists of a tag generation algorithm $\mathcal{G}$ and a verification algorithm $\mathcal{V}$. Both algorithms take a secret key K as a part of the input:

$$\mathcal{G}_K : \left\{ \begin{array}{l} \{0,1\}^* \to \mathcal{T} \\ M \mapsto T \end{array} \right. \quad \text{and} \quad \mathcal{V}_K : \left\{ \begin{array}{l} \{0,1\}^* \times \mathcal{T} \to \{\top, \bot\} \\ (M, T) \mapsto \top/\bot. \end{array} \right.$$

The tag generation algorithm returns a tag $T \in \mathcal{T}$, where the tag space $\mathcal{T}$ is a set of bit strings of a fixed length, for example, $\mathcal{T} = \{0,1\}^\tau$. The verification algorithm takes a message and a tag (M, T) as input, and returns either $\top$ or $\bot$. The output $\top$ corresponds to "accept", indicating (M, T) was originated from the sender, and $\bot$

Symmetric Cryptography 1,
coordinated by Christina BOURA and María NAYA-PLASENCIA. © ISTE Ltd 2023.

corresponds to "reject", indicating that (M, T) was manipulated during the transmission and was not originated from the sender. The correctness requirement is that, for any K and M, it holds that $\mathcal{V}_K(M, \mathcal{G}_K(M)) = \top$.

MACs can be constructed in many ways, and in this section, we will take a closer look at the provable security of a class of MACs called Wegman-Carter-Shoup authenticator (Shoup 1996), which is based on an earlier construction by Wegman and Carter (1981) and the work by Krawczyk (1994).

12.1.1. *WCS construction*

WCS authenticator (Shoup 1996) is a nonce-based MAC, where its tag generation algorithm takes a nonce N as input, in addition to the key K and a message M, and returns a tag T. The verification algorithm takes (K, N, M, T) as input, and returns either $\top$ or $\bot$.

This class of MACs makes use of a *universal hash function*. There are several types of universal hash functions, and we are interested in one of the constructions called an almost XOR universal hash function:

DEFINITION 12.1.– Let $H_L : \{0, 1\}^* \to \{0, 1\}^n$ be a keyed function with key $L \in \mathcal{L}$. H is an ε-almost XOR universal hash function, or an ε-AXU hash function, if for any distinct $x, x' \in \{0, 1\}^*$ and any $y \in \{0, 1\}^n$, it holds that

$$\Pr[H_L(x) \oplus H_L(x') = y] \le \varepsilon,$$

where the probability is taken over the random choice of the key $L \in \mathcal{L}$.

An example of an ε-AXU hash function is the GHASH function used in GMAC and GCM (McGrew and Viega 2004). We fix $n = 128$, and let $L \in \{0, 1\}^n$ be the key and $x = (x_1, \ldots, x_m)$ be the m-block input, where $x_i \in \{0, 1\}^n$ for $1 \le i \le m$. Then the GHASH value of x under the key L is defined as

$$\text{GHASH}_L(x) = L^m x_1 \oplus L^{m-1} x_2 \oplus \cdots \oplus L x_m, \qquad [12.1]$$

where the multiplication and the summation are defined over the finite field $\mathbb{F}_{2^n}$.

In the above definition, the input x is restricted to have length multiple of n bits. In order to cover an arbitrary length input $x \in \{0, 1\}^*$, let $\text{pad}(x) = x \| 0^j \| \text{len}(x)$, where $a \| b$ denotes the concatenation of bit strings a and b, j is the smallest non-negative integer such that $|x \| 0^j|$ is a multiple of n, and $\text{len}(x)$ denotes the n-bit binary representation of $|x|$. Here, $|x|$ is the bit length of x. Now we break $\text{pad}(x)$ into n-bit blocks as $(x_1, \ldots, x_m)$, and apply the GHASH function. Formally, we define the ε-AXU hash function H as

$$H_L(x) = \text{GHASH}_L(\text{pad}(x)).$$

To see that this function is an ε-AXU hash function for small ε, we first observe that the function pad is injective, that is, for any distinct $x, x' \in \{0,1\}^*$, we have $\text{pad}(x) \neq \text{pad}(x')$, since if they are different in length, then the last blocks of $\text{pad}(x)$ and $\text{pad}(x')$ must be different, and if $|x| = |x'|$, then there must be a difference in the first $|x| = |x'|$ bits of $\text{pad}(x)$ and $\text{pad}(x')$. Now we show that $\Pr[H_L(x) \oplus H_L(x') = y] \leq \max\{m, m'\}/2^n$, where $(x_1, \ldots, x_m) = \text{pad}(x)$ and $(x'_1, \ldots, x'_{m'}) = \text{pad}(x')$. Assume that $m \neq m'$. Then $H_L(x) \oplus H_L(x') = y$ is a non-trivial equation in L of degree at most $\max\{m, m'\}$, since there must be a difference in x_m and $x'_{m'}$. If $m = m'$, then $H_L(x) \oplus H_L(x') = y$ is also a non-trivial equation in L of degree at most $\max\{m, m'\}$, since there must be a difference between $x_1, \ldots, x_{m-1}$ and $x'_1, \ldots, x'_{m'-1}$. Therefore, at most $\max\{m, m'\}$ values of L out of 2^n choices satisfy $H_L(x) \oplus H_L(x') = y$.

Given an ε-AXU hash function $H_L : \{0,1\}^* \to \{0,1\}^n$ and a block cipher $E_K : \{0,1\}^n \to \{0,1\}^n$, WCS authenticator is defined as

$$\mathcal{G}_{L,K} : \begin{cases} \{0,1\}^n \times \{0,1\}^* \to \mathcal{T} \\ (N, M) \mapsto T \end{cases}$$

and

$$\mathcal{V}_{L,K} : \begin{cases} \{0,1\}^n \times \{0,1\}^* \times \mathcal{T} \to \{\top, \bot\} \\ (N, M, T) \mapsto \top/\bot, \end{cases}$$

where $T = H_L(M) \oplus E_K(N)$ in $\mathcal{G}_K$. $\mathcal{V}_K$ returns $\top$ if $T = H_L(M) \oplus E_K(N)$. Otherwise it returns $\bot$.

12.1.2. *Provable security*

There are several types of security definitions for MACs. Here, we consider a nonce-based MAC, for example, WCS authenticator, with key K, and the notion called *unforgeability against chosen message attacks*, where the adversary has oracle access to $\mathcal{G}_K$ and $\mathcal{V}_K$ for randomly chosen and unknown key K. Assume that the adversary $\mathcal{A}$ chooses i pairs $(N_1, M_1), \ldots, (N_i, M_i)$ of a nonce and a message, and has the corresponding i tags $T_1, \ldots, T_i$, where the jth nonce-message pair (N_j, M_j) can be chosen adaptively after obtaining T_{j-1}. A *forgery* is a tuple (N^*, M^*, T^*) of a nonce, message and a tag such that the receiver is convinced that this is originated from the sender, that is, $\mathcal{V}_K(N^*, M^*, T^*) = \top$ holds. The tuple (N^*, M^*, T^*) corresponds to a query to $\mathcal{V}_K$, and clearly, if (N^*, M^*, T^*) is one of (N_j, M_j, T_j) for some $1 \leq j \leq i$, then $\mathcal{V}_K$ outputs $\top$. However, this does not constitute a forgery. The goal of the adversary is to come up with (N^*, M^*, T^*) that is different from all

$(N_1, M_1, T_1), \ldots, (N_i, M_i, T_i)$ that the adversary obtains so far. Note that $N_1, \ldots, N_i$ are a nonce, meaning that these values are all distinct. However, these values could be used in the forgery.

Assume that the adversary outputs (N^*, M^*, T^*), which we call a forgery attempt, after obtaining $(N_1, M_1, T_1), \ldots, (N_i, M_i, T_i)$. If we require that M^* is different from all $M_1, \ldots, M_i$, then the forged message is "new", and we say that a MAC is *unforgeable* if the success probability of such a forgery attempt is sufficiently small. If we require that (N^*, M^*) is different from all $(N_1, M_1), \ldots, (N_i, M_i)$, then the forged message may not be "new", but we still consider this to be a forgery, since the pair (N^*, M^*) is not originated from the sender, and we say that a MAC is *strongly unforgeable* if the success probability of such a forgery attempt is sufficiently small. Let us write the success probability of this strong unforgeability game of an adversary $\mathcal{A}$ against a MAC as $\mathrm{Adv}^{\mathrm{su}}_{\mathrm{MAC}}(\mathcal{A})$. We formally define this as

$$\mathrm{Adv}^{\mathrm{su}}_{\mathrm{MAC}}(\mathcal{A}) = \Pr[\mathcal{A}^{\mathcal{G}_K, \mathcal{V}_K} \text{ forges}],$$

where the probability is taken over the random choice of K and $\mathcal{A}$'s internal coin, and $\mathcal{A}$ forges if $\mathcal{V}_K$ returns $\top$ for a verification query (N^*, M^*, T^*), which is not in the set of input–output pairs $\{(N_1, M_1, T_1), \ldots, (N_i, M_i, T_i)\}$ that $\mathcal{A}$ has obtained from $\mathcal{G}_K$ prior to making the verification query.

From a provable security view point, it is desirable that a MAC scheme is secure in the sense of strong unforgeability, since this implies the plain unforgeability. The goal of this section is to prove the following theorem.

THEOREM 12.1.– Let $\mathcal{A}$ be an adversary that makes q tag generation queries and v verification queries. Then WCS authenticator $\mathrm{WCS}[H, E]$ based on an ε-XOR universal hash function H and a block cipher E is strongly unforgeable under the assumption that ε is sufficiently small and the block cipher is a PRP. More precisely, we have

$$\mathrm{Adv}^{\mathrm{su}}_{\mathrm{WCS}[H,E]}(\mathcal{A}) \leq \mathrm{Adv}^{\mathrm{prp}}_E(\mathcal{B}) + \varepsilon v + \frac{0.5(q + v)^2}{2^n}$$

for some PRP adversary $\mathcal{B}$ against E that makes at most $q + v$ queries and whose computational complexity is almost the same as that of $\mathcal{A}$.

Proof. We consider a MAC that is obtained by replacing the block cipher E_K with a uniform random permutation P over $\{0, 1\}^n$, and then we replace P with a uniform random function F over $\{0, 1\}^n$. Let $\mathrm{WCS}[H, F]$ be the resulting MAC. From the assumption on E being a PRP and the permutation-to-function switch from Chapter 11, we have

$$\text{Adv}^{\text{su}}_{\text{WCS}[H,E]}(\mathcal{A}) - \text{Adv}^{\text{su}}_{\text{WCS}[H,F]}(\mathcal{A}) \leq \text{Adv}^{\text{prp}}_{E}(\mathcal{B}) + \frac{0.5(q+v)^2}{2^n},$$

since the number of block cipher calls is at most $q + v$. Now, it is sufficient to show $\text{Adv}^{\text{su}}_{\text{WCS}[H,F]}(\mathcal{A}) \leq \varepsilon v$.

We first consider a simple case of an adversary $\mathcal{A}_1$ that makes a single verification query. Without loss of generality, we may assume that the verification query is made after making all the q tag generation queries, since this assumption only increases the success probability of the forgery. Let $(N_1, M_1, T_1), \ldots, (N_q, M_q, T_q)$ be the input–output pairs of $\text{WCS}[H, F]$ that $\mathcal{A}$ obtains during the interaction with the tag generation oracle, and let (N^*, M^*, T^*) be the forgery attempt.

If $N^* \notin \{N_1, \ldots, N_q\}$, then we have $\text{Adv}^{\text{su}}_{\text{WCS}[H,F]}(\mathcal{A}_1) \leq 1/2^n$, since $\mathcal{A}_1$ needs to guess the value of $H_L(M^*) \oplus F(N^*)$, which is a random n-bit string that is independent of all other variables due the term $F(N^*)$.

If $N^* = N_i$ for some $1 \leq i \leq q$, then the event $T^* = H_L(M^*) \oplus F(N^*)$ implies $T^* \oplus T_i = H_L(M^*) \oplus H_L(M_i)$. Observe that we must have $M^* \neq M_i$, since otherwise $\mathcal{A}_1$ fails (in case $T^* \neq T_i$), or it breaks the rule of the game (in case $T^* = T_i$). We also observe that the tags other than T_i do not contribute to the success probability, since they are independent of this event due to the uniqueness of the nonce. Since $\Pr[T^* \oplus T_i = H_L(M^*) \oplus H_L(M_i)] \leq \varepsilon$ from the assumption on H, we have $\text{Adv}^{\text{su}}_{\text{WCS}[H,F]}(\mathcal{A}_1) \leq \varepsilon$.

We turn our attention to an adversary $\mathcal{A}$ that makes v verification queries. For any $\mathcal{A}$ that makes v verification queries, we claim that there exists an adversary $\mathcal{A}_1$ that makes a single verification query and $\text{Adv}^{\text{su}}_{\text{WCS}[H,F]}(\mathcal{A}) \leq v \cdot \text{Adv}^{\text{su}}_{\text{WCS}[H,F]}(\mathcal{A}_1)$. Given $\mathcal{A}$, we construct $\mathcal{A}_1$ as follows. The adversary $\mathcal{A}_1$ first chooses an index t uniformly at random from $\{1, \ldots, v\}$, and runs $\mathcal{A}$. If $\mathcal{A}$ makes a tag generation query (N_i, M_i), then $\mathcal{A}_1$ uses its own tag generation oracle to return T_i to $\mathcal{A}$. If $\mathcal{A}$ makes a verification query (N_j^*, M_j^*, T_j^*), then $\mathcal{A}_1$ returns $\perp$ to $\mathcal{A}$ if $j \neq t$. Otherwise $\mathcal{A}_1$ outputs (N_j^*, M_j^*, T_j^*) as its own forgery attempt. That is, $\mathcal{A}_1$ randomly guesses one of the v forgery attempts of $\mathcal{A}$ as its own forgery attempt.

Assume that $\mathcal{A}$ succeeds in forgery with (N_j^*, M_j^*, T_j^*), that is, the verification oracle returns $\top$ for this jth verification query, and returns $\perp$ for the first $j - 1$ verification queries. We see that if $j = t$, then the simulation of $\mathcal{A}_1$ is correct in that it returns $\perp$ for the first $j - 1$ queries, and we also see that the choice of t is independent of the rest of the variables. It follows that

$$\mathrm{Adv}^{\mathrm{su}}_{\mathrm{WCS}[H,F]}(\mathcal{A}_1) \geq \Pr[j = t] \times \Pr[\mathcal{A}\text{forges at the } j\text{-th forgery attempt}]$$

$$\geq \frac{1}{v} \cdot \mathrm{Adv}^{\mathrm{su}}_{\mathrm{WCS}[H,F]}(\mathcal{A}),$$

and this completes the proof.   □

REMARK 12.1.– The bound of theorem 12.1 is the so-called birthday bound, due to the term $0.5(q + v)^2/2^n$. For WCS authenticator, a stronger security bound is known (Bernstein 2005), which is also shown to be tight (Nandi 2018), that is, there exists an attack that matches the security bound.

12.2. Authenticated encryption

An encryption scheme like CBC mode or CTR mode does not provide authenticity. In fact, if a block in a ciphertext of CTR mode is modified, there is no way to detect this modification on the receiver side, and the receiver just decrypts the modified ciphertext into a wrong plaintext. We also see that a MAC does not provide privacy. A pair of a message and a tag (possibly with a nonce) is sent over the communication channel, and the message is visible to an adversary that monitors the channel.

In many use cases of a symmetric key cryptosystem, we often want to encrypt *and* authenticate data, and authenticated encryption can be used to efficiently achieve the goal. We have already seen several authenticated encryption schemes in Chapter 6, and in this section we look at an example of the provable security treatment of one of the constructions called GCM.

12.2.1. GCM, Galois/counter mode

GCM (McGrew and Viega 2004) is a nonce-based authenticated encryption with associated data (AEAD) scheme. It takes a plaintext and associated data as input, where the plaintext is encrypted and authenticated, and the associated data are the input that is authenticated but *not* encrypted. It internally uses GHASH as a universal hash function and AES as a block cipher.

Let us fix $n = 128$. The encryption algorithm of GCM takes a key K, a nonce N, associated data A and a plaintext M as input, and returns a ciphertext C and a tag T. The plaintext M is encrypted and authenticated, and the associated data A is authenticated but not encrypted. We write $\mathrm{GCM.Enc}_K(N, A, M) = (C, T)$. The key K is the AES key, the nonce length is 96 bits, M is any bit string of length at most $2^{39} - 256$ bits, A is any bit string of length at most $2^{64} - 1$ bits, C has the same length as M and the tag length is 128 bits. The nonce and tag lengths can take other values, but we focus on the above configuration.

We first run CTR mode to encrypt M into C, where $N\|0^{31}1$ is used as the initial value. We then compute the GHASH value of (A, C), which is XORed with $E_K(N\|0^{31}1)$ to obtain T, where $L = E_K(0^n)$ is used as the GHASH key. Formally, the encryption algorithm GCM.Enc is defined as follows:

GCM.Enc$_K(N, A, M)$
  1) $L \leftarrow E_K(0^n)$
  2) $C \leftarrow \text{CTR}_K(N\|0^{31}1, M)$
  3) $S \leftarrow \text{GHASH}_L(\text{pad}(A, C))$
  4) $T \leftarrow S \oplus E_K(N\|0^{31}1)$
  5) return (C, T)

CTR$_K(X, M)$
  1) $(M_1, \ldots, M_m) \leftarrow M$
  2) for $i = 1$ to m do
  3) $X \leftarrow \text{inc}(X)$
  4) $C_i \leftarrow E_K(X) \oplus M_i$
  5) return $C = (C_1, \ldots, C_m)$.

In GCM, the tag is used to authenticate both A and C, and they are encoded into a single bit string before applying the GHASH function (defined in equation [12.1]). We use the padding function pad defined as

$$\text{pad}(A, C) = A\|0^s\|C\|0^t\|\text{len}(A)\|\text{len}(C),$$

where s (respectively, t) is the smallest non-negative integer such that $|A\|0^s|$ (respectively, $|C\|0^t|$) is a multiple of 128, and $\text{len}(A)$ (respectively, $\text{len}(C)$) is the 64-bit binary representation of the bit length of A (respectively, C). We see that the result of the function pad is a bit string of length multiple of n bits, and it is easy to see that this function is injective. In CTR mode, we use the increment function $\text{inc}(X)$ for $X \in \{0, 1\}^n$ to update the counter. The first line breaks M into n-bit blocks $(M_1, \ldots, M_m)$, where the last block may have fewer than n bits. In this case, we use the first $|M_m|$ bits of $E_K(X)$ to obtain C_m.

To decrypt (N, A, C, T), the decryption algorithm GCM.Dec$_K(N, A, C, T)$ first computes $S \leftarrow \text{GHASH}_L(\text{pad}(A, C))$ and checks whether $T = S \oplus E_K(N\|0^{31}1)$ holds, in which case, the plaintext M obtained by the decryption of CTR mode is returned. Otherwise $\perp$ is returned. We write GCM.Dec$_K(N, A, C, T) = M$ or GCM.Dec$_K(N, A, C, T) = \perp$.

See Figure 12.1 for the process of encryption. The figure shows the case where $M = (M_1, M_2, M_3)$ has three full n-bit blocks. Observe that GCM is close to the encrypt-then-authenticate generic composition discussed in Chapter 6. The difference is that GCM takes a single AES key, and the key is used to encrypt M and to authenticate A and C, while in the generic composition, we use independent keys for encryption and authentication. We also observe the similarity of the MAC part, that is, the function $(N, A, C) \mapsto T$, to WCS construction. In GCM, GHASH and the "mask" $E_K(N\|0^{31}1)$ share the same key, while in WCS construction, the universal hash function has an independent key. However, it is useful to observe that the input 0^n to generate the GHASH key $L = E_K(0^n)$ is never used in other block cipher calls (even when $N = 0^{96}$), and hence the independence of L is almost maintained.

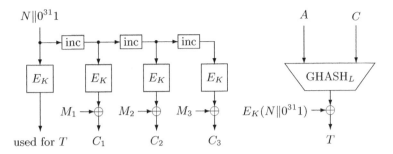

Figure 12.1. *The encryption algorithm of GCM*

12.2.2. *Provable security*

We consider the standard security notion for nonce-based AEAD. As AEAD has two functionalities of encryption and authentication, we consider both privacy and authenticity notions. In the privacy notion, we consider an adversary $\mathcal{A}$ that has either an encryption oracle $\mathcal{E}_K$ or a random bits oracle \$, where the goal of $\mathcal{A}$ is to distinguish the two oracles. For a query (N, A, M), the encryption oracle $\mathcal{E}_K$ returns $(C, T) \leftarrow$ GCM.Enc$_K(N, A, M)$, and the random bits oracle \$ returns a random string (C, T) of $|M| + n$ bits, which has the same length as the output of $\mathcal{E}_K$. We define the privacy advantage of an adversary $\mathcal{A}$ against GCM as

$$\mathrm{Adv}_{\mathrm{GCM}}^{\mathrm{priv}}(\mathcal{A}) = \Pr[\mathcal{A}^{\mathcal{E}_K} \Rightarrow 1] - \Pr[\mathcal{A}^{\$} \Rightarrow 1],$$

where the first probability is taken over the random choice of K and $\mathcal{A}$'s internal coin, and the last one is over \$ and $\mathcal{A}$. We assume that $\mathcal{A}$ is nonce-respecting, meaning that $\mathcal{A}$ does not repeat the same nonce twice or more. For the authenticity notion, we consider an adversary $\mathcal{A}$ that has an encryption oracle $\mathcal{E}_K$ and a decryption oracle $\mathcal{D}_K$, where $\mathcal{D}_K$ returns GCM.Dec$_K(N, A, C, T)$ for a query (N, A, C, T). We define the authenticity advantage of an adversary $\mathcal{A}$ against GCM as

$$\mathrm{Adv}_{\mathrm{GCM}}^{\mathrm{auth}}(\mathcal{A}) = \Pr[\mathcal{A}^{\mathcal{E}_K, \mathcal{D}_K} \text{ forges}],$$

where the probability is taken over the random choice of K and $\mathcal{A}$'s internal coin, and $\mathcal{A}$ forges if $\mathcal{D}_K$ returns a bit string that is not $\bot$ for a query (N, A, C, T). Here, for a decryption query (N, A, C, T), (C, T) cannot be the one that was previously returned from the encryption oracle for a query (N, A, M). We only consider $\mathcal{A}$ that is nonce-respecting, that is, $\mathcal{A}$ does not repeat the same nonce twice or more in encryption queries. Note that $\mathcal{A}$ can still reuse a nonce used in an encryption query for a decryption query.

The goal of this section is to prove theorems 12.2 and 12.3 that show the security of GCM based on a random permutation P over $\{0, 1\}^n$ as a block cipher, which we write GCM[P]. Theorem 12.2 shows the privacy result, and for an adversary that makes q encryption queries (N_i, A_i, M_i) for $1 \leq i \leq q$, if M_i has m_i blocks, then we define the total number of plaintext blocks as $\sum_{1 \leq i \leq q} m_i$.

THEOREM 12.2.– Let $\mathcal{A}$ be a privacy adversary against GCM[P] that makes q encryption queries such that the total number of plaintext blocks is at most σ. Then we have $\mathrm{Adv}^{\mathrm{priv}}_{\mathrm{GCM}[P]}(\mathcal{A}) \leq 0.5(\sigma + q + 1)^2/2^n$.

Proof. We replace the random permutation P with a uniform random function F over $\{0, 1\}^n$. Let GCM[F] be the resulting AEAD. From the permutation-to-function switch from Chapter 11, and since the total number of block cipher calls is at most $\sigma + q + 1$, we have $\mathrm{Adv}^{\mathrm{priv}}_{\mathrm{GCM}[P]}(\mathcal{A}) - \mathrm{Adv}^{\mathrm{priv}}_{\mathrm{GCM}[F]}(\mathcal{A}) \leq 0.5(\sigma + q + 1)^2/2^n$. Therefore, it is sufficient to show $\mathrm{Adv}^{\mathrm{priv}}_{\mathrm{GCM}[F]}(\mathcal{A}) = 0$.

For the ith query (N_i, A_i, M_i), if M_i has m_i blocks, then F takes $\mathrm{inc}^1(N_i\|0^{31}1), \mathrm{inc}^2(N_i\|0^{31}1), \ldots, \mathrm{inc}^{m_i}(N_i\|0^{31}1)$ as input to compute C_i, and $\mathrm{inc}^0(N_i\|0^{31}1)$ to compute T_i. We see that these $m_i + 1$ input values are all distinct. We also observe that these input values are never used in other encryption queries due to the uniqueness of the nonce. Therefore, for the ith query, $\mathcal{A}$ obtains a uniform random string of $|M_i| + n$ bits that has the same distribution as the output of the random bits oracle. □

Theorem 12.3 below shows the authenticity result, and for an adversary that makes q encryption queries (N_i, A_i, M_i) for $1 \leq i \leq q$ and v decryption queries $(N_j^*, A_j^*, C_j^*, T_j^*)$ for $1 \leq j \leq v$, we define the total number of plaintext blocks as $\sum_{1 \leq i \leq q} m_i$ as in theorem 12.2, and the maximum input length as $\max\{a_1 + m_1, \ldots, a_q + m_q, a_1^* + m_1^*, \ldots, a_v^* + m_v^*\}$, where A_i, M_i, A_j^* and C_j^* have a_i, m_i, a_j^* and m_j^* blocks, respectively.

THEOREM 12.3.– Let $\mathcal{A}$ be an authenticity adversary against GCM[P] that makes q encryption queries and v decryption queries such that the total number of plaintext blocks is at most σ and the maximum input length is at most ℓ. Then we have $\mathrm{Adv}^{\mathrm{auth}}_{\mathrm{GCM}[P]}(\mathcal{A}) \leq 0.5(\sigma + q + v + 1)^2/2^n + v(\ell + 1)/2^n$.

Proof. We first simplify the authenticity security game so that if $T^* = \mathrm{GHASH}_L(\mathrm{pad}(A^*, C^*)) \oplus E_K(N^*\|0^{31}1)$ holds for a decryption query (N^*, A^*, C^*, T^*), then we terminate the game declaring that $\mathcal{A}$ wins, without computing the corresponding plaintext M^*. This does not change the success provability of $\mathcal{A}$. We then replace the random permutation P with a uniform random function F over $\{0, 1\}^n$, and we consider GCM[F]. This step adds $0.5(\sigma + q + v + 1)^2/2^n$ to the security bound, since the total number of block cipher calls is at most $\sigma + q + v + 1$ (as we do not compute the plaintext when $\mathcal{A}$ succeeds in forgery). It remains to show $\mathrm{Adv}^{\mathrm{auth}}_{\mathrm{GCM}[F]}(\mathcal{A}) \leq v(\ell + 1)/2^n$, and the rest of the proof is similar to the proof of WCS construction.

Consider a simple case of an adversary $\mathcal{A}_1$ that makes a single decryption query, which is without loss of generality assumed to be made after making all the q encryption queries. Let $(N_1, A_1, M_1, C_1, T_1), \ldots, (N_q, A_q, M_q, C_q, T_q)$ be the input–output pairs of the encryption oracle $\mathcal{E}_K$ that $\mathcal{A}_1$ obtains during this phase, and let (N^*, A^*, C^*, T^*) be the decryption query.

If $N^* \notin \{N_1, \ldots, N_q\}$, then we have $\mathrm{Adv}^{\mathrm{auth}}_{\mathrm{GCM}[F]}(\mathcal{A}_1) \leq 1/2^n$, since in the equation $T^* = \mathrm{GHASH}_L(\mathrm{pad}(A^*, C^*)) \oplus F(N^*\|0^{31}1)$, the term $F(N^*\|0^{31}1)$ is a random n-bit string that is independent of all other variables.

If $N^* = N_i$ for some $1 \leq i \leq q$, then the event $T^* = \mathrm{GHASH}_L(\mathrm{pad}(A^*, C^*)) \oplus F(N^*\|0^{31}1)$ implies

$$T^* \oplus T_i = \mathrm{GHASH}_L(\mathrm{pad}(A^*, C^*)) \oplus \mathrm{GHASH}_L(\mathrm{pad}(A_i, C_i)) \,. \qquad [12.2]$$

We have $(A^*, C^*) \neq (A_i, C_i)$, since otherwise $\mathcal{A}$ does not succeed in forgery. Now the input–output pairs of the encryption oracle other than $(N_i, A_i, M_i, C_i, T_i)$ are irrelevant to the success probability from the uniqueness of the nonce, and we also observe that $L = F(0^n)$ is independent of the input–output pairs of the encryption oracle. Therefore, we have $\mathrm{Adv}^{\mathrm{auth}}_{\mathrm{GCM}[F]}(\mathcal{A}_1) \leq (\ell + 1)/2^n$, since equation [12.2] is a non-trivial equation in L of degree at most $\ell + 1$.

We then consider $\mathcal{A}$ that makes v decryption queries. For any $\mathcal{A}$ that makes v decryption queries, we construct an adversary $\mathcal{A}_1$ that makes a single decryption query and $\mathrm{Adv}^{\mathrm{auth}}_{\mathrm{GCM}[F]}(\mathcal{A}) \leq v \cdot \mathrm{Adv}^{\mathrm{auth}}_{\mathrm{GCM}[F]}(\mathcal{A}_1)$. The adversary $\mathcal{A}_1$ chooses an index t uniformly at random from $\{1, \ldots, v\}$, and runs $\mathcal{A}$. If $\mathcal{A}$ makes an encryption query (N_i, A_i, M_i), then $\mathcal{A}_1$ uses its own encryption oracle to return (C_i, T_i) to $\mathcal{A}$. If $\mathcal{A}$ makes a decryption query $(N_j^*, A_j^*, C_j^*, T_j^*)$, then $\mathcal{A}_1$ returns $\perp$ to $\mathcal{A}$ if $j \neq t$. Otherwise, $\mathcal{A}_1$ returns $(N_j^*, A_j^*, C_j^*, T_j^*)$ as its own decryption query.

Assume that $\mathcal{A}$ succeeds in forgery with $(N_j^*, A_j^*, C_j^*, T_j^*)$, that is, wins the authenticity game at the jth decryption query. We see that if $j = t$, then the simulation of $\mathcal{A}_1$ is correct as it returns $\perp$ to $\mathcal{A}$ for the first $j - 1$ decryption queries, and since the choice of t is independent of the rest of the variables, we have

$$\mathrm{Adv}^{\mathrm{auth}}_{\mathrm{GCM}[F]}(\mathcal{A}_1) \geq \Pr[j = t] \times \Pr[\mathcal{A} \text{ wins at the } j\text{th decryption query}]$$

$$\geq \frac{1}{v} \cdot \mathrm{Adv}^{\mathrm{auth}}_{\mathrm{GCM}[F]}(\mathcal{A}) \,,$$

and this completes the proof. $\square$

12.3. References

Bernstein, D.J. (2005). Stronger security bounds for Wegman-Carter-Shoup authenticators. In *EUROCRYPT 2005*, vol. 3494 of *Lecture Notes in Computer Science*, Cramer, R. (ed.). Springer.

Krawczyk, H. (1994). LFSR-based hashing and authentication. In *CRYPTO '94*, vol. 839 of *Lecture Notes in Computer Science*, Desmedt, Y. (ed.). Springer.

McGrew, D.A. and Viega, J. (2004). The security and performance of the Galois/counter mode (GCM) of operation. In *INDOCRYPT 2004*, vol. 3348 of *Lecture Notes in Computer Science*, Canteaut, A., Viswanathan, K. (eds). Springer.

Nandi, M. (2018). Bernstein bound on WCS is tight – Repairing Luykx-Preneel optimal forgeries. In *CRYPTO 2018, Part II*, vol. 10992 of *Lecture Notes in Computer Science*, Shacham, H., Boldyreva, A. (eds). Springer.

Shoup, V. (1996). On fast and provably secure message authentication based on universal hashing. In *CRYPTO '96*, vol. 1109 of *Lecture Notes in Computer Science*, Koblitz, N. (ed.). Springer.

Wegman, M.N. and Carter, L. (1981). New hash functions and their use in authentication and set equality. *J. Comput. Syst. Sci.*, 22(3), 265–279.

13

H-coefficients Technique

Yannick Seurin
ANSSI, Paris, France

This chapter is an introduction to the H-coefficients technique, a proof method allowing to upper bound the advantage of a computationally unbounded adversary in distinguishing between two random systems. Then, we present the Even-Mansour construction which defines a block cipher from a single permutation, and apply the H-coefficients technique to prove its security in the random permutation model.

13.1. The H-Coefficients technique

Some cryptographic schemes, such as one-time pad encryption or Wegman-Carter authentication, are information-theoretically secure, which means that they are secure against adversaries with unbounded computational capacities (this is also called, perhaps slightly misleadingly, *unconditional* security). However, they usually require very large keys and are therefore only suitable for very specific use cases. For the most part, as discussed in Chapter 10, symmetric cryptographic primitives such as block ciphers can only achieve security against computationally bounded adversaries. On the other hand, as explained in Chapters 5 and 11, primitives such as block ciphers are not used as is but rather in a mode of operation such as CTR for encryption or CBC-MAC for authentication. Analyzing the security of such modes is inherently information-theoretic. To illustrate, let us consider a mode of operation Mode for an arbitrary block cipher E. Concretely, this mode makes calls to E_K where K is a random secret key. A first generic step when proving security of Mode$[E]$ (for some security notion "sec") is to replace E_K by a uniformly random permutation P. This step can be justified using a reduction $\mathcal{A}'$ (as explained in Chapter 11) such that

$$\mathrm{Adv}^{\mathrm{sec}}_{\mathrm{Mode}[E]}(\mathcal{A}) \le \mathrm{Adv}^{(\mathrm{s})\mathrm{prp}}_{E}(\mathcal{A}') + \mathrm{Adv}^{\mathrm{sec}}_{\mathrm{Mode}^*}(\mathcal{A}),$$

where Mode^* denotes Mode with a uniformly random permutation P. While the first term reflects the (in)security of the block cipher E, the second term is intrinsically related to the mode itself, and can be upper bounded without any restriction on the time complexity of the adversary. We stress that, although the bulk of the security proof is information-theoretic, the cryptographic scheme $\mathrm{Mode}[E]$ is only secure against computationally bounded adversaries, as generic attacks on the underlying primitive E (such as exhaustive key search) always apply, thus ruling out unconditional security. Another important case where the analysis is information-theoretic in nature is when proving security in idealized models such as the ideal cipher model or the random permutation model (see section 13.3). Together with the game-playing approach (Bellare and Rogaway 2006), the H-coefficients technique is one of the major tools used to upper bound the advantage of an adversary against a symmetric cryptographic scheme in the information-theoretic setting.

In all the following, a (discrete) probability space is a non-empty set Ω endowed with a probability mass function $\mu \colon \Omega \to [0, 1]$ such that $\sum_{\omega \in \Omega} \mu(\omega) = 1$. We let $\omega \leftarrow_\$ \Omega$ denote the operation of sampling an element of Ω with probability distribution μ and assigning it to ω (we will keep μ implicit in all the following). A *probabilistic oracle* with randomness space Ω, domain X and range Y is a function $\mathcal{O} \colon \Omega \times X \to Y$, where Ω is a probability space and X and Y are finite non-empty sets. The most general setting for the H-coefficients technique considers two probabilistic oracles $\mathcal{O}_0 \colon \Omega_0 \times X \to Y$ and $\mathcal{O}_1 \colon \Omega_1 \times X \to Y$, with the same domain X and the same range Y, and the following distinguishing experiment involving a computationally unbounded (but possibly randomized, with probability space Ω) adversary $\mathcal{A}$ taking no input, interacting with either $\mathcal{O}_0(\omega_0, \cdot)$ for $\omega_0 \leftarrow_\$ \Omega_0$ or $\mathcal{O}_1(\omega_1, \cdot)$ for $\omega_1 \leftarrow_\$ \Omega_1$, and returning a single bit b'. The distinguishing advantage of $\mathcal{A}$ is defined as

$$\mathrm{Adv}^{\mathrm{dist}}_{\mathcal{O}_0, \mathcal{O}_1}(\mathcal{A}) = \left| \Pr_{\substack{\omega_0 \leftarrow_\$ \Omega_0 \\ \omega \leftarrow_\$ \Omega}} \left[1 \leftarrow \mathcal{A}^{\mathcal{O}_0(\omega_0, \cdot)}(\omega)\right] - \Pr_{\substack{\omega_1 \leftarrow_\$ \Omega_1 \\ \omega \leftarrow_\$ \Omega}} \left[1 \leftarrow \mathcal{A}^{\mathcal{O}_1(\omega_1, \cdot)}(\omega)\right] \right|.$$

Our final goal is to upper bound

$$\mathrm{Adv}^{\mathrm{dist}}_{\mathcal{O}_0, \mathcal{O}_1}(q) = \max_{\mathcal{A}} \left\{ \mathrm{Adv}^{\mathrm{dist}}_{\mathcal{O}_0, \mathcal{O}_1}(\mathcal{A}) \right\}$$

where the maximum is taken over all adversaries making at most q oracle queries.

A first observation is that it is sufficient to consider only *deterministic* adversaries. This is because

$$\max_{\mathcal{A}} \left\{ \mathrm{Adv}^{\mathrm{dist}}_{\mathcal{O}_0,\mathcal{O}_1}(\mathcal{A}) \right\} = \max_{\det \mathcal{A}} \left\{ \mathrm{Adv}^{\mathrm{dist}}_{\mathcal{O}_0,\mathcal{O}_1}(\mathcal{A}) \right\}$$

where the maximum in the left-hand side (LHS) is over all adversaries (randomized or deterministic) making at most q queries and the maximum in the right-hand side (RHS) is over the subset of all deterministic adversaries making at most q queries. The straightforward argument is as follows. Let $\mathcal{A}$ be a randomized adversary with probability space Ω. For every $\omega \in \Omega$, let $\mathcal{A}_\omega$ be the deterministic adversary obtained by running $\mathcal{A}$ with random coins ω. Let $\hat{\omega}$ be the random coins maximizing $\mathrm{Adv}^{\mathrm{dist}}_{\mathcal{O}_0,\mathcal{O}_1}(\mathcal{A}_\omega)$. Then

$$\mathrm{Adv}^{\mathrm{dist}}_{\mathcal{O}_0,\mathcal{O}_1}(\mathcal{A}) = \mathbb{E}_{\omega \xleftarrow{\$} \Omega} \left[\mathrm{Adv}^{\mathrm{dist}}_{\mathcal{O}_0,\mathcal{O}_1}(\mathcal{A}_\omega) \right] \leq \mathrm{Adv}^{\mathrm{dist}}_{\mathcal{O}_0,\mathcal{O}_1}(\mathcal{A}_{\hat{\omega}}).$$

In other words, for any adversary in the LHS, there is an adversary in the RHS with at least the same advantage, hence the result. One can also only consider without loss of generality adversaries always making *exactly q* queries.

REMARK 13.1.– In some cases, the cryptosystem being analyzed may offer two or more interfaces (e.g. when attacking an encryption scheme, the adversary might have access to both the encryption and the decryption functions). Our choice to restrict our attention to the case of $\mathcal{A}$ having access to a single oracle is obviously without loss of generality as one can always blend several oracles into a single one whose queries are prefixed with an integer indicating to which interface the query is intended. In such cases, one is often interested in characterizing the adversary's resources in a more fine-grained manner, typically by upper bounding the number of queries to each interface independently.

From now on, we fix a deterministic adversary $\mathcal{A}$ making exactly q queries to its oracle. The interaction between $\mathcal{A}$ and $\mathcal{O}_b$ ($b \in \{0,1\}$) defines a *transcript* $\tau = ((x_1, y_1), \ldots, (x_q, y_q))$ containing the ordered sequence of pairs (x_i, y_i) where $x_i \in X$ is the ith query made by $\mathcal{A}$ and $y_i \in Y$ is the corresponding answer returned by the oracle. Since $\mathcal{A}$ is deterministic, the transcript is a function of the random coins ω_b of $\mathcal{O}_b$. For $b \in \{0,1\}$, let T_b be the random variable representing the transcript when $\mathcal{A}$ interacts with $\mathcal{O}_b$. Formally, T_b is a function from Ω_b to $(X \times Y)^q$, where $T_b(\omega_b)$ is the transcript obtained by running $\mathcal{A}$ with oracle access to $\mathcal{O}_b(\omega_b, \cdot)$. The probability distribution of T_b results from the probability distribution of ω_b. As a first step, we observe that $\mathcal{A}$'s advantage is upper bounded by the statistical distance (defined below) between T_0 and T_1.

DEFINITION 13.1.– Let U and V be two random variables taking values in some finite set S. The *statistical distance* (or *total variation distance*) between U and V is

$$SD(U, V) = \frac{1}{2} \sum_{s \in S} \left| \Pr\left[U = s\right] - \Pr\left[V = s\right] \right|$$

$$= \sum_{s \in S:\ \Pr[U=s] > \Pr[V=s]} \left(\Pr\left[U = s\right] - \Pr\left[V = s\right]\right).$$

The equivalence between the two definitions can be proven easily. Let us show that as claimed above,

$$\mathrm{Adv}^{\mathrm{dist}}_{\mathcal{O}_0, \mathcal{O}_1}(\mathcal{A}) \leq SD(T_0, T_1). \qquad [13.1]$$

Let $\mathcal{T}$ denote the set of all transcripts τ that can possibly be obtained when $\mathcal{A}$ interacts with either $\mathcal{O}_0$ or $\mathcal{O}_1$, that is, such that $\max\{\Pr\left[T_0 = \tau\right], \Pr\left[T_1 = \tau\right]\} > 0$. Since $\mathcal{A}$ is deterministic, its output b' is a function $\phi_{\mathcal{A}}$ of the transcript τ. For $b' \in \{0, 1\}$, let $\Theta_{b'} \subseteq \mathcal{T}$ be the subset of transcripts τ such that $\phi_{\mathcal{A}}(\tau) = b'$. Then for $b, b' \in \{0, 1\}$,

$$\Pr_{\omega_b \leftarrow \$ \Omega_b}\left[b' \leftarrow \mathcal{A}^{\mathcal{O}_b(\omega_b, \cdot)}\right] = \sum_{\tau \in \Theta_{b'}} \Pr\left[T_b = \tau\right]. \qquad [13.2]$$

By definition of the distinguishing advantage,

$$\mathrm{Adv}^{\mathrm{dist}}_{\mathcal{O}_0, \mathcal{O}_1}(\mathcal{A}) = \left| \Pr_{\omega_0 \leftarrow \$ \Omega_0}\left[1 \leftarrow \mathcal{A}^{\mathcal{O}_0(\omega_0, \cdot)}\right] - \Pr_{\omega_1 \leftarrow \$ \Omega_1}\left[1 \leftarrow \mathcal{A}^{\mathcal{O}_1(\omega_1, \cdot)}\right] \right|$$

$$= \left| \Pr_{\omega_0 \leftarrow \$ \Omega_0}\left[0 \leftarrow \mathcal{A}^{\mathcal{O}_0(\omega_0, \cdot)}\right] - \Pr_{\omega_1 \leftarrow \$ \Omega_1}\left[0 \leftarrow \mathcal{A}^{\mathcal{O}_1(\omega_1, \cdot)}\right] \right|.$$

Injecting [13.2] in the first equality, we obtain

$$\mathrm{Adv}^{\mathrm{dist}}_{\mathcal{O}_0, \mathcal{O}_1}(\mathcal{A}) = \left| \sum_{\tau \in \Theta_1} \left(\Pr\left[T_0 = \tau\right] - \Pr\left[T_1 = \tau\right]\right) \right| \qquad [13.3]$$

$$\leq \sum_{\tau \in \Theta_1} \left| \Pr\left[T_0 = \tau\right] - \Pr\left[T_1 = \tau\right] \right|. \qquad [13.4]$$

Similarly, using the second expression of the advantage, we have

$$\mathrm{Adv}^{\mathrm{dist}}_{\mathcal{O}_0, \mathcal{O}_1}(\mathcal{A}) \leq \sum_{\tau \in \Theta_0} \left| \Pr\left[T_0 = \tau\right] - \Pr\left[T_1 = \tau\right] \right|. \qquad [13.5]$$

Combining [13.4] and [13.5] and using that $\mathcal{T}$ is the disjoint union of Θ_0 and Θ_1,

$$\text{Adv}_{\mathcal{O}_0,\mathcal{O}_1}^{\text{dist}}(\mathcal{A}) \leq \frac{1}{2} \sum_{\tau \in \mathcal{T}} |\Pr[T_0 = \tau] - \Pr[T_1 = \tau]| = \text{SD}(T_0, T_1).$$

The central result of the H-coefficients technique is the following theorem.

THEOREM 13.1 (H-coefficients technique).– Let $\mathcal{A}$ be an adversary interacting with one of two probabilistic oracles $\mathcal{O}_0$ and $\mathcal{O}_1$. Let $\mathcal{T}_1$ be the set of transcripts that can be obtained with non-zero probability when $\mathcal{A}$ interacts with $\mathcal{O}_1$. Assume that there exists a subset $\mathcal{T}_{\text{good}} \subseteq \mathcal{T}_1$ and $\varepsilon \geq 0$ such that for every $\tau \in \mathcal{T}_{\text{good}}$,

$$\frac{\Pr[T_0 = \tau]}{\Pr[T_1 = \tau]} \geq 1 - \varepsilon, \qquad\qquad\qquad [13.6]$$

and let $\mathcal{T}_{\text{bad}} = \mathcal{T}_1 \setminus \mathcal{T}_{\text{good}}$. Then $\text{Adv}_{\mathcal{O}_0,\mathcal{O}_1}^{\text{dist}}(\mathcal{A}) \leq \Pr[T_1 \in \mathcal{T}_{\text{bad}}] + \varepsilon$.

Proof. Starting from the second definition of the statistical distance, we have

$$\text{SD}(T_0, T_1) = \sum_{\tau \in \mathcal{T}:\ \Pr[T_1=\tau]>\Pr[T_0=\tau]} (\Pr[T_1 = \tau] - \Pr[T_0 = \tau])$$

$$= \sum_{\tau \in \mathcal{T}:\ \Pr[T_1=\tau]>\Pr[T_0=\tau]} \Pr[T_1 = \tau]\left(1 - \frac{\Pr[T_0 = \tau]}{\Pr[T_1 = \tau]}\right)$$

$$\leq \sum_{\tau \in \mathcal{T}_1} \Pr[T_1 = \tau]\left(1 - \frac{\Pr[T_0 = \tau]}{\Pr[T_1 = \tau]}\right)$$

$$\leq \sum_{\tau \in \mathcal{T}_{\text{bad}}} \Pr[T_1 = \tau] + \sum_{\tau \in \mathcal{T}_{\text{good}}} \Pr[T_1 = \tau]\varepsilon$$

$$\leq \Pr[T_1 \in \mathcal{T}_{\text{bad}}] + \varepsilon,$$

where the third line follows from $\{\tau \in \mathcal{T}:\ \Pr[T_1 = \tau] > \Pr[T_0 = \tau]\} \subseteq \mathcal{T}_1$ and the fourth line follows from equation [13.6]. The result follows from equation [13.1]. $\square$

How do we use the H-coefficients theorem? Upper bounding $\Pr[T_1 \in \mathcal{T}_{\text{bad}}]$ is usually the easy part, as $\mathcal{O}_1$, being the ideal counterpart of the cryptographic scheme being analyzed (e.g. a uniformly random permutation when analyzing a block cipher), often has a very simple distribution (one casually refers to it as the *ideal world*, by opposition to $\mathcal{O}_0$ which is usually called the *real world*). An important insight of the H-coefficients technique is that, although the distribution of T_0 and T_1 depends on the adversary, one has $\Pr[T_0 = \tau] \in \{0, p_0(\tau)\}$ where $p_0 \colon (X \times Y)^q \to [0, 1]$ is a function that depends on $\mathcal{O}_0$ but not on $\mathcal{A}$ (and similarly for $\Pr[T_1 = \tau]$). To show this, let us fix some potential q-queries transcript $\tau \in (X \times Y)^q$. We say that $\omega_0 \in \Omega_0$ is *compatible* with τ if for every $i = 1, \ldots, q$, $\mathcal{O}_0(\omega_0, x_i) = y_i$. In other words, if queries $x_1, \ldots, x_q$ are asked to $\mathcal{O}_0(\omega_0, \cdot)$, then answers are $y_1, \ldots, y_q$. Let $\mathrm{comp}_0(\tau)$ denote the set of random coins $\omega_0 \in \Omega_0$ compatible with a transcript τ, and define $p_0(\tau) = \Pr_{\omega_0 \twoheadleftarrow \$ \Omega_0}[\omega_0 \in \mathrm{comp}_0(\tau)]$. Given a deterministic adversary $\mathcal{A}$, running $\mathcal{A}^{\mathcal{O}_0(\omega_0, \cdot)}$ for $\omega_0 \in \mathrm{comp}_0(\tau)$ will not necessarily produce τ as, for example, $\mathcal{A}$'s first query might be different from x_1. However, if $\Pr[T_0 = \tau] > 0$, then necessarily $\Pr[T_0 = \tau] = p_0(\tau)$. Indeed, in that case, running $\mathcal{A}^{\mathcal{O}_0(\omega_0, \cdot)}$ produces τ if and only if $\omega_0 \in \mathrm{comp}_0(\tau)$. For the "only if" part, observe that running $\mathcal{A}^{\mathcal{O}_0(\omega_0, \cdot)}$ for $\omega_0 \notin \mathrm{comp}_0(\tau)$ cannot produce τ as $\mathcal{O}_0(\omega_0, x) \neq y$ for some $(x, y) \in \tau$. For the "if" part, observe that since $\Pr[T_0 = \tau] > 0$, there exists $\omega_0' \in \Omega_0$ such that running $\mathcal{A}^{\mathcal{O}_0(\omega_0', \cdot)}$ produces τ, and that running $\mathcal{A}^{\mathcal{O}_0(\omega_0, \cdot)}$ for any $\omega_0 \in \mathrm{comp}_0(\tau)$ will result in exactly the same sequence of queries and answers as running $\mathcal{A}^{\mathcal{O}_0(\omega_0', \cdot)}$ since $\mathcal{A}$ is deterministic, hence will produce transcript τ as well. As a result, condition [13.6] can be equivalently written as

$$\frac{\Pr_{\omega_0 \twoheadleftarrow \$ \Omega_0}[\omega_0 \in \mathrm{comp}_0(\tau)]}{\Pr_{\omega_1 \twoheadleftarrow \$ \Omega_1}[\omega_1 \in \mathrm{comp}_1(\tau)]} \geq 1 - \varepsilon.$$

This expression is independent of the adversary and hence easier to reason about. Again, $\Pr_{\omega_1 \twoheadleftarrow \$ \Omega_1}[\omega_1 \in \mathrm{comp}(\tau)]$ is usually simple to compute due to the simplicity of the ideal world. The technically delicate part of the proof is often to derive a good lower bound for $\Pr_{\omega_0 \twoheadleftarrow \$ \Omega_0}[\omega_0 \in \mathrm{comp}(\tau)]$.

History: Patarin (1991, 2003, 2004) pioneered the H-coefficients technique (and explicitly named it according to the notation used to denote the quantity $|\mathrm{comp}_0(\tau)|$) in his PhD dissertation (1991, in French) and subsequently used it in a number of works analyzing the Feistel construction. He presented the technique in a systematic way in Patarin (2008). Concurrently, several authors independently used very similar approaches (Bernstein 1999; Naor and Reingold 1999). The technique was popularized by its exposition in Chen and Steinberger (2014) and since then has been used in a quickly growing number of papers.

13.2. A worked out example: the three-round Feistel construction

Let us put the H-coefficients technique to work by proving that the 3-round Feistel construction is pseudorandom. Fix an integer $n \geq 1$ and let f_1, f_2, and f_3 be three functions from $\{0, 1\}^n$ to $\{0, 1\}^n$. The three-round Feistel construction associates to (f_1, f_2, f_3) a permutation $\Phi_3[f_1, f_2, f_3]$ of $(\{0, 1\}^n)^2$ mapping (x_0, x_1) to (x_3, x_4) defined by the following equations:

$$x_2 = x_0 \oplus f_1(x_1), \quad x_3 = x_1 \oplus f_2(x_2), \quad x_4 = x_2 \oplus f_3(x_3).$$

THEOREM 13.2.– The advantage of any adversary making at most q queries to a permutation oracle in distinguishing $\Phi_3[f_1, f_2, f_3]$ with uniformly random and independent functions from a truly random permutation P satisfies

$$\text{Adv}_{\Phi_3}^{\text{prp}}(q) \leq \frac{q^2}{2^n} + \frac{q^2}{2^{2n+1}}.$$

Proof. Let $\mathcal{A}$ be a deterministic adversary making exactly q distinct queries. Let $\mathcal{F}$ denote the set of all functions from $\{0,1\}^n$ to $\{0,1\}^n$ and $\mathcal{P}$ denote the set of all permutations of $(\{0,1\}^n)^2$. Then the probability spaces we consider are $\Omega_0 = \mathcal{F}^3$ and $\Omega_1 = \mathcal{P}$, both endowed with the uniform distribution, and for $(x_0, x_1) \in (\{0,1\}^n)^2$ one has $\mathcal{O}_0((f_1, f_2, f_3), (x_0, x_1)) = \Phi_3[f_1, f_2, f_3](x_0, x_1)$ and $\mathcal{O}_1(P, (x_0, x_1)) = P(x_0, x_1)$. Let $\tau = (((x_0^{(1)}, x_1^{(1)}), (x_3^{(1)}, x_4^{(1)})), \ldots, ((x_0^{(q)}, x_1^{(q)}), (x_3^{(q)}, x_4^{(q)})))$ denote the transcript of the interaction of $\mathcal{A}$ with its oracle where $(x_0^{(i)}, x_1^{(i)})$ is the ith query and $(x_3^{(i)}, x_4^{(i)})$ the corresponding answer. For $b \in \{0,1\}$, let T_b denote the random variable representing the transcript when $\mathcal{A}$ interacts with $\mathcal{O}_b$, and let $\mathcal{T}_1$ denote the set of transcripts that can be obtained with non-zero probability when $\mathcal{A}$ interacts with $\mathcal{O}_1$. We say that a transcript is bad if there exists $i \neq j$ such that $x_3^{(i)} = x_3^{(j)}$. We let $\mathcal{T}_{\text{bad}}$ denote the set of bad transcripts and $\mathcal{T}_{\text{good}} = \mathcal{T}_1 \setminus \mathcal{T}_{\text{bad}}$ be the set of good transcripts. Then

$$\Pr[T_1 \in \mathcal{T}_{\text{bad}}] \leq \frac{q(q-1)(2^n - 1)}{2(2^{2n} - 1)} \leq \frac{q^2}{2^{n+1}}. \tag{13.7}$$

Indeed, for each pair (i,j), $i \neq j$, $\text{Left}(P(x_0^{(i)}, x_1^{(i)})) = \text{Left}(P(x_0^{(j)}, x_1^{(j)}))$ with probability at most $(2^n - 1)/(2^{2n} - 1)$ over the draw of $P \leftarrow_\$ \mathcal{P}$, where $\text{Left}((x,y)) = x$. The result follows by the union bound over all pairs (i,j).

We must now lower bound $\Pr[T_0 = \tau] / \Pr[T_1 = \tau]$ for good transcripts τ. Let $\text{comp}_0(\tau)$ be the set of $(f_1, f_2, f_3) \in \Omega_0$ compatible with τ, that is, such that $\Phi_3[f_1, f_2, f_3](x_0^{(i)}, x_1^{(i)}) = (x_3^{(i)}, x_4^{(i)})$ for every $i \in \{1, \ldots, q\}$ and let $\text{comp}_1(\tau)$ be the set of $P \in \Omega_1$ compatible with τ, that is, such that $P(x_0^{(i)}, x_1^{(i)}) = (x_3^{(i)}, x_4^{(i)})$ for every $i \in \{1, \ldots, q\}$. Then for every transcript $\tau \in \mathcal{T}_1$ (good or bad),

$$\Pr_{P \leftarrow_\$ \Omega_1}[P \in \text{comp}_1(\tau)] = \frac{1}{2^{2n}(2^{2n} - 1) \cdots (2^{2n} - q + 1)}. \tag{13.8}$$

Consider now a good transcript τ. Let S be the set of $f_1 \in \mathcal{F}$ such that the values $x_2^{(i)} = x_0^{(i)} \oplus f_1(x_1^{(i)})$, $1 \leq i \leq q$, are distinct. Then $\Pr[f_1 \in S] \geq (1 - q^2/2^{n+1})$. Indeed, for $i \neq j$, either $x_1^{(i)} = x_1^{(j)}$, in which case $x_0^{(i)} \neq x_0^{(j)}$ (since the adversary does not repeat queries) so that $x_2^{(i)} \neq x_2^{(j)}$, or $x_1^{(i)} \neq x_1^{(j)}$, in which case $x_2^{(i)} = x_2^{(j)}$ holds with probability $1/2^n$. By the union bound, $\Pr[f_1 \in S] \leq q(q-1)/2^{n+1}$. Conditioned on $f_1 \in S$, equalities $f_2(x_2^{(i)}) = x_1^{(i)} \oplus x_3^{(i)}$, $1 \leq i \leq q$, are satisfied with probability $1/(2^n)^q$, and similarly for equalities $f_3(x_3^{(i)}) = x_2^{(i)} \oplus x_4^{(i)}$. Hence,

$$\Pr_{(f_1,f_2,f_3) \leftarrow\$ \Omega_0} [(f_1, f_2, f_3) \in \mathrm{comp}_0(\tau)] \geq \left(1 - \frac{q^2}{2^{n+1}}\right) \frac{1}{2^{2nq}}. \qquad [13.9]$$

Combining equations [13.8] and [13.9], we obtain

$$\frac{\Pr[T_0 = \tau]}{\Pr[T_1 = \tau]} = \frac{\Pr_{(f_1,f_2,f_3) \leftarrow\$ \Omega_0} [(f_1, f_2, f_3) \in \mathrm{comp}_0(\tau)]}{\Pr_{P \leftarrow\$ \Omega_1} [P \in \mathrm{comp}_1(\tau)]} \geq 1 - \frac{q^2}{2^{n+1}} - \frac{q^2}{2^{2n+1}},$$

where we used $\prod_{i=0}^{q-1}(1 - i/2^{2n}) \geq 1 - q^2/2^{2n+1}$. Applying the H-coefficients theorem with $\varepsilon = q^2/2^{n+1} + q^2/2^{2n+1}$ and equation [13.7] yields the result. $\qquad\square$

13.3. The Even-Mansour construction

The Even-Mansour construction (Even and Mansour 1997) is a very simple way to build a block cipher from a public permutation P. Fix an integer $n \geq 1$ and let P be an efficiently computable permutation on n-bit strings. The Even-Mansour cipher associated with P, denoted $\mathsf{EM}[P]$ and depicted below, is the block cipher with block space $\{0,1\}^n$ and key space $(\{0,1\}^n)^2$ which encrypts plaintext $x \in \{0,1\}^n$ under key $(k_0, k_1) \in (\{0,1\}^n)^2$ as $\mathsf{EM}[P]_{(k_0,k_1)}(x) = k_1 \oplus P(x \oplus k_0)$. Decryption of a ciphertext y under key $(k_0, k_1) \in (\{0,1\}^n)^2$ is obtained as $x = k_0 \oplus P^{-1}(y \oplus k_1)$.

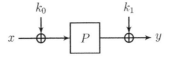

Obviously, not all choices of permutation P will provide a secure block cipher. For example, if P is a translation $x \mapsto x \oplus c$ for some public constant $c \in \{0,1\}^n$, the Even-Mansour cipher is linear; in particular, the value of $k_0 \oplus k_1$ can be retrieved with a single plaintext/ciphertext pair. However, for a "complex enough" permutation P, one might hope to obtain a secure block cipher.

The Even-Mansour construction is minimal in the sense that removing any component makes it insecure: omitting the XOR of the key k_0 allows an attacker to retrieve k_1 from a single plaintext/ciphertext pair (x, y) as $k_1 = y \oplus P(x)$; similarly, omitting the XOR of the last key k_1 allows an attacker to retrieve k_0 from a single plaintext/ciphertext pair (x, y) as $k_0 = x \oplus P^{-1}(y)$; finally, omitting the permutation P makes the cipher linear and trivially insecure. It has been shown in Dunkelman et al. (2012) that the construction offers a similar level of security when using a single n-bit key k and letting $k_0 = k_1 = k$. This variant is called the *single-key* Even-Mansour construction.

13.3.1. *H-coefficients security proof*

We now provide the standard security proof for the (single-key) Even-Mansour construction, using the H-coefficients technique presented in section 13.3. The analysis is carried in the *random permutation model* (RPM), meaning that the inner permutation P on which the construction is based is modeled as a uniformly random permutation to which the distinguisher has two-sided (i.e. it can query both P and P^{-1}) black-box access: a random permutation oracle. Hence, the standard indistinguishability experiment defining the (strong) pseudorandom permutation property of a block cipher, in which the distinguisher has access to a permutation oracle (and its inverse) implementing either the block cipher keyed with a uniformly random key or a uniformly random permutation Q, is modified as follows: the distinguisher must tell apart the four-interfaces oracle $\mathcal{O}_0 = (\mathsf{EM}[P]_k, (\mathsf{EM}[P]_k)^{-1}, P, P^{-1})$ where P is a uniformly random permutation of $\{0, 1\}^n$ and k is chosen uniformly at random in $\{0, 1\}^n$ (the "real world"), from $\mathcal{O}_1 = (Q, Q^{-1}, P, P^{-1})$ where Q and P are uniformly random and independent permutations of $\{0, 1\}^n$ (the "ideal world"). We will refer to queries to the first two interfaces $(\mathsf{EM}[P]_k/(\mathsf{EM}[P]_k)^{-1}$ or Q/Q^{-1} depending on which world we consider) as *construction queries* and queries to the last two interfaces (P/P^{-1}) as *primitive queries*.

THEOREM 13.3.– Let $\mathsf{EM}[P]$ be the single-key Even-Mansour construction where the inner permutation P is modeled as a random permutation oracle. Then any adversary against the SPRP security of $\mathsf{EM}[P]$ making at most q_c construction queries and at most q_p primitive queries has distinguishing advantage at most $2q_c q_p / 2^n$.

Proof. Let us fix an adversary $\mathcal{A}$. As explained in section 13.1, we can restrict our attention to deterministic adversaries making exactly q_c construction queries and q_p primitive queries. We also assume without loss of generality that the adversary never makes redundant queries, meaning that it never repeats any query nor queries, that is, $P(x)$ obtaining answer y and then queries $P^{-1}(y)$ (and similarly for other interfaces). Finally, we slightly modify the security experiment by augmenting it with a special interface (taking no input) that the adversary can only query *after* its q_c construction queries and its q_p primitive queries and behaves as follows: in the real world, it returns the key k, while in the ideal world, it returns a uniformly random "dummy" key k. Let $\mathcal{P}$ denote the set of all permutations of $\{0,1\}^n$. Then the probability space for the real-world oracle $\mathcal{O}_0$ is $\Omega_0 = \mathcal{P} \times \{0,1\}^n$, while the randomness space for the ideal world oracle $\mathcal{O}_1$ is $\Omega_1 = (\mathcal{P})^2 \times \{0,1\}^n$, both endowed with the uniform distribution. The transcript of the interaction of the adversary with the oracle consists in a sequence of triples (i, w, w'), where $i \in \{1, 2, 3, 4\}$ indicates which interface is queried, w is the actual query and w' the oracle answer (e.g. triple $(4, y, x)$ means that $\mathcal{A}$ queried $P^{-1}(y)$ and received answer x) followed by key k. For notational simplicity, we encode the transcript as a tuple $\tau = (\Gamma_{\mathrm{c}}, \Gamma_{\mathrm{p}}, k)$ such that Γ_{c} contains all pairs (u, v) such that the adversary either queried $(1, u)$ and received answer v or queried $(2, v)$ and received answer u and Γ_{p} contains all pairs (x, y) such that the adversary either queried $(3, x)$ and received answer y or queried $(4, y)$ and received answer x. Because the adversary is deterministic, there is a one-to-one correspondence between the original transcript and this more convenient form. As in section 13.1, for $b \in \{0, 1\}$ we let T_b denote the random variable representing the transcript when $\mathcal{A}$ interacts with $\mathcal{O}_b$ and define $\mathcal{T}_1$ as the set of transcripts that can be obtained with non-zero probability when $\mathcal{A}$ interacts with $\mathcal{O}_1$. We say that a transcript is bad if there exists $(u, v) \in \Gamma_{\mathrm{c}}$ and $(x, y) \in \Gamma_{\mathrm{p}}$ such that $u \oplus x = k$ or $v \oplus y = k$ and we let $\mathcal{T}_{\mathrm{bad}}$ denote the set of bad transcripts and $\mathcal{T}_{\mathrm{good}} = \mathcal{T}_1 \setminus \mathcal{T}_{\mathrm{bad}}$ denote the set of good transcripts. Since in the ideal world, the key is uniformly random from $\{0,1\}^n$ and independent of the adversary's queries and oracle's answers, for each $(u, v) \in \Gamma_{\mathrm{c}}$ and $(x, y) \in \Gamma_{\mathrm{p}}$, $u \oplus x = k \vee v \oplus y = k$ holds with probability at most $2/2^n$. By the union bound, and since $|\Gamma_{\mathrm{c}}| = q_{\mathrm{c}}$ and $|\Gamma_{\mathrm{p}}| = q_{\mathrm{p}}$, we have

$$\Pr[T_1 \in \mathcal{T}_{\mathrm{bad}}] \leq 2q_{\mathrm{c}}q_{\mathrm{p}}/2^n. \tag{13.10}$$

It remains to lower bound $\Pr[T_0 = \tau] / \Pr[T_1 = \tau]$ for transcripts $\tau \in \mathcal{T}_{\mathrm{good}}$. In the following, for integers $1 \leq a \leq b$ we write $(b)_a = b(b - 1) \cdots (b - a + 1)$. Recall that, as explained in section 13.1, an element $\omega_b \in \Omega_b$ is said compatible with a transcript τ if for every $(z, z') \in \tau$, $\mathcal{O}_b(\omega_b, z) = z'$ and that if $\Pr[T_b = \tau] > 0$, then $\Pr[T_b = \tau] = \Pr_{\omega_b \leftarrow \$ \Omega_b}[\omega_b \in \mathrm{comp}_b(\tau)]$, where $\mathrm{comp}_b(\tau)$ is the set of $\omega_b \in \Omega_b$ compatible with τ. In our case, this translates as follows. An element $(Q, P, k^*) \in \Omega_1$ is compatible with a transcript $\tau = (\Gamma_{\mathrm{c}}, \Gamma_{\mathrm{p}}, k)$ if $Q(u) = v$ for every $(u, v) \in \Gamma_{\mathrm{c}}$, $P(x) = y$ for every $(x, y) \in \Gamma_{\mathrm{p}}$, and $k^* = k$. Then for $\tau \in \mathcal{T}_1$ (good or bad),

$$\Pr_{(Q,P,k^*) \leftarrow \$ \Omega_1}[(Q, P, k^*) \in \mathrm{comp}_1(\tau)] = \frac{1}{(2^n)_{q_{\mathrm{c}}}} \cdot \frac{1}{(2^n)_{q_{\mathrm{p}}}} \cdot \frac{1}{2^n}. \tag{13.11}$$

Similarly, an element $(P, k^*) \in \Omega_0$ is compatible with a transcript $\tau = (\Gamma_{\mathrm{c}}, \Gamma_{\mathrm{p}}, k)$ if $\mathrm{EM}[P]_k(u) = v$ for every $(u, v) \in \Gamma_{\mathrm{c}}$, $P(x) = y$ for every $(x, y) \in \Gamma_{\mathrm{p}}$, and $k^* = k$. Consider now a good transcript $\tau = (\Gamma_{\mathrm{c}}, \Gamma_{\mathrm{p}}, k)$. Then, by definition, for every $(u, v) \in \Gamma_{\mathrm{c}}$ and every $(x, y) \in \Gamma_{\mathrm{p}}$, we have $u \oplus k \neq x$ and $v \oplus k \neq y$. Hence, the condition that $\mathsf{EM}[P]_k(u) = v$ for every $(u, v) \in \Gamma_c$ translates to q_c equations $P(u \oplus k) = v \oplus k$ which together with the q_p equations $P(x) = y$ for $(x, y) \in \Gamma_p$ yields $q_c + q_p$ consistent equations on P. Hence,

$$\Pr_{(P, k^*) \xleftarrow{\$} \Omega_0} [(P, k^*) \in \mathsf{comp}_0(\tau)] = \frac{1}{(2^n)_{q_c + q_p}} \cdot \frac{1}{2^n}. \tag{13.12}$$

Hence, combining Eqs. [13.11] and [13.12],

$$\frac{\Pr[T_0 = \tau]}{\Pr[T_1 = \tau]} = \frac{\Pr_{(P, k^*) \xleftarrow{\$} \Omega_0} [(P, k^*) \in \mathsf{comp}_0(\tau)]}{\Pr_{(Q, P, k^*) \xleftarrow{\$} \Omega_1} [(Q, P, k^*) \in \mathsf{comp}_1(\tau)]} = \frac{(2)_{q_c}(2^n)_{q_p}}{(2^n)_{q_c + q_p}} \geq 1.$$

Applying the H-coefficients theorem with $\varepsilon = 0$ and equation [13.10] yields the result. $\qquad\square$

13.3.2. *Extension to multiple rounds*

The Even-Mansour construction can be generalized to multiple rounds: given integers $n, \kappa, r \geq 1$, r permutations $P_1, \ldots, P_r$ on n-bit strings, and $r + 1$ functions $f_0, \ldots, f_r$ from $\{0, 1\}^\kappa$ to $\{0, 1\}^n$, the *iterated Even-Mansour* (IEM) construction, depicted below, defines a block cipher with block space $\{0, 1\}^n$ and key space $\{0, 1\}^\kappa$ which maps a plaintext $x \in \{0, 1\}^n$ and a key $k \in \{0, 1\}^\kappa$ to ciphertext y computed as

$$y = k_r \oplus P_r \left(k_{r-1} \oplus P_{r-1} \left(\cdots P_2 \big(k_1 \oplus P_1(k_0 \oplus x) \big) \cdots \right) \right),$$

where $k_i = f_i(k)$ for $i = 0, \ldots, r$. The IEM construction captures the high-level structure of so-called *key-alternating* ciphers such as AES. A large number of papers have studied the security properties of this construction in the RPM depending on the number of rounds and the distribution of permutations $P_1, \ldots, P_r$ and round keys $k_0, \ldots, k_r$. In particular, for independent random permutations and independent random round keys, it has been shown that any adversary must make at least about $2^{rn/(r+1)}$ oracle queries to break the strong pseudorandomness of the r-round IEM construction with constant advantage (Chen and Steinberger 2014).

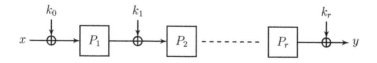

13.4. References

Bellare, M. and Rogaway, P. (2006). The security of triple encryption and a framework for code-based game-playing proofs. In *EUROCRYPT 2006*, vol. 4004 of *Lecture Notes in Computer Science*, Vaudenay, S. (ed.). Springer.

Bernstein, D.J. (1999). How to stretch random functions: The security of protected counter sums. *J. Cryptol.*, 12(3), 185–192.

Chen, S. and Steinberger, J.P. (2014). Tight security bounds for key-alternating ciphers. In *EUROCRYPT 2014*, vol. 8441 of *Lecture Notes in Computer Science*, Nguyen, P.Q., Oswald, E. (eds). Springer.

Dunkelman, O., Keller, N., Shamir, A. (2012). Minimalism in cryptography: The Even-Mansour scheme revisited. In *EUROCRYPT 2012*, vol. 7237 of *Lecture Notes in Computer Science*, Pointcheval, D., Johansson, T. (eds). Springer.

Even, S. and Mansour, Y. (1997). A construction of a cipher from a single pseudorandom permutation. *J. Cryptol.*, 10(3), 151–162.

Naor, M. and Reingold, O. (1999). On the construction of pseudorandom permutations: Luby-Rackoff revisited. *J. Cryptol.*, 12(1), 29–66.

Patarin, J. (1991). New results on pseudorandom permutation generators based on the DES scheme. In *CRYPTO '91*, vol. 576 of *Lecture Notes in Computer Science*, Feigenbaum, J. (ed.). Springer.

Patarin, J. (2003). Luby-Rackoff: 7 rounds are enough for $2^{n(1-epsilon)}$ security. In *CRYPTO 2003*, vol. 2729 of *Lecture Notes in Computer Science*, Boneh, D. (ed.). Springer.

Patarin, J. (2004). Security of random Feistel schemes with 5 or more rounds. In *CRYPTO 2004*, vol. 3152 of *Lecture Notes in Computer Science*, Franklin, M.K. (ed.). Springer.

Patarin, J. (2008). The coefficients H technique. In *SAC 2008*, vol. 5381 of *Lecture Notes in Computer Science*, Avanzi, R.M., Keliher, L., Sica, F. (eds). Springer.

14

Chi-square Method

Mridul Nandi

Indian Statistical Institute, Kolkata, India

Different tools from probability and statistics are now heavily used in cryptography. Among them, the χ^2-method is a recent addition in cryptographic literature. The idea was introduced to cryptography in Dai et al. (2017), who showed pseudorandom function security (PRF-security) of two constructions, namely the sum of random permutations (Patarin 2008, 2010; Bellare and Impagliazzo 1999; Lucks 2000) and encrypted Davies-Meyer (EDM) (Cogliati and Seurin 2016; Mennink and Neves 2017). Stam (1978) described a very similar method in a statistical context. The χ^2-method sometimes helps to obtain tight and simplified proofs for certain constructions where earlier proof techniques were not fully satisfactory. In this chapter, we will discuss the χ^2-method and apply this technique to the PRF-security of the truncated random permutation construction (Stam 1978; Hall et al. 1998; Bellare and Impagliazzo 1999; Gilboa and Gueron 2015, 2016; Gilboa et al. 2018). We also sketch the proof of PRF-security of the sum of two random permutations and discuss some other applications.

14.1. Introduction

χ^2-method in statistics: the χ^2-distance, a popular statistic for hypothesis testing, is an implicit backbone of the χ^2-method. It has its origin in mathematical statistics dating back to Pearson (see Liese and Vajda (1987) for some history). Although it is not a metric (as it is not symmetric), it is useful for bounding the statistical distance.

Suppose we observe a sample $x_1, x_2, \ldots, x_n$ and we believe that the distribution is $\mathbf{P_0}$ (null hypothesis). We divide the space into some disjoint intervals $I_1, \ldots, I_k$. Let n_j denote the number of samples in the interval I_j and $n'_j := \mathbf{P_0}(I_j) \cdot n$ denote the expected number of samples observed provided the samples indeed follow $\mathbf{P_0}$. When n is large, and under a reasonable regularity assumption, the χ^2-test statistic

$$\chi^2 := \sum_{i=1}^{k} \frac{(n_j - n'_j)^2}{n'_j}$$

follows a distribution very close to the χ^2-distribution (a well-known distribution in statistics) given that the sample is actually sampled under the null hypothesis. This motivates the definition of a distance-like measurement. In what follows, we use the convention $0/0 = 0$.

DEFINITION 14.1.– The χ^2-distance between distributions $\mathbf{P_0}$ and $\mathbf{P_1}$ (over a sample space Ω) with $\mathbf{P_0} \ll \mathbf{P_1}$ (i.e. the support of $\mathbf{P_0}$ is contained in the support of $\mathbf{P_1}$) is defined as

$$d_{\chi^2}(\mathbf{P_0}, \mathbf{P_1}) := \sum_{x \in \Omega} \frac{(\mathbf{P_0}(x) - \mathbf{P_1}(x))^2}{\mathbf{P_1}(x)}.$$

In other words, the χ^2-test is used to compare the observed probability distribution of a given sample with the probability distribution under the hypothesis. Thus, it measures a kind of *distance* between two probability distributions. The condition $\mathbf{P_0} \ll \mathbf{P_1}$ ensures that whenever the denominator is zero, the numerator is also zero (and hence according to convention the ratio is defined as zero). Thus, the sum can be taken over all x in the support of $\mathbf{P_1}$.

Statistical distance: the *distinguishing advantage* of a family of keyed functions is bounded by the *statistical distance* between the output distribution of the family and the output distribution of a random function (for more details, see section 14.2.1). The statistical distance (which, unlike the χ^2-distance, is a metric) between two probability distributions $\mathbf{P_0}$ and $\mathbf{P_1}$ over a sample space Ω, denoted $d_{\mathrm{TV}}(\mathbf{P_0}, \mathbf{P_1})$, is defined as half of the L_1-norm

$$d_{\mathrm{TV}}(\mathbf{P_0}, \mathbf{P_1}) = \frac{1}{2} \cdot \|\mathbf{P_0} - \mathbf{P_1}\|_1 = \frac{1}{2} \cdot \sum_{x \in \Omega} |\mathbf{P_0}(x) - \mathbf{P_1}(x)|.$$

An equivalent definition of statistical distance is $d_{\mathrm{TV}}(\mathbf{P_0}, \mathbf{P_1}) = \max_{\mathcal{E} \subseteq \Omega}(\mathbf{P_0}(\mathcal{E}) - \mathbf{P_1}(\mathcal{E}))$. If X and Y are two random variables following distributions $\mathbf{P_0}$ and $\mathbf{P_1}$, respectively, we write $d_{\mathrm{TV}}(\mathsf{X}, \mathsf{Y}) := \frac{1}{2} \cdot \|\mathbf{P_0} - \mathbf{P_1}\|_1$.

χ^2-Method: in Dai et al. (2017), the authors revisited a variation of the additivity property of the Kullback-Leibler divergence between two joint distributions. The authors termed it the χ^2-method. When $\mathbf{P_0}$ and $\mathbf{P_1}$ are joint distributions, this method provides an upper bound on $\|\mathbf{P_0} - \mathbf{P_1}\|_1$ based on the χ^2-distance between the conditional distributions of $\mathbf{P_0}$ and $\mathbf{P_1}$.

Let $\mathsf{X} = (\mathsf{X}_1, \ldots, \mathsf{X}_q)$ and $\mathsf{Y} = (\mathsf{Y}_1, \ldots, \mathsf{Y}_q)$ be two multivariate random variables taking values from Ω^q, following $\mathbf{P_0}$ and $\mathbf{P_1}$, respectively. In order to simplify the notation, we denote by X^{i-1} the joint random variable $(\mathsf{X}_1, \ldots, \mathsf{X}_{i-1})$, and similar for Y^{i-1}. Let $\mathbf{P_0}_{x_1,\ldots,x_{i-1}}$ denote the conditional probability distribution of X_i given $\mathsf{X}_1 = x_1, \ldots, \mathsf{X}_{i-1} = x_{i-1}$. We similarly write $\mathbf{P_1}_{x_1,\ldots,x_{i-1}}$ for the distribution of Y_i given $\mathsf{Y}_1 = x_1, \ldots, \mathsf{Y}_{i-1} = x_{i-1}$. Then, the χ^2-method guarantees that

$$d_{\mathrm{TV}}(\mathsf{X}, \mathsf{Y}) \leq \left(\frac{1}{2} \sum_{i=1}^{q} \mathbf{Ex}(\chi^2(\mathsf{X}_1, \ldots, \mathsf{X}_{i-1})) \right)^{\frac{1}{2}}, \qquad [14.1]$$

where the $\chi^2(\cdots)$ function is defined as

$$\chi^2(x_1, \ldots, x_{i-1}) = d_{\chi^2}(\mathbf{P_0}_{x_1,\ldots,x_{i-1}}, \mathbf{P_1}_{x_1,\ldots,x_{i-1}}), \qquad [14.2]$$

and for all $x_1, \ldots, x_{i-1}$, $\mathbf{P_0}_{x_1,\ldots,x_{i-1}} \ll \mathbf{P_1}_{x_1,\ldots,x_{i-1}}$. Note that we need the latter condition to be able to define $d_{\chi^2}(\mathbf{P_0}_{x_1,\ldots,x_{i-1}}, \mathbf{P_1}_{x_1,\ldots,x_{i-1}})$ in the first place.

14.2. Preliminaries

Notation and convention: we use the shorthand notation X^t to denote a tuple $(X_1, \ldots, X_t)$. We use notations $\mathsf{X}, \mathsf{Y}, \mathsf{Z}, \ldots$ (possibly with suffixes) to represent random variables over some sets. We use $\mathcal{E}, \mathcal{S}, \mathcal{T}, \ldots$ (possibly with suffixes) to denote sets. $\mathcal{A}$ will always represent an adversary. By $\mathsf{X} \leftarrow_\$ \mathcal{S}$ we mean that X is sampled uniformly from a finite set $\mathcal{S}$. For positive integers m and n, perm_n denotes the set of all permutations on $\{0,1\}^n$ and $\mathrm{func}_{n \to m}$ the set of all functions from $\{0,1\}^n$ to $\{0,1\}^m$.

14.2.1. *PRF-security definition*

A pseudorandom function (PRF) is a very popular security notion in cryptography. Let m and n be positive integers. Consider a function $f : \mathcal{K} \times \{0,1\}^n \to \{0,1\}^m$ that for a fixed key from $\mathcal{K}$ maps inputs from $\{0,1\}^n$ to $\{0,1\}^m$. We define the *PRF-advantage* of f by how good it "behaves" like a random function $\mathsf{RF}_{n \to m} \leftarrow_\$ \mathrm{func}_{n \to m}$.

DEFINITION 14.2 (PRF-advantage).– Let $\mathcal{A}$ be an adversary (oracle algorithm) and $f : \mathcal{K} \times \{0,1\}^n \to \{0,1\}^m$. Then, the PRF-advantage of $\mathcal{A}$ against f is defined as

$$\mathbf{Adv}_f^{\mathrm{prf}}(\mathcal{A}) = |\mathbf{Pr}(\mathcal{A}^{f_{\mathsf{K}}} \to 1 \; : \; \mathsf{K} \leftarrow_{\!\$} \mathcal{K}) - \mathbf{Pr}(\mathcal{A}^{\mathsf{RF}_{n \to m}} \to 1 \; : \;$$
$$\mathsf{RF}_{n \to m} \leftarrow_{\!\$} \mathrm{func}_{n \to m})|.$$

Without loss of generality, we will assume the following conventions:

1) As we restrict to only deterministic keyed functions (i.e. functions which give the same output on the same input), we can assume, without loss of generality, that the adversary does not repeat its queries.

2) We can also assume that $\mathcal{A}$ is deterministic whenever we deal with unbounded time adversaries. Note that it can always run with the best random coins that maximizes the advantage (see also Chapter 13).

Suppose $\mathcal{A}$ makes q distinct queries adaptively, denoted $Q_1, \ldots, Q_q$. If $\mathcal{A}$ is interacting with $\mathsf{RF}_{n \to m}$, the outputs are uniformly and independently distributed over $\{0,1\}^m$, which we denote as $U_1, \ldots, U_q \leftarrow_{\!\$} \{0,1\}^m$. Similarly, let $X_1 := f_{\mathsf{K}}(U_1), \ldots, X_q := f_{\mathsf{K}}(U_q)$, which denote the outputs of f_{K} where $\mathsf{K} \leftarrow_{\!\$} \mathcal{K}$. We denote the probability distributions associated with $U_1, \ldots, U_q$ and $X_1, \ldots, X_q$ by $\mathbf{P_1}$ and $\mathbf{P_0}$, respectively. Thus,

$$\mathbf{Adv}_f^{\mathrm{prf}}(\mathcal{A}) = |\mathbf{P_1}(\mathcal{E}) - \mathbf{P_0}(\mathcal{E})|$$
$$\leq d_{\mathrm{TV}}(\mathbf{P_0}, \mathbf{P_1}),$$

where $\mathcal{E}$ is the set of all q-tuple of responses $x^q := (x_1, \ldots, x_q) \in (\{0,1\}^m)^q$ for which $\mathcal{A}$ returns 1. Thus, the main cryptographic objective (that of determining the PRF-advantage $\mathbf{Adv}_f^{\mathrm{prf}}(\mathcal{A})$) turns out to be a purely probability problem.

14.2.2. *Hypergeometric distribution*

Suppose a box contains N balls of which K balls are blue. We draw a ball randomly and we call it *success* if the color of the ball is blue. The binomial distribution describes the probability of k successes in n trials with replacement. The hypergeometric distribution describes the probability of k successes in n trials without replacement. In case of sampling without replacement, the possible value of k must satisfy

$$n + K - N \leq k \leq \min(n, K).$$

We list some useful properties of the random variable H, the number of successes, following the hypergeometric distribution as described above. The probability mass function can be written as follows:

$$\mathbf{Pr}(H = k) = \frac{\binom{K}{k} \cdot \binom{N-K}{n-k}}{\binom{N}{n}}. \tag{14.3}$$

We simply write H $\sim$ HG(N, n, K). The expected value of hypergeometric distribution is

$$\mathbf{Ex}(H) = \frac{nK}{N},$$

and the variance is

$$\mathbf{Var}(H) = \frac{nK}{N} \cdot \left(1 - \frac{K}{N}\right) \cdot \frac{N-n}{N-1}.$$

Similar to the binomial distribution, K/N represents the proportion of success in the original configuration. The expected value of success is exactly the same as the binomial distribution. As an aside, we mention that the factor $\frac{N-n}{N-1}$ is also known as the *finite sampling correction factor*. Up to this factor, the expression of variance is the same as that of the binomial distribution.

14.3. Truncation of random permutation

Before discussing the truncation construction and its analysis let us note the following point about a random permutation $RP_n \leftarrow_{\$} perm_n$. If all queries to a random permutation RP_n are distinct and depend only on the previous responses (which is the case for an adversary), the outputs $V_1, \ldots, V_q$ behave like a random sample without replacement (WOR) from $\{0, 1\}^n$. We write $V_1, \ldots, V_q \leftarrow_{wor} \{0, 1\}^n$ to denote this. More formally, for all *distinct* $x_1, \ldots, x_q \in \{0, 1\}^n$, $\mathbf{Pr}(V_1 = x_1, \ldots V_q = x_q) = \frac{1}{(N)_q}$, where $(N)_q = N(N-1) \cdots (N-q+1)$. Now, we briefly describe the truncation construction.

trRP **Construction**: let $m \leq n$, and let $trunc_m : \{0, 1\}^n \to \{0, 1\}^m$ denote the *truncation function* which returns the first m bits of its input. The truncated random permutation construction is the composition of a random permutation followed by the truncation function. More formally, we define for every $x \in \{0, 1\}^n$,

$$trRP_m(x) = trunc_m(RP_n(x)).$$

See also Figure 14.1(a). Note that this is a function family, keyed by the random permutation, mapping the set of all n-bit sequences to the set of all m-bit sequences.

14.3.1. *PRF-security of truncation*

The PRF-security of truncation has been studied by Stam (1978), though in a different and broader context, and later by others (e.g. Hall et al. 1998; Bellare and Impagliazzo 1999; Gilboa and Gueron 2015, 2016; Gilboa et al. 2018). In particular, let $V_1, \ldots, V_q \leftarrow_{\text{wor}} \{0,1\}^n$ and $X_i = \text{trunc}_m(V_i)$, for $i \in [q]$. Let $U_1, \ldots, U_q \leftarrow_\$ \{0,1\}^m$. Let $\mathbf{P_0}$ and $\mathbf{P_1}$ denote the probability distributions of X^q and U^q, respectively. Stam proved the following statement (stated in terms of our notation):

$$d_{\text{TV}}(\mathbf{P_0}, \mathbf{P_1}) \leq \frac{q}{2^{n+1-\frac{m}{2}}}. \tag{14.4}$$

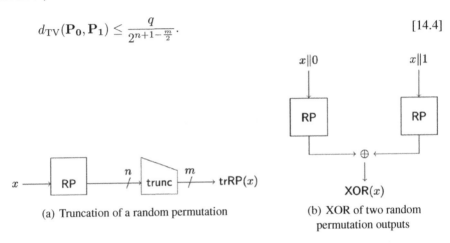

(a) Truncation of a random permutation   (b) XOR of two random permutation outputs

Figure 14.1. *Two PRF-constructions*

We will describe his proof in the context of the χ^2-method.

Proof. (Proof of Stam's theorem) We write $M = 2^m$, $N = 2^n$ and $K = N/M$. For any $i \in [q]$ and $x \in \{0,1\}^m$, let $\mathcal{S}_{i,x}(x^{i-1}) = \{v \in \{0,1\}^n : \exists j < i \ \text{trunc}_m(v) = x_j\}$. Then,

$$\mathbf{P}_{0|x^{i-1}}(x) = \mathbf{Pr}(X_i = x \mid X_1 = x_1, \ldots, X_{i-1} = x_{i-1})$$
$$= \mathbf{Pr}(V_i \notin \mathcal{S}_{i,x}(x^{i-1}))$$
$$= \frac{K - N_{i,x}(x^{i-1})}{N - i + 1},$$

where $N_{i,x}(x^{i-1}) := |\mathcal{S}_{i,x}(x^{i-1})|$. Clearly, $\mathbf{P}_{1|x^{i-1}}(x) = 1/M$. Thus, using equation [14.2],

$$\chi^2(x^{i-1}) = \sum_{x \in [M]} \frac{\left(\frac{\frac{N}{M} - N_{i,x}(x^{i-1})}{N-i+1} - \frac{1}{M} \right)^2}{\frac{1}{M}}$$

$$= \sum_{x \in [M]} M \left(\frac{\frac{N}{M} - N_{i,x}(x^{i-1})}{N-i+1} - \frac{1}{M} \right)^2$$

$$= \sum_{x \in [M]} \frac{M}{(N-i+1)^2} \cdot \left(N_{i,x}(x^{i-1}) - \frac{i-1}{M} \right)^2 .$$

We can observe that $\mathsf{H} := N_{i,x}(\mathsf{X}^{i-1})$ follows $\mathrm{HG}(N, K, (i-1))$ with mean $(i-1)/M$ and variance $\frac{i-1}{M} \cdot \left(1 - \frac{1}{M}\right) \cdot \frac{N-i+1}{N-1}$. Hence, if we take the expectation of above term (see equation [14.1]), we obtain:

$$\mathbf{Ex}(\chi^2(\mathsf{X}^{i-1})) = \mathbf{Ex}\left(\sum_{x \in [M]} \frac{M}{(N-i+1)^2} \cdot \left(\mathsf{H} - \frac{i-1}{M} \right)^2 \right)$$

$$= \sum_{x \in [M]} \frac{M}{(N-i+1)^2} \cdot \mathbf{Var}[\mathsf{H}]. \qquad [14.5]$$

$$= \frac{M^2}{(N-i+1)^2} \cdot \frac{i-1}{M} \cdot \left(1 - \frac{1}{M}\right) \cdot \frac{N-i+1}{N-1} \qquad [14.6]$$

$$= \frac{(M-1)(i-1)}{(N-1)(N-i+1)}. \qquad [14.7]$$

By using the χ^2-method (see equation [14.1]), we thus obtain

$$d_{\mathrm{TV}}(\mathbf{P_0}, \mathbf{P_1}) \leq \left(\frac{1}{2} \sum_{i=1}^{q} \mathbf{Ex}(\chi^2(\mathsf{X}^{i-1})) \right)^{\frac{1}{2}}$$

$$\leq \frac{1}{2} \left(\frac{(M-1)q(q-1)}{(N-1)(N-q+1)} \right)^{\frac{1}{2}}$$

$$\leq 2^{(m-n)/2-1} \left(\frac{q(q-1)}{N-q+1} \right)^{\frac{1}{2}}$$

$$\leq 2^{(m-n)/2-1} \left(\frac{2q(q-1)}{N} \right)^{\frac{1}{2}},$$

using that $\frac{M-1}{N-1} \leq \frac{M}{N}$ and $\frac{q-1}{N-q+1} \leq \frac{2q}{N}$ for $q \leq N/2$. We subsequently obtain:

$$d_{\mathrm{TV}}(\mathbf{P_0}, \mathbf{P_1}) \leq \frac{q}{\sqrt{2}} \cdot 2^{-n+\frac{m}{2}}. \qquad \square$$

This result immediately implies PRF-security of the truncated random permutation construction.

COROLLARY 14.1.– For any adversary $\mathcal{A}$ making q queries, we have

$$\mathbf{Adv}^{\mathrm{prf}}_{\mathrm{trRP}_m}(\mathcal{A}) \leq \frac{q}{2^{n-\frac{m-1}{2}}}.$$

14.4. XOR of random permutations

Below, we briefly outline other results obtained using the χ^2-method. Recall that $\mathrm{RP}_n \leftarrow_\$ \mathrm{perm}_n$ is a random permutation of $\{0,1\}^n$. One of the important applications of the χ^2-method is in the analysis of PRF-security of the XOR construction or its variants. In particular, we mention and outline the following result from Dai et al. (2017).

XOR **Construction**: define $\mathrm{XOR}_{\mathrm{RP}} : \{0,1\}^{n-1} \to \{0,1\}^n$ to be the construction that takes random permutation as a key, and on input $x \in \{0,1\}^{n-1}$ it returns $\mathrm{RP}(x\|0) \oplus \mathrm{RP}(x\|1)$. Thus, the XOR construction based on a random permutation RP_n returns $X_1, \ldots, X_q$ where $X_1 := V_1 \oplus V_2, \ldots, X_q := V_{2q-1} \oplus V_{2q}$ and $V_1, \ldots, V_{2q} \leftarrow_{\mathrm{wor}} \{0,1\}^n$. The construction is depicted in Figure 14.1(b).

THEOREM 14.1 (Dai et al. (2017)).– Fix an integer $n \geq 8$ and let $N = 2^n$. For any adversary $\mathcal{A}$ that makes $q \leq \frac{N}{32}$ queries, we have

$$\mathbf{Adv}^{\mathrm{prf}}_{\mathrm{XOR}}(\mathcal{A}) \leq \left(\frac{q}{N}\right) + 3\left(\frac{q}{N}\right)^{\frac{3}{2}}.$$

Proof sketch. The main part of the proof of theorem 14.1 consists of computing an upper bound on $d_{\mathrm{TV}}(\mathbf{P_0}, \mathbf{P_1})$, where the distributions $\mathbf{P_0}$, and $\mathbf{P_1}$ are as follows. Let $U_1, \ldots, U_q \leftarrow_\$ \{0,1\}^n \setminus \{0^n\}$ and $X_1 := V_1 \oplus V_2, \ldots, X_q := V_{2q-1} \oplus V_{2q}$, where $V_1, \ldots, V_{2q} \leftarrow_{\mathrm{wor}} \{0,1\}^n$. Then $\mathbf{P_0}$ and $\mathbf{P_1}$ denote the distributions of $U := (U_1, \ldots, U_q)$ and $X := (X_1, \ldots, X_q)$, respectively. Here, the χ^2-method is applied to show that

$$d_{\mathrm{TV}}(\mathbf{P_0}, \mathbf{P_1}) \leq 3\left(\frac{q}{N}\right)^{\frac{3}{2}}.$$

Then, the upper bound on $\mathbf{Adv}_{\mathrm{XOR}}^{\mathrm{prf}}(\mathcal{A})$ follows by a triangle inequality on the distributions $\mathbf{P_0}$, $\mathbf{P_1}$, and the output distribution of the random function. Now, for every non-zero $x_1, \ldots, x_i$, we clearly have $\mathbf{P}_{\mathbf{0}|x^{i-1}}(x_i) = 1/(N-1)$. For simplicity, let us denote by $Y_{i,x}$ the conditional probability $\mathbf{P}_{\mathbf{1}|x^{i-1}}(x)$, which is also a function over x^{i-1}. When x^{i-1} is chosen following the distribution of X^{i-1}, we denote $Y_{i,x}$ as $Y_{i,x}$ From the definition of the χ^2-function corresponding to $(\mathsf{V}_1, \ldots, \mathsf{V}_q)$ and $(\mathsf{U}_1, \ldots, \mathsf{U}_q)$, we have

$$\chi^2(\mathsf{X}^{i-1}) = \sum_{x \neq 0^n} (N-1) \cdot \left(Y_{i,x} - \frac{1}{N-1} \right)^2. \qquad [14.8]$$

Similarly, let $\mathsf{W}_{i,x}$ denote the random variable $\mathbf{Pr}\left(\{\}\mathsf{X}_i = x \mid \mathsf{V}_1, \ldots, \mathsf{V}_{2i-2}\right)$ (i.e. $\mathsf{W}_{i,x}$ is a random variable that depends on $\mathsf{V}_1, \ldots, \mathsf{V}_{2i-2}$). Then by Jensen's inequality (see Dai et al. (2017) for details), it follows that

$$\mathbf{Ex}\left(\left(Y_{i,x} - \frac{1}{N-1} \right)^2 \right) \leq \mathbf{Ex}\left(\left(\mathsf{W}_{i,x} - \frac{1}{N-1} \right)^2 \right).$$

Now, denoting by S the set $\{\mathsf{V}_1, \ldots, \mathsf{V}_{2i-2}\}$, letting $\mathsf{D}_{i,x} = \{u \in \{0,1\}^n | u, u \oplus x \in \mathsf{S}\}$, and by using principle of inclusion and exclusion, we have

$$\mathsf{W}_{i,x} = \frac{N - 4(i-1) + \mathsf{D}_{i,x}}{(N - 2i + 1)(N - 2i + 2)}. \qquad [14.9]$$

After some algebraic manipulation, it can be shown that

$$\mathbf{Ex}(\chi^2(\mathsf{X}^{i-1})) \leq \sum_{x \neq 0^n} N \cdot \mathbf{Ex}\left(\left(\mathsf{W}_{i,x} - \frac{1}{N-1} \right)^2 \right) \qquad [14.10]$$

$$\leq \sum_{x \neq 0^n} \frac{12(i-1)^2}{N^5} + \frac{3}{N^3} \cdot \mathbf{Ex}\left(\left(\mathsf{D}_{i,x} - \frac{4(i-1)^2}{N} \right)^2 \right). \qquad [14.11]$$

Here, note that $\mathsf{D}_{i,x}$ is a function of $\mathsf{V}_1, \mathsf{V}_2, \ldots, \mathsf{V}_{2i-2}$, and the expectation is taken over the choices of $\mathsf{V}_1, \mathsf{V}_2, \ldots, \mathsf{V}_{2i-2}$ sampled uniformly without replacement from $\{0,1\}^n$. Next, for any $x \in \{0,1\}^n \setminus \{0^n\}$, it can be shown that

$$\mathbf{Ex}\left(\left(\mathsf{D}_{i,x} - \frac{4(i-1)^2}{N} \right)^2 \right) \leq \frac{16(i-1)^2}{N}.$$

Entering this value in equation [14.11] for $n \geq 8$ yields

$$\mathbf{Ex}(\chi^2(\mathsf{X}^{i-1})) \leq \frac{54(i-1)^2}{N^3}.$$

Finally, by the χ^2-method (see equation [14.1]), the obtained bound is

$$d_{\mathrm{TV}}(\mathbf{P_0}, \mathbf{P_1}) \leq \left(\frac{1}{2} \sum_{i=1}^{q} \mathbf{Ex}(\chi^2(\mathsf{X}^{i-1})) \right)^{\frac{1}{2}}$$

$$\leq 3 \left(\frac{q}{N} \right)^{\frac{3}{2}}. \qquad \square$$

14.5. Other applications of the chi-squared method

1) In Mennink (2019), the author studies a generalized truncation function. More precisely, the function is given by

$$\mathsf{GTrunc}^P(x) = \mathsf{post}(x, \mathsf{RP}_n(x)),$$

where $\mathsf{post} : \{0,1\}^n \times \{0,1\}^n \mapsto \{0,1\}^m$ is a post-processing function. Here, it may be noted that the post-processing function post takes the input (to the construction) as one of its inputs. When post is balanced (i.e. when each point in its image has the same number of preimages), the author proves the following bound:

THEOREM 14.2 (Mennink (2019)).– For any adversary $\mathcal{A}$ making at most q queries, we have

$$\mathbf{Adv}_{\mathsf{GTrunc}}^{\mathrm{prf}}(\mathcal{A}) \leq \frac{1}{2} \left(\frac{(2^m - 1)q(q-1)}{(2^n - 1)(2^n - q + 1)} \right)^{\frac{1}{2}}.$$

A similar type of bound was also shown for the case when post is not balanced.

2) In Chen et al. (2017), the authors introduced a length doubling construction[1] using tweakable block ciphers, that is, LDT. They showed birthday bound (i.e. $\frac{n}{2}$-bit) security of the construction. They also gave an attack in $2^{n-\frac{s}{2}}$ queries, where s is a parameter of the construction. In Chen et al. (2018), the authors used the χ^2-method to show that the construction, in fact, achieves beyond birthday bound security under certain conditions; the achieved security level goes up to $\frac{2n}{3}$-bit. Further, they showed that three-round LDT (the original LDT construction of Chen et al. (2017) is composed of two rounds) achieves n-bit security under certain conditions.

---

1 An enciphering scheme that can encrypt any bit string of length $[n \ldots 2n - 1]$ as opposed to the ordinary block cipher that can encrypt a fixed length (n) string.

14.6. Acknowledgments

The major part of the chapter is based on Bhattacharya and Nandi (2018).

14.7. References

Bellare, M. and Impagliazzo, R. (1999). A tool for obtaining tighter security analyses of pseudorandom function based constructions, with applications to PRP to PRF conversion. *IACR Cryptology ePrint Archive*, 1999, 24.

Bhattacharya, S. and Nandi, M. (2018). A note on the chi-square method: A tool for proving cryptographic security. *Cryptogr. Commun.*, 10(5), 935–957.

Chen, Y.L., Luykx, A., Mennink, B., Preneel, B. (2017). Efficient length doubling from tweakable block ciphers. *IACR Trans. Symmetric Cryptol.*, 2017(3), 253–270.

Chen, Y.L., Mennink, B., Nandi, M. (2018). Short variable length domain extenders with beyond birthday bound security. In *ASIACRYPT 2018, Part I*, vol. 11272 of *Lecture Notes in Computer Science*, Peyrin, T., Galbraith, S.D. (eds). Springer.

Cogliati, B. and Seurin, Y. (2016). EWCDM: An efficient, beyond-birthday secure, nonce-misuse resistant MAC. In *CRYPTO 2016, Part I*, vol. 9814 of *Lecture Notes in Computer Science*, Robshaw, M., Katz, J. (eds). Springer.

Dai, W., Hoang, V.T., Tessaro, S. (2017). Information-theoretic indistinguishability via the chi-squared method. *Lecture Notes in Computer Science*, Katz, J., Shacham, H. (eds), Springer, 10403, 497–523.

Gilboa, S. and Gueron, S. (2015). Distinguishing a truncated random permutation from a random function. *IACR Cryptology ePrint Archive*, 2015, 773.

Gilboa, S. and Gueron, S. (2016). The advantage of truncated permutations. *CoRR* [Online]. Available at: http://arxiv.org/abs/1610.02518.

Gilboa, S., Gueron, S., Morris, B. (2018). How many queries are needed to distinguish a truncated random permutation from a random function? *J. Cryptol.*, 31(1), 162–171.

Hall, C., Wagner, D.A., Kelsey, J., Schneier, B. (1998). Building PRFs from PRPs. In *CRYPTO '98*, vol. 1462 of *Lecture Notes in Computer Science*, Krawczyk, H. (ed.). Springer.

Liese, F. and Vajda, I. (1987). *Convex Statistical Distances*. Teubner.

Lucks, S. (2000). The sum of PRPs is a secure PRF. In *EUROCRYPT 2000*, vol. 1807 of *Lecture Notes in Computer Science*, Preneel, B. (ed.). Springer.

Mennink, B. (2019). Linking Stam's bounds with generalized truncation. In *CT-RSA 2019*, vol. 11405 of *Lecture Notes in Computer Science*, Matsui, M. (ed.). Springer.

Mennink, B. and Neves, S. (2017). Encrypted Davies-Meyer and its dual: Towards optimal security using mirror theory. In *CRYPTO 2017, Part III*, vol. 10403 of *Lecture Notes in Computer Science*, Katz, J., Shacham, H. (eds). Springer.

Patarin, J. (2008). A proof of security in $o(2^n)$ for the Xor of two random permutations. In *ICITS 2008*, vol. 5155 of *Lecture Notes in Computer Science*, Safavi-Naini, R. (ed.). Springer.

Patarin, J. (2010). Introduction to mirror theory: Analysis of systems of linear equalities and linear non equalities for cryptography [Online]. Available at: http://eprint.iacr.org/2010/287.

Stam, A.J. (1978). Distance between sampling with and without replacement. *Statistica Neerlandica*, 32(2), 81–91.

PART 3

Appendices

Appendix 1

Data Encryption Standard (DES)

Christina Boura

University of Paris-Saclay, UVSQ, CNRS, Versailles, France

The goal of this chapter is to provide the specifications of some of the most well-known symmetric primitives. The four algorithms presented here, three block ciphers (DES, AES, Present) and one hash function (Keccak/SHA-3), are mentioned in different chapters of this book and their specifications are thus given here for completeness. We start by describing the block cipher DES. This algorithm is now deprecated and should not be used any more, but its design influenced many succeeding ciphers and inspired what should soon become some of the most important attacks against block ciphers. The other three algorithms to be described next are all actual standards.

DES was first published in 1975. This algorithm, developed internally at IBM during the period 1973–1974, was based on an initial design by Horst Feistel that was called *Lucifer*. After modifications made to this first version (notably by the NSA), DES became a federal standard in August 1976 and was published as FIPS PUB 46 in January 1977 (National Institute of Standards and Technology 1977). DES encrypts and decrypts blocks of 64 bits by using a 56-bit key. The cipher follows a classical Feistel structure (see Chapter 3) and iterates a round function 16 times. The bits are labeled from 1 (leftmost bit) to 64 (rightmost bit). Even if today we tend to label bits starting from 0, we will follow here, for historical reasons, the original specification of DES, as given in the original FIPS documentation (National Institute of Standards and Technology 1977).

A1.1. Initial and final permutations

An initial bitwise permutation IP of the 64-bit input block is applied before encryption starts. To maintain the convenient property of Feistel ciphers that the encryption circuit can be used for decryption, the inverse permutation IP^{-1} is applied to the state just before outputting the ciphertext. The permutation IP and its inverse are given in Table A1.1. This table indicates that the first bit (bit 1) after the permutation will contain the content of bit 58 before the permutation. In the same way, the second bit (bit 2) will contain the bit 50 and the last bit (bit 64) will contain the content of bit 7.

IP									FP							
58	50	42	34	26	18	10	2		40	8	48	16	56	24	64	32
60	52	44	36	28	20	12	4		39	7	47	15	55	23	63	31
62	54	46	38	30	22	14	6		38	6	46	14	54	22	62	30
64	56	48	40	32	24	16	8		37	5	45	13	53	21	61	29
57	49	41	33	25	17	9	1		36	4	44	12	52	20	60	28
59	51	43	35	27	19	11	3		35	3	43	11	51	19	59	27
61	53	45	37	29	21	13	5		34	2	42	10	50	18	58	26
63	55	47	39	31	23	15	7		33	1	41	9	49	17	57	25

Table A1.1. *The permutation IP (on the left) and its inverse FP (on the right)*

A1.2. Round function of DES

After the application of the initial permutation IP, the 64-bit block is divided into two 32-bit halves: a left half L_0 and a right half R_0. The same round function is then iterated 16 times. The datapath of the computation is depicted in Figure A1.2. At round i, $1 \leq i \leq 16$, a function f takes as input the 32-bit right half of the state R_{i-1} together with the 48-bit subkey K_i and produces a 32-bit output that is then XORed to the 32-bit left half L_{i-1}. The right and left branches are then swapped:

$$L_i = R_{i-1}$$
$$R_i = L_{i-1} \oplus f(R_{i-1}, K_i),$$

for $1 \leq i \leq 16$. The preoutput block, input to the FP permutation, is $R_{16}||L_{16}$.

A1.2.1. The function f

The function f takes as input at round i a 32-bit value R_{i-1} and a 48-bit subkey K_i. The following transformations (see Figure A1.2) are then applied:

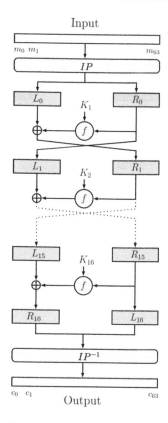

Figure A1.1. DES *encryption*

1) The first operation of f is the application of a bitwise expansion E to the value R_{i-1}. The goal of this application is the expansion of the 32-bit value R_{i-1} to a 48-bit intermediate value. This is done by duplicating 16 of the input bits so that they appear twice in the output. The action of E can be represented by the left part in Table A1.2. This table should be read in the same way as the tables for IP and FP. For example, we can see that the first 3 bits of the intermediate 48-bit register after the application of E will contain the bits 32, 1 and 2 before the application.

2) The generated 48-bit output after the application of E is XORed with the 48-bit subkey K_i.

3) The 48-bit result of the above operation is then divided into eight 6-bit words, and a different S-box is applied to each word. The eight different S-boxes, denoted by $S_1, S_2, \ldots, S_8$ are given in Table A1.3. Each S-box takes as input 6 bits and outputs 4 bits. By concatenating the outputs of all the S-boxes, we get a 32-bit intermediate value.

4) A bit-permutation P is finally applied to the 32-bit output of the previous step. This permutation is given in Table A1.2 and should be interpreted as all previously given tables.

E					
32	1	2	3	4	5
4	5	6	7	8	9
8	9	10	11	12	13
12	13	14	15	16	17
16	17	18	19	20	21
20	21	22	23	24	25
24	25	26	27	28	29
28	29	30	31	32	1

P			
16	7	20	21
29	12	28	17
1	15	23	26
5	18	31	10
2	8	24	14
32	27	3	9
19	13	30	6
22	11	4	25

Table A1.2. *E Bit-selection table (on the left) and permutation P (on the right)*

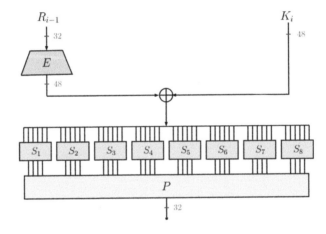

Figure A1.2. *Function f used in DES*

S-boxes: the eight S-boxes of DES are very important for the security of DES as they are the only nonlinear components of the cipher. The S-boxes finally used in DES were chosen by the NSA and were different than those presented in the first version of the algorithm. We know today that the S-boxes were notably manipulated in order for DES to resist the differential attack, 15 years before this attack was publicly discovered and published by Biham and Shamir. All S-boxes are different but have similar cryptographic properties (e.g. all of them are of algebraic degree 5). The eight S-boxes are described in Table A1.3. Each table should be interpreted in the following way. The 6-bit input to each S-box is split into two parts. First, the two outer bits, concatenated as a 2-bit value, are used to choose a row in the Table: (00 for row 0, 01 for row 1, 10 for row 2 and 11 for row 3). Then, the four inner bits are used to choose a column of the table. Let us take as example the S-box S_1 and suppose the input to the S-box is $(110101)_2$. The two outer bits 11 point to the row 3, while the four inner bits 1010 form the hexadecimal value a. Thus, the output is the hexadecimal value 3, or 0011 if seen in binary: $S_1[110101] = 0011$. It has to be noted that due to the action of E, the bits entering an S-box are shared among two neighboring S-boxes.

	0 1 2 3 4 5 6 7 8 9 a b c d e f		0 1 2 3 4 5 6 7 8 9 a b c d e f
	S_1		S_5
0	e 4 d 1 2 f b 8 3 a 6 c 5 9 0 7	0	2 c 4 1 7 a b 6 8 5 3 f d 0 e 9
1	0 f 7 4 e 2 d 1 a 6 c b 9 5 3 8	1	e b 2 c 4 7 d 1 5 0 f a 3 9 8 6
2	4 1 e 8 d 6 2 b f c 9 7 3 a 5 0	2	4 2 1 b a d 7 8 f 9 c 5 6 3 0 e
3	f c 8 2 4 9 1 7 5 b 3 e a 0 6 d	3	b 8 c 7 1 e 2 d 6 f 0 9 a 4 5 3
	S_2		S_6
0	f 1 8 e 6 b 3 4 9 7 2 d c 0 5 a	0	c 1 a f 9 2 6 8 0 d 3 4 e 7 5 b
1	3 d 4 7 f 2 8 e c 0 1 a 6 9 b 5	1	a f 4 2 7 c 9 5 6 1 d e 0 b 3 8
2	0 e 7 b a 4 d 1 5 8 c 6 9 3 2 f	2	9 e f 5 2 8 c 3 7 0 4 a 1 d b 6
3	d 8 a 1 3 f 4 2 b 6 7 c 0 5 e 9	3	4 3 2 c 9 5 f a b e 1 7 6 0 8 d
	S_3		S_7
0	a 0 9 e 6 3 f 5 1 d c 7 b 4 2 8	0	4 b 2 e f 0 8 d 3 c 9 7 5 a 6 1
1	d 7 0 9 3 4 6 a 2 8 5 e c b f 1	1	d 0 b 7 4 9 1 a e 3 5 c 2 f 8 6
2	d 6 4 9 8 f 3 0 b 1 2 c 5 a e 7	2	1 4 b d c 3 7 e a f 6 8 0 5 9 2
3	1 a d 0 6 9 8 7 4 f e 3 b 5 2 c	3	6 b d 8 1 4 a 7 9 5 0 f e 2 3 c
	S_4		S_8
0	7 d e 3 0 6 9 a 1 2 8 5 b c 4 f	0	d 2 8 4 6 f b 1 a 9 3 e 5 0 c 7
1	d 8 b 5 6 f 0 3 4 7 2 c 1 a e 9	1	1 f d 8 a 3 7 4 c 5 6 b 0 e 9 2
2	a 6 9 0 c b 7 d f 1 3 e 5 2 8 4	2	7 b 4 1 9 c e 2 0 6 a d f 3 5 8
3	3 f 0 6 a 1 d 8 9 4 5 b c 7 2 e	3	2 1 e 7 4 a 8 d f c 9 0 3 5 6 b

Table A1.3. *DES S-boxes*

A1.3. Key schedule of DES

This section describes the key schedule algorithm of DES. This algorithm takes as input the 56-bit master key K of DES and outputs the sixteen 48-bit round keys $K_1, \ldots, K_{16}$. The master key of DES contains 56 randomly generated bits, embedded into a 64-bit register. The remaining 8 bits of this register, in positions 8, 16, 24, ..., 64, are *parity bits*, meaning that the value of each of those bits is such that the parity of the corresponding byte (XOR of all bits inside the byte) is odd. This feature could for example be used to detect errors in key generation, transfer or storage.

The first operation inside the key schedule is the application of the bit-permutation *Permuted Choice 1* ($PC1$ for short), described in Table A1.4. We see notably from this table that the eight parity bits are ignored. The remaining 56 bits, after being permuted, are loaded into two 28-bit registers, C and D. The bits loaded in the register C are the ones corresponding to the four upmost rows of the table, while those loaded to D are the ones in the four remaining rows. Then, both registers C and D are rotated to the left by 1 or 2 positions. This number of rotation positions that depends on the round i, is denoted by r_i, $1 \leq i \leq 16$ and is given in Table A1.4. Finally, 48 bits are extracted by the registers C and D following a table known as *Permuted Choice 2* ($PC2$) and that it is also described in Table A1.4. For this, the registers C and D are concatenated as a unique 56-bit register $C||D$ and $PC2$ chooses 48 bits among $C||D$ to form the round subkey. For example, bit 1 of the round subkey K_i is the bit 14 of the register C, while the last bit of K_i is the bit 32 of $C||D$, that is bit 4 of register D.

PC1						
57	49	41	33	25	17	9
1	58	50	42	34	26	18
10	2	59	51	43	35	27
19	11	3	60	52	44	36
63	55	47	39	31	23	15
7	62	54	46	38	30	22
14	6	61	53	45	37	29
21	13	5	28	20	12	4

PC2					
14	17	11	24	1	5
3	28	15	6	21	10
23	19	12	4	26	8
16	7	27	20	13	2
41	52	31	37	47	55
30	40	51	45	33	48
44	49	39	56	34	53
46	42	50	36	29	32

round	1	2	3	4	5	6	7	8	9	10	11	12	13	14	15	16
r_i	1	1	2	2	2	2	2	2	1	2	2	2	2	2	2	1

Table A1.4. *Permutations PC1 and PC2. The last table contains the round-dependent constants r_i*

We conclude this section with a summary of the most important cryptanalysis results against DES.

A1.4. Best attacks against DES

The invention of the differential cryptanalysis by Biham and Shamir (1990) in the 1990 permitted to break all 16 rounds of DES. This attack, although having a particularly low time complexity, was not implemented because of the relatively high number of chosen plaintext/ciphertext pairs needed for its execution. The invention of linear cryptanalysis by Tardy-Corfdir and Gilbert (1991) and Matsui (1993) permitted to Matsui to mount a practical key-recovery attack against DES and to recover the secret key after a few days of computation (Matsui 1994). Since these cryptanalysis results, DES was considered as broken and successful brute force attacks between 1997 and 1999 demonstrated that the key-length of DES started to be too short for current machines. Some improvements and refinements of the seminal linear attack on DES appeared after 2000. All these attacks are summarized in Table A1.5.

Year	Cryptanalysis	Data	Time	Attack Scenario	Reference
1990	Differential	2^{47}	2^{37}	Chosen Plaintext	(Biham and Shamir 1990)
1994	Linear	2^{43}	2^{43}	Known Plaintext	(Matsui 1994)
2001	Linear	2^{43}	2^{41}	Known Plaintext	(Junod 2001)
2017	Multiple linear	$2^{42.78}$	$2^{38.86}$	Known Plaintext	(Bogdanov and Vejre 2017)
2017	Multiple linear	2^{41}	$2^{49.76}$	Known Plaintext	(Bogdanov and Vejre 2017)

Table A1.5. *All known cryptanalysis results against full DES*

Withdrawal: in the late 1990s, many practical demonstrations showed that the key-length of DES was way too short for new machines, but the standard was officially withdrawn only in 2004. In 2018, the NIST also deprecated 3DES for all new applications. Its usage should be disallowed after 2023.

A1.5. References

Biham, E. and Shamir, A. (1990). Differential cryptanalysis of DES-like cryptosystems. In *CRYPTO '90*, vol. 537 of *Lecture Notes in Computer Science*, Menezes, A., Vanstone, S.A. (eds). Springer.

Bogdanov, A. and Vejre, P.S. (2017). Linear cryptanalysis of DES with asymmetries. In *ASIACRYPT 2017, Part I*, vol. 10624 of *Lecture Notes in Computer Science*, Takagi, T., Peyrin, T. (eds). Springer.

Junod, P. (2001). On the complexity of Matsui's attack. In *SAC 2001*, vol. 2259 of *Lecture Notes in Computer Science*, Vaudenay, S., Youssef, A.M. (eds). Springer.

Matsui, M. (1993). Linear cryptanalysis method for DES cipher. In *EUROCRYPT '93*, vol. 765 of *Lecture Notes in Computer Science*, Helleseth, T. (ed.). Springer.

Matsui, M. (1994). The first experimental cryptanalysis of the data encryption standard. In *CRYPTO '94*, vol. 839 of *Lecture Notes in Computer Science*, Desmedt, Y. (ed.). Springer.

National Institute of Standards and Technology (1977). Data encryption standard. Federal Information Processing Standard (FIPS), Publication 46 [Online]. Available at: https://csrc.nist.gov/csrc/media/publications/fips/46/3/archive/1999-10-25/documents/fips46-3.pdf.

Tardy-Corfdir, A. and Gilbert, H. (1991). A known plaintext attack of FEAL-4 and FEAL-6. In *CRYPTO '91*, vol. 576 of *Lecture Notes in Computer Science*, Feigenbaum, J. (ed.) Springer.

Appendix 2

Advanced Encryption Standard (AES)

Christina Boura[1] and Orr Dunkelman[2]
[1]University of Paris-Saclay, UVSQ, CNRS, Versailles, France
[2]Computer Science Department, University of Haifa, Israel

In the mid-1990s and after the success of several brute-force efforts against DES, it became clear that a new symmetric cipher was needed to replace the old standard. Between 1997 and 2000, the American National Institute of Standards and Technology (NIST) organized a public competition with the goal to replace DES by a new secure block cipher. The candidate designs to this competition should have a publicly available and royalty-free design, support keys of 128, 192 and 256 bits and offer at minimum a security level equal to that of the two-key triple-DES.

In total, 15 designs were accepted for the first round of the competition and five among them were selected in August 1999 for the final phase. On October 2, 2000, the NIST announced that RIJNDAEL, a block cipher designed by Joan Daemen and Vincent Rijmen won the competition and should become the advanced encryption standard (AES).

We offer in this section a description of this standard. We alert the reader that this is a concise description, and thus, we do not give here the full design criteria (some of which were discussed in Chapter 3). A more detailed description of both the cipher's specifications and its design criteria can for example be found in Knudsen and Robshaw (2011). Furthermore, we forewarn the reader that implementing AES is indeed a straightforward matter, but building a secure and efficient implementation may not be as trivial as one would expect from the simple description. We encourage readers to familiarize themselves with constant-time implementations of AES before pursuing such efforts.

A2.1. Finite field arithmetic

Understanding arithmetic in the finite field $\mathbb{F}_{2^n}$ is essential for computing with the AES. The AES is a byte-oriented design, and its state can be seen as a 4×4 matrix of bytes. Each byte can be represented as a binary vector $(a_7, a_6, a_5, a_4, a_3, a_2, a_1, a_0)$ (the rightmost bit is the least significant one) or can alternatively been expressed as a polynomial of degree 7 in the variable X:

$$a_7 X^7 + a_6 X^6 + a_5 X^5 + a_4 X^4 + a_3 X^3 + a_2 X^2 + a_1 X + a_0.$$

This polynomial representation is very convenient for doing mathematical operations, notably the operations of addition and multiplication.

A2.1.1. *Addition*

To add two bytes $a = (a_7, a_6, \ldots, a_0)$ and $b = (b_7, b_6, \ldots, b_0)$, we add the two corresponding polynomials:

$$a_7 X^7 + a_6 X^6 + a_5 X^5 + a_4 X^4 + a_3 X^3 + a_2 X^2 + a_1 X + a_0$$
$$+ b_7 X^7 + b_6 X^6 + b_5 X^5 + b_4 X^4 + b_3 X^3 + b_2 X^2 + b_1 X + b_0$$
$$= (a_7 \oplus b_7) X^7 + (a_6 \oplus b_6) X^6 + (a_5 \oplus b_5) X^5 + (a_4 \oplus b_4) X^4$$
$$+ (a_3 \oplus b_3) X^3 + (a_2 \oplus b_2) X^2 + (a_1 \oplus b_1) X + (a_0 \oplus b_0).$$

Thus, the result of the addition operation is the XOR between the corresponding bits in the two binary representations:

$$(a_7 \oplus b_7, a_6 \oplus b_6, a_5 \oplus b_5, a_4 \oplus b_4, a_3 \oplus b_3, a_2 \oplus b_2, a_1 \oplus b_1, a_0 \oplus b_0).$$

A2.1.2. *Multiplication*

Multiplication is a slightly more complex operation. When multiplying two polynomials of degree 7, the degree of the resulting polynomial will potentially be higher than the degrees of the input polynomials. For this reason, we need to reduce the product polynomial back to a degree at most 7 with the help of an irreducible polynomial R_p. For AES, this polynomial equals:

$$R_p = X^8 + X^4 + X^3 + X + 1,$$

and is better known as the *Rijndael polynomial*.

EXAMPLE.– [Multiplying two bytes] Suppose we want to multiply the polynomials $X^5 + X^3 + X + 1$ and $X^3 + X^2$, corresponding to the byte values 0x2b and 0x0c, respectively. The computation is done as follows:

$$
\begin{aligned}
(X^5 &+ X^3 + X + 1)(X^3 + X^2) \\
&= X^8 + X^7 + X^6 + X^5 + X^4 + X^3 + X^3 + X^2 \\
&= (X^4 + X^3 + X + 1) + X^7 + X^6 + X^5 + X^4 + X^2 \quad \bmod R_p \\
&= X^7 + X^6 + X^5 + X^3 + X^2 + X + 1,
\end{aligned}
$$

and this result corresponds to the byte value 0xef. As one can see, the monomial X^8 in the second row is replaced by $X^4 + X^3 + X + 1$, because $X^8 \equiv X^4 + X^3 + X + 1$ mod R_p.

A2.2. Round function of AES

The AES (Daemen and Rijmen 2020) is a substitution-permutation network, which has 128-bit plaintexts and 128-, 192-, or 256-bit keys. The internal state is treated as a byte matrix $(s_{i,j})$, $0 \le i, j < 4$, of size 4×4, where each byte represents a value in $\mathbb{F}_{2^8}$:

$s_{0,0}$	$s_{0,1}$	$s_{0,2}$	$s_{0,3}$
$s_{1,0}$	$s_{1,1}$	$s_{1,2}$	$s_{1,3}$
$s_{2,0}$	$s_{2,1}$	$s_{2,2}$	$s_{2,3}$
$s_{3,0}$	$s_{3,1}$	$s_{3,2}$	$s_{3,3}$

Figure A2.1. AES *state representation*

An AES round applies the following four operations to this state matrix: SubBytes (SB), ShiftRows (SR), MixColumns (MC) and AddRoundKey (ARK).

A2.2.1. SubBytes (SB)

This operation applies the same 8-bit to 8-bit invertible S-box 16 times in parallel on each byte of the state. This S-box is based on the inversion operation over the field $\mathbb{F}_{2^8}$, and is inspired by the work of Knudsen and Nyberg in proving security against differential and linear cryptanalysis. More precisely, for an input byte x,

$$S(x) = L \cdot x^{(-1)} + c,$$

where L is the 8×8 $\mathbb{F}_2$-matrix

$$L = \begin{pmatrix} 1 & 0 & 0 & 0 & 1 & 1 & 1 & 1 \\ 1 & 1 & 0 & 0 & 0 & 1 & 1 & 1 \\ 1 & 1 & 1 & 0 & 0 & 0 & 1 & 1 \\ 1 & 1 & 1 & 1 & 0 & 0 & 0 & 1 \\ 1 & 1 & 1 & 1 & 1 & 0 & 0 & 0 \\ 0 & 1 & 1 & 1 & 1 & 1 & 0 & 0 \\ 0 & 0 & 1 & 1 & 1 & 1 & 1 & 0 \\ 0 & 0 & 0 & 1 & 1 & 1 & 1 & 1 \end{pmatrix},$$

c is the constant 01100011 = 0x63, and $x^{(-1)}$ is the modified inversion operation in $\mathbb{F}_{2^8}$, corresponding to the multiplicative inversion for all $x \neq 0$ and for which we set $x^{-1}(0) \triangleq 0$. The table representation of this S-box is given in Table A2.1 From this table, we have for example that the image of 0x1a by the S-box is 0xa2 as this is the value in the intersection of the row 0x10 and the column 0x0a.

A2.2.2. ShiftRows (SR)

This operation cyclically shifts the ith row by i bytes to the left, where 0 is the upmost row and 3 is the row in the bottom, as seen in Figure A2.2.

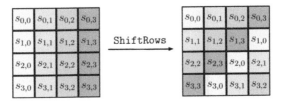

Figure A2.2. *The ShiftRows operation*

	00	01	02	03	04	05	06	07	08	09	0a	0b	0c	0d	0e	0f
00	63	7c	77	7b	f2	6b	6f	c5	30	01	67	2b	fe	d7	ab	76
10	ca	82	c9	7d	fa	59	47	f0	ad	d4	a2	af	9c	a4	72	c0
20	b7	fd	93	26	36	3f	f7	cc	34	a5	e5	f1	71	d8	31	15
30	04	c7	23	c3	18	96	05	9a	07	12	80	e2	eb	27	b2	75
40	09	83	2c	1a	1b	6e	5a	a0	52	3b	d6	b3	29	e3	2f	84
50	53	d1	00	ed	20	fc	b1	5b	6a	cb	be	39	4a	4c	58	cf
60	d0	ef	aa	fb	43	4d	33	85	45	f9	02	7f	50	3c	9f	a8
70	51	a3	40	8f	92	9d	38	f5	bc	b6	da	21	10	ff	f3	d2
80	cd	0c	13	ec	5f	97	44	17	c4	a7	7e	3d	64	5d	19	73
90	60	81	4f	dc	22	2a	90	88	46	ee	b8	14	de	5e	0b	db
a0	e0	32	3a	0a	49	06	24	5c	c2	d3	ac	62	91	95	e4	79
b0	e7	c8	37	6d	8d	d5	4e	a9	6c	56	f4	ea	65	7a	ae	08
c0	ba	78	25	2e	1c	a6	b4	c6	e8	dd	74	1f	4b	bd	8b	8a
d0	70	3e	b5	66	48	03	f6	0e	61	35	57	b9	86	c1	1d	9e
e0	e1	f8	98	11	69	d9	8e	94	9b	1e	87	e9	ce	55	28	df
f0	8c	a1	89	0d	bf	e6	42	68	41	99	2d	0f	b0	54	bb	16

Table A2.1. *The AES S-box*

A2.2.3. MixColumns (MC)

This operation consists of a multiplication of each column by a constant 4×4 matrix over the field $GF(2^8)$. This matrix is usually written as (see also Chapter 7):

$$M_{\text{AES}} = \begin{pmatrix} 2 & 3 & 1 & 1 \\ 1 & 2 & 3 & 1 \\ 1 & 1 & 2 & 3 \\ 3 & 1 & 1 & 2 \end{pmatrix},$$

where 1, 2 and 1 represent elements of the finite field $\mathbb{F}_{2^8}$, using an hexadecimal notation for the bitwise representation of finite fields elements. More precisely, 2 and 3 denote elements α and $\alpha \oplus 1$, respectively, with α a root of the Rijndael polynomial R_p.

The ShiftRows and the MixColumns operations are the ones that constitute the linear diffusion layer.

A2.2.4. AddRoundKey (ARK)

During this last operation, the state is XORed with a 128-bit subkey produced by the key schedule algorithm.

An additional AddRoundKey operation is applied before the first round (as otherwise the first round can be easily computed, even without the knowledge of the secret key). In the last round, the `MixColumns` operation is omitted (as its impact on security is negligible, and it helps making the decryption similar to the encryption).

The number of rounds Nr in AES depends on the key length: 10 rounds for 128-bit keys, 12 rounds for 192-bit keys and 14 rounds for 256-bit keys. The rounds are numbered $0, \ldots, Nr - 1$.

A computation example for one round of AES can be visualized in Figure A2.3.

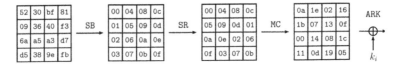

Figure A2.3. *Example of computation of an* AES *round*

A2.3. Key schedule of AES

The key schedule of AES transforms the Nk-word key[1] into $Nr + 1$ 128-bit subkeys. We denote the subkey array by $W[0, \ldots, 4 \cdot Nr + 3]$, where each word of $W[\cdot]$ consists of 32 bits. The length of the key is Nk 32-bit words, the user supplied key is loaded into the first Nk words of $W[\cdot]$, and the remaining words of $W[\cdot]$ are updated according to the following rule:

– For $i = Nk, \ldots, 4 \cdot Nr + 3$, do

- if $i \equiv 0 \bmod Nk$ then $W[i] = W[i - Nk] \oplus \mathrm{SB}(W[i - 1] \lll 8) \oplus RCON[i/Nk]$,

- else if $Nk = 8$ and $i \equiv 4 \bmod 8$ then $W[i] = W[i - 8] \oplus \mathrm{SB}(W[i - 1])$,

- otherwise $W[i] = W[i - 1] \oplus W[i - Nk]$,

where $\lll$ denotes rotation of the word by 8 bits to the left, and $RCON[\cdot]$ is a 32-bit array of predetermined constants, given in the form $RCON[i] = [rc_i, 00, 00, 00]$, where rc_i is a byte whose value in hexadecimal notation is given in Table A2.2.

The key schedule of AES-128 is graphically depicted in Figure A2.4, while those of AES-192 and AES-256 are illustrated in Figures A2.5 and A2.6, respectively.

---

1 We adopt the original description of AES, even if it is somewhat confusing. The key schedule treats the key as Nk words of 32 bits each, i.e., $Nk = 4$ for AES with 128-bit keys, $Nk = 6$ for 192-bit keys, and $Nk = 8$ for 256-bit keys.

i	1	2	3	4	5	6	7	8	9	10
rc_i	01	02	04	08	10	20	40	80	1b	36

Table A2.2. *The constants rc_i, for $i = 1, \ldots, 10$.*

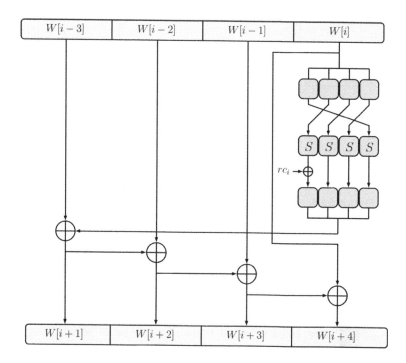

Figure A2.4. *The key schedule of* AES-128. *For a color version of this figure, see www.iste.co.uk/boura/symmetric1.zip*

A2.4. Decryption with the AES

For decrypting with AES, the inverse operation of all implied transformations must be specified. First, for the SUBBYTES step, the inverse S-box of the one used for encryption must be applied. This inverse S-box is given in Table A2.3.

Next, one will need the inverse of the MDS matrix given in section A2.2. The inverse of this matrix is

$$M_{\text{AES}}^{-1} = \begin{pmatrix} e & b & d & 9 \\ 9 & e & b & d \\ d & 9 & e & b \\ b & d & 9 & e \end{pmatrix}.$$

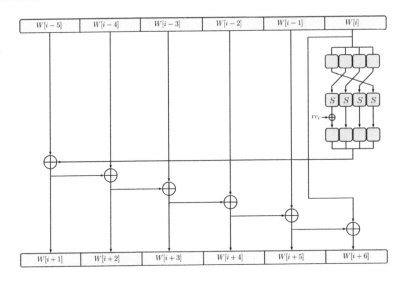

Figure A2.5. *The key schedule of* AES-192. *For a color version of this figure, see www.iste.co.uk/boura/symmetric1.zip*

	00	01	02	03	04	05	06	07	08	09	0a	0b	0c	0d	0e	0f
00	52	09	6a	d5	30	36	a5	38	bf	40	a3	9e	81	f3	d7	fb
10	7c	e3	39	82	9b	2f	ff	87	34	8e	43	44	c4	de	e9	cb
20	54	7b	94	32	a6	c2	23	3d	ee	4c	95	0b	42	fa	c3	4e
30	08	2e	a1	66	28	d9	24	b2	76	5b	a2	49	6d	8b	d1	25
40	72	f8	f6	64	86	68	98	16	d4	a4	5c	cc	5d	65	b6	92
50	6c	70	48	50	fd	ed	b9	da	5e	15	46	57	a7	8d	9d	84
60	90	d8	ab	00	8c	bc	d3	0a	f7	e4	58	05	b8	b3	45	06
70	d0	2c	1e	8f	ca	3f	0f	02	c1	af	bd	03	01	13	8a	6b
80	3a	91	11	41	4f	67	dc	ea	97	f2	cf	ce	f0	b4	e6	73
90	96	ac	74	22	e7	ad	35	85	e2	f9	37	e8	1c	75	df	6e
a0	47	f1	1a	71	1d	29	c5	89	6f	b7	62	0e	aa	18	be	1b
b0	fc	56	3e	4b	c6	d2	79	20	9a	db	c0	fe	78	cd	5a	f4
c0	1f	dd	a8	33	88	07	c7	31	b1	12	10	59	27	80	ec	5f
d0	60	51	7f	a9	19	b5	4a	0d	2d	e5	7a	9f	93	c9	9c	ef
e0	a0	e0	3b	4d	ae	2a	f5	b0	c8	eb	bb	3c	83	53	99	61
f0	17	2b	04	7e	ba	77	d6	26	e1	69	14	63	55	21	0c	7d

Table A2.3. *The inverse of the AES S-box*

Finally, for the SHIFTROWS operation, each row has to be rotated in the opposite direction by the same offset, as shown in Figure A2.7.

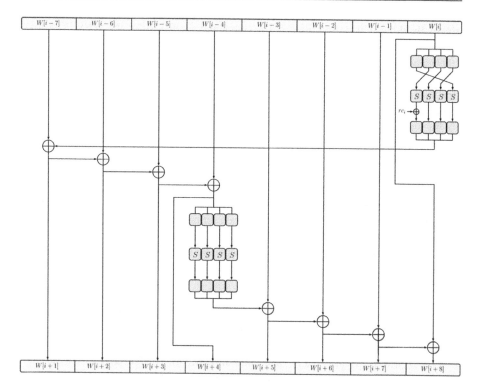

Figure A2.6. *The key schedule of* AES-256. *For a color version of this figure, see www.iste.co.uk/boura/symmetric1.zip*

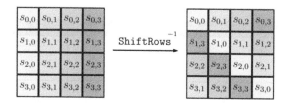

Figure A2.7. *The inverse of the* ShiftRows *operation. For a color version of this figure, see www.iste.co.uk/boura/symmetric1.zip*

A2.5. Best attacks against the AES

The AES is probably the most well-studied and widely deployed symmetric-key cipher. Understanding its security is therefore crucial. Since the introduction of RIJNDAEL and AES, reduced-round variants were analyzed using multiple cryptanalytic methods, even if the progress has been slow. There have been principally three major directions in the cryptanalysis history of the AES. The first line of research was developed around the square attack introduced in Daemen et al. (1997) and further explored in Ferguson et al. (2000). Then, Gilbert and Minier developed further the idea of square attacks to present a 7-round collision attack on AES Gilbert and Minier (2000). This attack had a complexity of 2^{32} chosen plaintexts, a memory complexity of 2^{80} and a time complexity of $2^{146.3}$ for the 192-bit and 256-bit versions. The idea behind the Gilbert-Minier attack was then generalized by Demirci and Selçuk (2008) by using meet-in-the-middle (MITM) techniques. MITM attacks are considered today as an important direction in AES cryptanalysis (Dunkelman et al. 2010; Derbez and Fouque 2013; Derbez et al. 2013; Bonnetain et al. 2019). Finally, a third important analysis direction is impossible differential cryptanalysis. The first results in this line of research are due to Biham and Keller (2000). These first results were then refined and improved in a long series of articles (Lu et al. 2008; Mala et al. 2010; Boura et al. 2018; Leurent and Pernot 2021). Impossible differential attacks managed notably to break seven rounds of AES-128, while MITM attacks permitted to reach up to eight rounds for AES-192 and up to nine rounds for AES-256.

In 2018, Bar-On et al. (2018) provided low data and memory complexity attacks against five, six and seven rounds of AES, with interesting results on the 192 and 256-bit versions. These attacks improved and refined the multiple-of-8 property (Grassi et al. 2017) and the mixture of differential cryptanalysis technique (Grassi 2018), new cryptanalysis methods introduced by Grassi et al. The techniques of Bar-On et al. (2018) permitted among others to improve the data and memory complexity of the Gilbert and Minier attack. Finally, in 2020, Dunkelman et al. (2020) provided a five-round attack against AES with a key recovery complexity of only $2^{16.5}$.

Version	# Rounds	Cryptanalysis	Data	Time	Memory	Reference
	MITM	7	2^{97}	2^{99}	2^{98}	(Derbez et al. 2013)
128	MITM	7	2^{105}	2^{105}	2^{81}	(Bonnetain et al. 2019)
	ID	7	$2^{104.9}$	$2^{110.9}$	$2^{71.9}$	(Leurent and Pernot 2021)
192	MD-based	7	2^{26}	$2^{146.3}$	2^{40}	(Bar-On et al. 2018)
	MITM	8	2^{107}	2^{172}	2^{96}	(Derbez et al. 2013)
	MITM	7	2^{97}	2^{99}	2^{98}	(Derbez et al. 2013)
256	MD-based	7	2^{26}	$2^{146.3}$	2^{40}	(Bar-On et al. 2018)
	MITM	8	2^{107}	2^{196}	2^{96}	(Derbez et al. 2013)
	MITM	9	2^{120}	2^{203}	2^{203}	(Derbez et al. 2013)

MITM: Meet-In-The-Middle   ID: Impossible Differential   MD-based: Mixture-Differential-based

Table A2.4. *Results covering the highest number of rounds against AES in the single-key model*

The most important attacks among those covering the highest number of rounds in the single key model are summarized in Table A2.4. Note that other data/time/memory trade-offs exist for most of the mentioned attacks and can be found in the respective articles.

It has to be noted that in the related-key model (a restricted version of it), in which an attacker can exploit the relation between two or more keys, the two biggest versions of AES were fully broken in 2009 (Biryukov and Khovratovich 2009; Biryukov et al. 2009). These attacks exploit essentially properties of the key schedule. The key schedule of AES-128 being different, this version was not affected by this type of attacks.

A2.6. References

Bar-On, A., Dunkelman, O., Keller, N., Ronen, E., Shamir, A. (2018). Improved key recovery attacks on reduced-round AES with practical data and memory complexities. In *CRYPTO 2018, Part II*, vol. 10992 of *Lecture Notes in Computer Science*, Shacham, H., Boldyreva, A. (eds). Springer.

Biham, E. and Keller, N. (2000). Cryptanalysis of reduced variants of Rijndael. Technical Report, Computer Science Department, Technion-Israel Institute of Technology.

Biryukov, A. and Khovratovich, D. (2009). Related-key cryptanalysis of the full AES-192 and AES-256. In *ASIACRYPT 2009*, vol. 5912 of *Lecture Notes in Computer Science*, Matsui, M. (ed.). Springer.

Biryukov, A., Khovratovich, D., Nikolic, I. (2009). Distinguisher and related-key attack on the full AES-256. In *CRYPTO 2009*, vol. 5677 of *Lecture Notes in Computer Science*, Halevi, S. (ed.). Springer.

Bonnetain, X., Naya-Plasencia, M., Schrottenloher, A. (2019). Quantum security analysis of AES. *IACR Trans. Symmetric Cryptol.*, 2019(2), 55–93.

Boura, C., Lallemand, V., Naya-Plasencia, M., Suder, V. (2018). Making the impossible possible. *J. Cryptol.*, 31(1), 101–133.

Daemen, J. and Rijmen, V. (2020). *The Design of Rijndael – The Advanced Encryption Standard (AES)*, 2nd ed. Information Security and Cryptography. Springer.

Daemen, J., Knudsen, L.R., Rijmen, V. (1997). The block cipher square. In *FSE '97*, vol. 1267 of *Lecture Notes in Computer Science*, Biham, E. (ed.), Springer.

Demirci, H. and Selçuk, A.A. (2008). A meet-in-the-middle attack on 8-round AES. In *FSE 2008*, vol. 5086 of *Lecture Notes in Computer Science*, Nyberg, K. (ed.). Springer.

Derbez, P. and Fouque, P. (2013). Exhausting Demirci-Selçuk meet-in-the-middle attacks against reduced-round AES. In *FSE 2013*, vol. 8424 of *Lecture Notes in Computer Science*, Moriai, S. (ed.). Springer.

Derbez, P., Fouque, P., Jean, J. (2013). Improved key recovery attacks on reduced-round AES in the single-key setting. In *EUROCRYPT 2013*, vol. 7881 of *Lecture Notes in Computer Science*, Johansson, T., Nguyen, P.Q. (eds). Springer.

Dunkelman, O., Keller, N., Shamir, A. (2010). Improved single-key attacks on 8-round AES-192 and AES-256. In *ASIACRYPT 2010*, vol. 6477 of *Lecture Notes in Computer Science*, Abe, M. (ed.). Springer.

Dunkelman, O., Keller, N., Ronen, E., Shamir, A. (2020). The retracing boomerang attack. In *EUROCRYPT 2020*, Part I, vol. 12105 of *Lecture Notes in Computer Science*, Canteaut, A., Ishai, Y. (eds). Springer.

Ferguson, N., Kelsey, J., Lucks, S., Schneier, B., Stay, M., Wagner, D.A., Whiting, D. (2000). Improved cryptanalysis of Rijndael. In *FSE 2000*, vol. 1978 of *Lecture Notes in Computer Science*, Schneier, B. (ed.). Springer.

Gilbert, H. and Minier, M. (2000). A collision attack on 7 rounds of Rijndael. In *The Third Advanced Encryption Standard Candidate Conference*. National Institute of Standards and Technology.

Grassi, L. (2018). Mixture differential cryptanalysis: A new approach to distinguishers and attacks on round-reduced AES. *IACR Trans. Symmetric Cryptol.*, 2018(2), 133–160.

Grassi, L., Rechberger, C., Rønjom, S. (2017). A new structural-differential property of 5-round AES. In *EUROCRYPT 2017, Part II*, vol. 10211 of *Lecture Notes in Computer Science*, Coron, J., Nielsen, J.B. (eds), Springer.

Knudsen, L.R. and Robshaw, M.J.B. (2011). *The Block Cipher Companion*. Springer.

Leurent, G. and Pernot, C. (2021). New representations of the AES key schedule. In *EUROCRYPT 2021, Part I*, vol. 12696 of *Lecture Notes in Computer Science*, Canteaut, A., Standaert, F. (eds). Springer.

Lu, J., Dunkelman, O., Keller, N., Kim, J. (2008). New impossible differential attacks on AES. In *INDOCRYPT 2008*, vol. 5365 of *Lecture Notes in Computer Science*, Chowdhury, D.R., Rijmen, V., Das, A. (eds). Springer.

Mala, H., Dakhilalian, M., Rijmen, V., Modarres-Hashemi, M. (2010). Improved impossible differential cryptanalysis of 7-round AES-128. In *INDOCRYPT 2010*, vol. 6498 of *Lecture Notes in Computer Science*, Gong, G., Gupta, K.C. (eds). Springer.

Appendix 3

PRESENT

Christina BOURA

University of Paris-Saclay, UVSQ, CNRS, Versailles, France

PRESENT is an ultra-lightweight block cipher designed by Bogdanov et al. in 2007 (Bogdanov et al. 2007). It is among the oldest, and most well-known lightweight symmetric ciphers.

A3.1. Some history

Since the design of RIJNDAEL and its selection as the advanced encryption standard (AES) in 2000, the design of new block ciphers slowed temporarily down. Indeed, the new standard had all of the characteristics of a secure cipher and could be employed in different scenarios. However, some years later it became evident that the design of the AES is not suitable for extremely constrained environments such as RFID tags or sensor networks. Therefore, the need for a more *lightweight* block cipher but with a similar level of security emerged. PRESENT was designed in 2007 with hardware efficiency in mind. It had the characteristics of a lightweight cipher, as it could be implemented with only 1570 GE and had a low-power design. To achieve this, the designers of PRESENT opted for components that could be implemented in hardware for a low cost, such as a small 4-bit S-box and bitwise permutations. The reason we chose PRESENT as one of the ciphers to be described, is that since its design, PRESENT has shown to be one of the most popular and well-studied lightweight designs. This is notably demonstrated by the fact that PRESENT is since many years an ISO/IEC standard.

A3.2. The design of PRESENT

PRESENT has a classical SPN structure. It encrypts blocks of 64 bits and supports two different key lengths: 80 and 128 bits. Both versions consist of 31 rounds. At round i, $1 \le i \le 31$, a 64-bit subkey K_i is first XORed to the state. Then a 4-bit S-box S is applied in parallel (sBoxLayer step) and finally the state is permuted by a bitwise permutation P (pLayer state). The subkey K_{32} is used for post-whitening before outputting the ciphertext. A pseudo-code of the encryption procedure is given in Algorithm 1 and two rounds of encryption are depicted in Figure A3.1.

Require: A 64-bit plaintext block m and 32 subkeys K_i, $1 \le i \le 32$, generated by PRESENT's key-schedule algorithm.
Ensure: A 64-bit ciphertext block c
    State $\leftarrow m$
    for $i = 1 \ldots 31$ **do**
        State $\leftarrow$ State $\oplus K_i$
        State $\leftarrow$ sBoxLayer(State)
        State $\leftarrow$ pLayer(State)
    end for
    State $\leftarrow$ State $\oplus K_{32}$
    $c \leftarrow$ State

Algorithm 1. *Encryption with PRESENT*

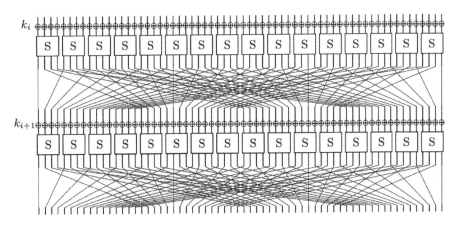

Figure A3.1. *Two rounds of PRESENT (Bogdanov et al. 2007)*

The details of the nonlinear and linear layers of PRESENT are now given as follows:

– sBoxLayer: the nonlinear layer of PRESENT consists of the application in parallel of a 4-bit S-box $S : \mathbb{F}_2^4 \rightarrow \mathbb{F}_2^4$, whose table representation in hexadecimal notation is given in Table A3.1.

x	0 1 2 3 4 5 6 7 8 9 a b c d e f
S[x]	c 5 6 b 9 0 a d 3 e f 8 4 7 1 2

Table A3.1. *S-box of* PRESENT

– pLayer: the linear layer of the round function consists of a bitwise permutation P, whose description is given in Table A3.2. This operation has the advantage of being almost free to implement in hardware.

i	0	1	2	3	4	5	6	7	8	9	10	11	12	13	14	15
$P(i)$	0	16	32	48	1	17	33	49	2	18	34	50	3	19	35	51
i	16	17	18	19	20	21	22	23	24	25	26	27	28	29	30	31
$P(i)$	4	20	36	52	5	21	37	53	6	22	38	54	7	23	39	55
i	32	33	34	35	36	37	38	39	40	41	42	43	44	45	46	47
$P(i)$	8	24	40	56	9	25	41	57	10	26	42	58	11	27	43	59
i	48	49	50	51	52	53	54	55	56	57	58	59	60	61	62	63
$P(i)$	12	28	44	60	13	29	45	61	14	30	46	62	15	31	47	63

Table A3.2. *Linear permutation P of* PRESENT. *The bit i of the state, $0 \leq i < 64$, is moved to position $P(i)$ after the permutation*

A3.3. The key schedule of PRESENT

We describe here the key schedule algorithms for both versions of the algorithm: PRESENT-80 and PRESENT-128. Both descriptions follow closely the algorithms given in the original paper (Bogdanov et al. 2007).

A3.3.1. PRESENT-80

The master key is stored in an 80-bit register K and is represented as $k_{79}k_{78} \ldots k_0$. At round i, $1 \leq i \leq 31$, the 64-bit subkey K_i consists of the following 64 bits of the register K:

$$K_i = k_{79}k_{38} \ldots k_{17}k_{16}.$$

After the round subkey has been extracted from register K, the register is updated as follows:

1) $[k_{79}k_{78}\ldots k_1 k_0] = [k_{18}k_{17}\ldots k_{20}k_{19}]$;

2) $[k_{79}k_{78}k_{77}k_{76}] = S[k_{79}k_{78}k_{77}k_{76}]$;

3) $[k_{19}k_{18}k_{17}k_{16}k_{15}] = [k_{19}k_{18}k_{17}k_{16}k_{15}] \oplus \texttt{round\_counter}$.

In the first step described above, the register is rotated by 61 positions to the left. In the second step, the same 4-bit S-box as the one used in the sBoxLayer step is applied to the four leftmost bits of the register. Finally, the bits $k_{19}k_{18}k_{17}k_{16}k_{15}$ of the register are XORed with the binary representation of a round-dependent constant corresponding to the round number. For example, for round 1, round_counter = (00001); for round 2, round_counter = (00010), etc.

A3.3.2. PRESENT-128

For this version, the master key is stored in a 128-bit register K and is represented as $k_{127}k_{126}\ldots k_0$. As for the 80-bit variant, at round i, $1 \leq i \leq 31$, the 64-bit subkey K_i consists of the following 64 bits of the register K:

$$K_i = k_{79}k_{38}\ldots k_{17}k_{16}.$$

After the round subkey has been extracted from register K, the register is updated in the following way:

1) $[k_{127}k_{126}\ldots k_1 k_0] = [k_{66}k_{65}\ldots k_{68}k_{67}]$;

2) $[k_{127}k_{126}k_{125}k_{124}] = S[k_{127}k_{126}k_{125}k_{124}]$;

3) $[k_{123}k_{122}k_{121}k_{120}] = S[k_{123}k_{122}k_{121}k_{120}]$;

4) $[k_{66}k_{65}k_{64}k_{63}k_{62}] = [k_{66}k_{65}k_{64}k_{63}k_{62}] \oplus \texttt{round\_counter}$;

Here again, the register is first rotated by 61 positions to the left. Next, the 4-bit S-box is applied a first time to the four leftmost bits of the register and at a second time to the following four bits. Finally, the bits $k_{66}k_{65}k_{64}k_{63}k_{62}$ of the register are XORed with the binary representation of a round-dependent constant corresponding to the round number, exactly as done for the 80-bit variant.

A3.4. Best attacks against PRESENT

Since its design in 2007, PRESENT has been the target of numerous cryptanalysis attempts, with linear cryptanalysis being the most successful analysis technique against reduced-round versions of this primitive. The most successful attacks against PRESENT are linear ones. The first noteworthy result in this direction is due to Ohkuma that is presented in 2009 (Ohkuma 2009), a weak-key linear attack against

24-round PRESENT. The same year, Collard and Standaert (2009) published a statistical saturation attack against 26 rounds of the primitive while a multidimensional attack on the same number of rounds but with a higher success probability was presented by Cho (2010) in 2010. Much later, first (Zheng and Zhang 2015) and then (Bogdanov et al. 2018) gave 27-round linear attacks against PRESENT, while the first attack on 28 rounds is due to Flórez-Gutiérrez and Naya-Plasencia (2020). At the time of writing, the attacks given in Flórez-Gutiérrez and Naya-Plasencia (2020) are the best attacks against PRESENT.

Table A3.3, taken from Flórez-Gutiérrez and Naya-Plasencia (2020), summarizes the above attacks.

# Rounds	Key size	# KR rounds	# Approxim	Capacity	Data	Time	Memory	Success prob.	Reference
	80	2	2295 (MD)	$2^{-55.38}$	2^{64} KP	2^{72}	2^{32}	0.95	(Cho 2010)
	80	2	2295 (MD)	$2^{-55.38}$	$2^{63.8}$ KP	2^{72}	2^{32}	0.51	(Cho 2010; Blondeau and Nyberg 2016)
26	80	4	135	$2^{-55.47}$	2^{63} KP	$2^{68.6}$	2^{48}	0.95	(Bogdanov et al. 2018)
	80	4	128	$2^{-54.11}$	$2^{61.1}$ KP	$2^{68.2}$	2^{44}	0.95	(Flórez-Gutiérrez and Naya-Plasencia 2020)
	80	4	128	$2^{-54.11}$	$2^{60.8}$ KP	$2^{71.8}$	2^{44}	0.95	(Flórez-Gutiérrez and Naya-Plasencia 2020)
	80	2	405 (MD)	$2^{-55.33}$	2^{64} KP	2^{74}	2^{67}	0.95	(Zheng and Zhang 2015)
27	80	4	135	$2^{-58.06}$	$2^{63.8}$ DKP	$2^{77.3}$	2^{48}	0.95	(Bogdanov et al. 2018)
	80	4	128	$2^{-56.71}$	$2^{63.4}$ DKP	2^{72}	2^{44}	0.95	(Flórez-Gutiérrez and Naya-Plasencia 2020)
28	80	4	296	$2^{-57.8}$	2^{64} DKP	$2^{77.4}$	2^{51}	0.95	(Flórez-Gutiérrez and Naya-Plasencia 2020)
	80	4	128	$2^{-56.71}$	2^{64} DKP	2^{122}	$2^{84.6}$	0.95	(Flórez-Gutiérrez and Naya-Plasencia 2020)

Table A3.3. *Most important attacks against reduced-round* PRESENT. *KP stands for known plaintexts and DKP for distinct known plaintexts*

A3.5. References

Blondeau, C. and Nyberg, K. (2016). Improved parameter estimates for correlation and capacity deviates in linear cryptanalysis. *IACR Trans. Symmetric Cryptol.*, 2016(2), 162–191.

Bogdanov, A., Knudsen, L.R., Leander, G., Paar, C., Poschmann, A., Robshaw, M.J.B., Seurin, Y., Vikkelsoe, C. (2007). PRESENT: An ultra-lightweight block cipher. In *CHES 2007*, vol. 4727 of *Lecture Notes in Computer Science*, Paillier, P., Verbauwhede, I. (eds). Springer.

Bogdanov, A., Tischhauser, E., Vejre, P.S. (2018). Multivariate profiling of hulls for linear cryptanalysis. *IACR Trans. Symmetric Cryptol.*, 2018(1), 101–125.

Cho, J.Y. (2010). Linear cryptanalysis of reduced-round PRESENT. In *CT-RSA 2010*, vol. 5985 of *Lecture Notes in Computer Science*, Pieprzyk, J. (ed.). Springer.

Collard, B. and Standaert, F. (2009). A statistical saturation attack against the block cipher PRESENT. In *CT-RSA 2009*, vol. 5473 of *Lecture Notes in Computer Science*, Fischlin, M. (ed.). Springer.

Flórez-Gutiérrez, A. and Naya-Plasencia, M. (2020). Improving key-recovery in linear attacks: Application to 28-round PRESENT. In *EUROCRYPT 2020, Part I*, vol. 12105 of *Lecture Notes in Computer Science*, Canteaut, A., Ishai, Y. (eds). Springer.

Ohkuma, K. (2009). Weak keys of reduced-round PRESENT for linear cryptanalysis. In *SAC 2009*, vol. 5867 of *Lecture Notes in Computer Science*, Jacobson Jr., H.J., Rijmen, V., Safavi-Naini, R. (eds). Springer.

Zheng, L. and Zhang, S. (2015). Fft-based multidimensional linear attack on PRESENT using the 2-bit-fixed characteristic. *Secur. Commun. Networks*, 8(18), 3535–3545.

Appendix 4

KECCAK

Christina Boura

University of Paris-Saclay, UVSQ, CNRS, Versailles, France

KECCAK is a versatile cryptographic function designed by Bertoni (et al.) in 2008 (Bertoni et al. 2013). It can be used as a hash function, an authenticated encryption scheme or a pseudo-random number generator. KECCAK is based on the sponge construction (Bertoni et al. 2007) and applies internally a cryptographic permutation called KECCAK-f. KECCAK is notably the winner of the NIST SHA-3 competition and has been standardized in 3GPP TS 35.231 for mobile telephony (TUAK), and in NIST standards FIPS 202 and SP 800-185. The description given in this chapter is a more detailed specification of the brief description given in Chapter 4.

A4.1. The KECCAK-f permutation

The KECCAK-f permutation is applied on a $5 \times 5 \times w$-bit state, where $w = 1, 2, 4, 8, 16, 32, 64$, that can be represented by a three-dimensional matrix $a[x][y][z]$, with $0 \leq x, y < 5$ and $0 \leq z < w$. Thus, the state can be seen as a collection of w slices, each slice containing five rows and five columns. The round function is iterated 24 times.

Each round R is composed of a sequence of five permutations, θ, ρ, π, χ and ι that modify the state:

$$R = \iota \circ \chi \circ \pi \circ \rho \circ \theta.$$

Symmetric Cryptography 1,
coordinated by Christina BOURA and María NAYA-PLASENCIA. © ISTE Ltd 2023.

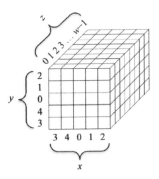

Figure A4.1. *The KECCAK-f state (Bertoni et al. 2011)*

Each transformation plays a different role in order to ensure to the final permutation a high nonlinearity and a good diffusion in all directions of the three-dimension state. They are briefly described in the following.

θ: this function is a linear transformation that XORs to bit $a[x][y][z]$ of the state the parity of the two columns $a[x-1][\cdot][z]$ and $a[x][\cdot][z+1]$:

$$a[x][y][z] = a[x][y][z] + \sum_{i=0}^{4} a[x-1][i][z] + \sum_{i=0}^{4} a[x][i][z+1].$$

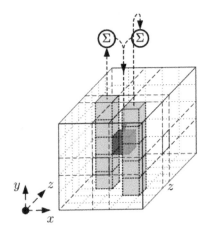

Figure A4.2. *The action of θ (Bertoni et al. 2011) to a 200-bit state*

This kind of transformation was later called a *column-parity mixer* and the properties of those transformations were analyzed in detail in Stoffelen and Daemen (2018).

ρ: the role of this transformation is to rotate bits along the z axis. Each bit is rotated by a certain offset that depends on the x and y coordinates of the lane to which it belongs. Therefore, the z coordinate of each bit is modified by adding to it the corresponding offset modulo the lane size w ($w = 64$ for the classical 1600-bit permutation). The offsets for each lane are given in Table A4.1.

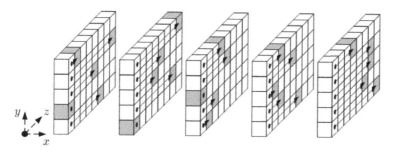

Figure A4.3. *The action of ρ (Bertoni et al. 2011)*

	$x = 3$	$x = 4$	$x = 0$	$x = 1$	$x = 2$
$y = 2$	153	231	3	10	171
$y = 1$	55	276	36	300	6
$y = 0$	28	91	0	1	190
$y = 4$	120	78	210	66	253
$y = 3$	21	136	105	45	15

Table A4.1. *Offsets of ρ*

π: this is another linear transformation whose role is to permute the bits inside a slice, or differently speaking, to rearrange the position of the lanes. Its action can be simply described by the formula $a'[x][y][z] = a[(x + 3y) \mod 5, x, z]$ and depicted in Figure A4.4, where a' is the state after the application of π to the state a.

χ: this permutation is the only nonlinear transformation of KECCAK-f. It applies a 5×5 S-box S (often called χ, similar to the whole non-linear transformation itself) in parallel to each row of the state. This function is quadratic and the algebraic normal form (ANF) of each of its coordinates is given by:

$$S : \mathbb{F}_2^5 \to \mathbb{F}_2^5$$

$$(x_0, x_1, x_2, x_3, x_4, x_5) \mapsto (x_0 x_2 + x_1 + x_2,$$

$$x_1 x_3 + x_2 + x_3,$$

$$x_2 x_4 + x_3 + x_4,$$

$$x_3 x_0 + x_4 + x_0,$$

$$x_4 x_1 + x_0 + x_1).$$

ι: this function adds a constant to certain bits of the state to break symmetry. In particular, only the bits of the lane $(x, y) = (0, 0)$ are affected by ι.

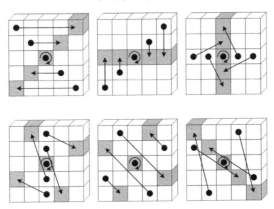

Figure A4.4. *The transformation π applied to a single slide (Bertoni et al. 2011)*

A4.1.1. *Best attacks against KECCAK/SHA-3*

The KECCAK hash function was the winner of the SHA-3 competition and was standardized in 2015 by the NIST. As the algorithm was public since 2008, it received a lot of attention from the community and was thoroughly analyzed since the beginning.

The first results were dedicated to the analysis of the internal permutation KECCAK-f, in particular by exhibiting *zero-sum distinguishers* (Aumasson and Meier 2009; Boura and Canteaut 2010a, 2010b; Boura et al. 2011; Duan and Lai 2011; Yan et al. 2019). The existence of zero-sum distinguishers for the whole permutation KECCAK-f was notably the reason that pushed the designers of KECCAK to increase the number of rounds from 18 to 24, even if it remains quite unclear how the existence of this type of properties can affect the security of the global design.

Kuila et al. (2014) exhibited low-complexity distinguishers for up to six-rounds of KECCAK-f by considering self-symmetric states. Other differential-like distinguishers were proposed by Duc et al. (2012) and Jean and Nikolic (2015).

In parallel, different cryptanalysis efforts targeted the collision and preimage security of the different variants of KECCAK and later the SHA-3 standard. The SHA-3 family of is composed of four hash functions with different but fixed output lengths: SHA-3-224, SHA-3-256, SHA-3-384 and SHA-3-512 as well as two XOFs: SHAKE128 and SHAKE256. The KECCAK variants are denoted as KECCAK$[r, c]_n$ where r is the rate, c the capacity and n the output length. Much of the first published third-party analysis was devoted into finding collisions for reduced-round versions of the algorithm. First, Naya-Plasencia et al. constructed two practical two-round collision attacks against KECCAK$[1088, 512]_{256}$ and KECCAK$[1152, 448]_{224}$. Then, Dinur et al. (2012) presented practical collision attacks against four-rounds of the same two KECCAK variants. This was done by mean of algebraic techniques by using a three-round low-weight characteristic together with a one-round connector. One year later, the same authors constructed in Dinur et al. (2013) practical collisions on four-round KECCAK$[832, 768]_{384}$ and five-round KECCAK$[1088, 512]_{256}$ using the technique of internal differentials. In 2017, Qiao et al. (2017) presented a powerful framework for collision attacks against SHA-3 based on S-box linearization techniques. This framework was further improved in Song et al. (2017) (see also Guo et al. (2020) for a journal joint version of these both works) and permitted to find practical collision attacks against five-round SHA-3-224 and five-round SHA-3-256. Recently, a collision attack against 4-round SHA-3-384 was given in Huang et al. (2022) with a time complexity much lower than the previous best attack (Dinur et al. 2013) against this version of KECCAK/SHA-3. Finally, Guo et al. presented in 2022 the first collision attack against six rounds of the KECCAK variant with output length 256 (SHAKE-128).

Other works focused on the preimage security of KECCAK/SHA-3. First, Bernstein proposed second preimage attacks for six, seven and eight rounds of KECCAK at the cost however of a huge memory amount (Bernstein 2010). Then, in 2013 the first four-round preimage attacks were published against all versions of the standard (Morawiecki et al. 2013) by applying rotational cryptanalysis. Further preimage attacks up to four-rounds were published later in Guo et al. (2016) by exploiting the technique of linear structures. In 2019, Li and Sun (2019) exploit a new idea for producing preimage attacks by targeting 2 blocks. This method was then further improved in He et al. (2021). A different more algebraic method was used recently in Wei et al. (2021) to produce four-round preimages. The above attacks together with their corresponding complexities are summarized in Table A4.3. Note that this table only mentions the longest attacks. Most of the mentioned works also present attacks on a smaller number of rounds.

Target $[r, c]$	n	# Rounds	Time	Reference
KECCAK[576,1024]	512	3	Practical	(Dinur et al. 2013)
KECCAK[832,768]	384	3	Practical	(Dinur et al. 2013)
		4	2^{147}	(Dinur et al. 2013)
		4	$2^{59.65}$	(Huang et al. 2022)
KECCAK[1088,512]	256	4	Practical	(Dinur et al. 2012)
		5	2^{115}	(Dinur et al. 2013)
		5	Practical	(Qiao et al. 2017)
		6	$2^{123.5}$	(Guo et al. 2022)
KECCAK[1152,448]	224	4	Practical	(Dinur et al. 2012)
		5	Practical	(Qiao et al. 2017)

Table A4.2. *Summary of collision attacks on* KECCAK

Target $[r, c]$	n	# Rounds	Time	Memory	Reference
KECCAK[576,1024]	512	4	2^{506}	Negligible	(Morawiecki et al. 2013)
		6	2^{506}	2^{176}	(Bernstein 2010)
		7	2^{507}	2^{230}	(Bernstein 2010)
		8	$2^{511.5}$	2^{508}	(Bernstein 2010)
KECCAK[832,768]	384	4	2^{378}	Negligible	(Morawiecki et al. 2013)
KECCAK[1088,512]	256	4	2^{252}	Negligible	(Morawiecki et al. 2013)
		4	2^{251}	Negligible	(Guo et al. 2016)
		4	2^{239}	Negligible	(Li and Sun 2019)
		4	2^{218}	Negligible	(He et al. 2021)
		4	2^{214}	Negligible	(Wei et al. 2021)
KECCAK[1152,448]	224	4	2^{221}	Negligible	(Morawiecki et al. 2013)
		4	2^{213}	Negligible	(Guo et al. 2016)
		4	2^{207}	Negligible	(Li and Sun 2019)
		4	2^{192}	Negligible	(He et al. 2021)
		4	2^{182}	Negligible	(Wei et al. 2021)

Table A4.3. *Summary of the longest preimage attacks on* KECCAK

Many results have also been published against keyed versions of KECCAK. We decided not to treat these results here, but they can be found at https://keccak.team/third_party.html.

A4.2. References

Aumasson, J.-P., Meier, W. (2009). Zero-sum distinguishers for reduced KECCAK-f and for the core functions of Luffa and Hamsi [Online]. Available at: https://www.aumasson.jp/data/papers/AM09.pdf.

Bernstein, D.J. (2010). Second preimages for 6 (7? (8??)) rounds of KECCAK? NIST mailing list [Online]. Available at: http://ehash.iaik.tugraz.at/uploads/6/65/NIST-mailing-list_Bernstein-Daemen.txt.

Bertoni, G., Daemen, J., Peeters, M., Van Assche, G. (2007). Sponge functions, Ecrypt Hash Workshop 2007, Barcelona, Spain.

Bertoni, G., Daemen, J., Peeters, M., Van Assche, G. (2011). The KECCAK reference, version 3.0 [Online]. Available at: http://keccak.noekeon.org/Keccak-reference-3.0.pdf.

Bertoni, G., Daemen, J., Peeters, M., Van Assche, G. (2013). In *EUROCRYPT 2013*, vol. 7881 of *Lecture Notes in Computer Science*, Johansson, T., Nguyen, P.Q. (eds). Springer.

Boura, C. and Canteaut, A. (2010a). Zero-sum distinguishers for iterated permutations and application to Keccak-*f* and Hamsi-256. In *SAC 2010*, vol. 6544 of *Lecture Notes in Computer Science*, Biryukov, A., Gong, G., Stinson, D.R. (eds). Springer.

Boura, C. and Canteaut, A. (2010b). A zero-sum property for the KECCAK-f permutation with 18 rounds. In *ISIT 2010*. IEEE.

Boura, C., Canteaut, A., De Cannière, C. (2011). Higher-order differential properties of KECCAK and *Luffa*. In *FSE 2011*, vol. 6733 of *Lecture Notes in Computer Science*, Joux, A. (ed.). Springer.

Dinur, I., Dunkelman, O., Shamir, A. (2012). New attacks on KECCAK-224 and KECCAK-256. In *FSE 2012*, vol. 7549 of *Lecture Notes in Computer Science*, Canteaut, A. (ed.). Springer.

Dinur, I., Dunkelman, O., Shamir, A. (2013). Collision attacks on up to 5 rounds of SHA-3 using generalized internal differentials. In *FSE 2013*, vol. 8424 of *Lecture Notes in Computer Science*, Moriai, S. (ed.). Springer.

Duan, M. and Lai, X. (2011). Improved zero-sum distinguisher for full round KECCAK-f permutation. *IACR Cryptol. ePrint Arch.*, 23.

Duc, A., Guo, J., Peyrin, T., Wei, L. (2012). Unaligned rebound attack: Application to KECCAK. In *FSE 2012*, vol. 7549 of *Lecture Notes in Computer Science*, Canteaut, A. (ed.). Springer.

Guo, J., Liu, M., Song, L. (2016). Linear structures: Applications to cryptanalysis of round-reduced KECCAK. In *ASIACRYPT 2016, Part I*, vol. 10031 of *Lecture Notes in Computer Science*, Cheon, J.H., Takagi, T. (eds), Springer.

Guo, J., Liao, G., Liu, G., Liu, M., Qiao, K., Song, L. (2020). Practical collision attacks against round-reduced SHA-3. *J. Cryptol.*, 33(1), 228–270.

Guo, J., Liu, G., Song, L., Tu, Y. (2022). Exploring SAT for cryptanalysis: (Quantum) collision attacks against 6-round SHA-3. *IACR Cryptol. ePrint Arch.*, 184.

He, L., Lin, X., Yu, H. (2021). Improved preimage attacks on 4-round KECCAK-224/256. *IACR Trans. Symmetric Cryptol.*, 2021(1), 217–238.

Huang, S., Ben-Yehuda, O.A., Dunkelman, O., Maximov, A. (2022). Finding collisions against 4-round SHA3-384 in practical time. Cryptology ePrint Archive, Paper 2022/194 [Online]. Available at: https://eprint.iacr.org/2022/194.

Jean, J. and Nikolic, I. (2015). Internal differential boomerangs: Practical analysis of the round-reduced KECCAK-f permutation. In *FSE 2015*, vol. 9054 of *Lecture Notes in Computer Science*, Leander, G. (ed.). Springer.

Kuila, S., Saha, D., Pal, M., Chowdhury, D.R. (2014). Practical distinguishers against 6-round KECCAK-f exploiting self-symmetry. In *AFRICACRYPT 2014*, vol. 8469 of *Lecture Notes in Computer Science*, Pointcheval, D., Vergnaud, D. (eds). Springer.

Li, T. and Sun, Y. (2019), Preimage attacks on round-reduced KECCAK-224/256 via an allocating approach. In *EUROCRYPT 2019, Part III*, vol. 11478 of *Lecture Notes in Computer Science*, Ishai, Y., Rijmen, V. (eds). Springer.

Morawiecki, P., Pieprzyk, J., Srebrny, M. (2013). Rotational cryptanalysis of round-reduced KECCAK. In *FSE 2013*, vol. 8424 of *Lecture Notes in Computer Science*, Moriai, S. (ed.). Springer.

Qiao, K., Song, L., Liu, M., Guo, J. (2017). New collision attacks on round-reduced KECCAK. In *EUROCRYPT 2017, Part III*, vol. 10212 of *Lecture Notes in Computer Science*, Coron, J.-S., Nielsen, J.B. (eds). Springer.

Song, L., Liao, G., Guo, J. (2017). Non-full Sbox linearization: Applications to collision attacks on round-reduced KECCAK. In *CRYPTO 2017, Part II*, vol. 10402 of *Lecture Notes in Computer Science*, Katz, J., Shacham, H. (eds). Springer.

Stoffelen, K. and Daemen, J. (2018). Column parity mixers. *IACR Trans. Symmetric Cryptol.*, 2018(1), 126–159.

Wei, C., Wu, C., Fu, X., Dong, X., He, K., Hong, J., Wang, X. (2021). Preimage attacks on 4-round KECCAK by solving multivariate quadratic systems. In *ICISC 2021* of *Lecture Notes in Computer Science*, Park, J.H., Seo, S-H. (eds), Springer, 13218, 195–216.

Yan, H., Lai, X., Wang, L., Yu, Y., Xing, Y. (2019). New zero-sum distinguishers on full 24-round Keccak-f using the division property. *IET Inf. Secur.*, 13(5), 469–478.

List of Authors

Christina BOURA
University of Paris-Saclay
UVSQ
CNRS
Versailles
France

Joan DAEMEN
Radboud University
Nijmegen
The Netherlands

Orr DUNKELMAN
Computer Science Department
University of Haifa
Israel

Maria EICHLSEDER
Graz University of Technology
Austria

Tetsu IWATA
Nagoya University
Japan

Gaëtan LEURENT
Inria
Paris
France

Chaoyun LI
imec-COSIC
Department of Electrical
Engineering (ESAT)
KU Leuven
Belgium

Bart MENNINK
Radboud University
Nijmegen
The Netherlands

Mridul NANDI
Indian Statistical Institute
Kolkata
India

María NAYA-PLASENCIA
Inria
Paris
France

Léo PERRIN
Inria
Paris
France

Yannick SEURIN
ANSSI
Paris
France

Bart PRENEEL
imec-COSIC
Department of Electrical
Engineering (ESAT)
KU Leuven
Belgium

Gilles VAN ASSCHE
STMicroelectronics
Belgium

Index

Summary of Volume 2

Chapter 3. Impossible Differential Cryptanalysis

Christina BOURA and Maria NAYA-PLASENCIA

Chapter 4. Zero-Correlation Cryptanalysis

Vincent RIJMEN

Chapter 5. Differential-Linear Cryptanalysis
Yosuke TODO

5.1. Brief introduction of differential-linear attacks
5.2. How to estimate correlations of a differential-linear distinguisher
5.3. On the key recovery
5.4. State of the art for differential-linear attacks
    5.4.1. Differential-linear connecting table
    5.4.2. Three techniques to improve differential-linear attacks
5.5. References

Chapter 6. Boomerang Cryptanalysis
Ling SONG

6.1. Basic boomerang attack
6.2. Variants and refinements
6.3. Tricks and failures
6.4. Formalize the dependency
6.5. References

Chapter 7. Meet-in-the-Middle Cryptanalysis
Brice MINAUD

7.1. Introduction
7.2. Basic meet-in-the-middle framework
    7.2.1. The 2DES attack
    7.2.2. Algorithmic framework
    7.2.3. Complexity analysis and memory usage
7.3. Meet-in-the-middle techniques
    7.3.1. Filtering
    7.3.2. Splice-and-cut
    7.3.3. Bicliques
7.4. Automatic tools
7.5. References

Chapter 8. Meet-in-the-Middle Demirci-Selçuk Cryptanalysis
Patrick DERBEZ

8.1. Original Demirci-Selçuk attack
8.2. Improvements
    8.2.1. Data/time/memory trade-off
    8.2.2. Difference instead of value
    8.2.3. Multiset
    8.2.4. Linear combinations
    8.2.5. Differential enumeration technique

Chapter 12. Correlation Attacks on Stream Ciphers
Thomas JOHANSSON

Chapter 13. Addition, Rotation, XOR
Leo PERRIN

Chapter 14. SHA-3 Contest Related Cryptanalysis
Yu SASAKI

Chapter 18. New Fields in Symmetric Cryptography
Léo PERRIN

Chapter 19. Deck-function-based Cryptography
Joan DAEMEN

.

Printed and bound by CPI Group (UK) Ltd, Croydon, CR0 4YY

27/10/2024

14580732-0004